# ICE!

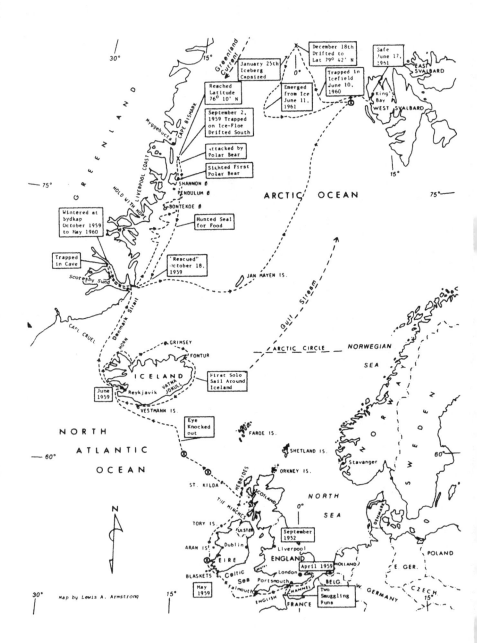

December 18th
Drifted to
Lat 79° 42' N

Safe
June 17,
1961

EAST
SVALBARD

January 25th
Iceberg
Capsized

Trapped in
Icefield
June 10, 1960

Reached
Latitude
76° 10' N

Emerged
from Ice
June 11,
1961

King's
Bay
WEST SVALBARD

September 2,
1959 Trapped
on Ice-Floe
Drifted South

Attacked by
Polar Bear

Sighted First
Polar Bear

SHANNON Ø
PENDULUM Ø

ARCTIC OCEAN

75°

BONTEKOE Ø

Wintered at
Sydkap
October 1959
to May 1960

Hunted Seal
for Food

G R E E N L A N D

Trapped
in Cave

"Rescued"
October 18,
1959

Scoresby Sund

JAN MAYEN IS.

Gulf Stream

CARL CRUEL

Denmark Strait

ARCTIC CIRCLE    NORWEGIAN

GRIMSEY

FONTUR

SEA

I C E L A N D

First Solo
Sail Around
Iceland

VATNA
JOKULL

June
1959

Reykjavik

VESTMANN IS.

Eye
Knocked
out

N O R W A Y

N O R T H

FAROE IS.

ATLANTIC

SHETLAND IS.

Stavanger

S W E D E N

60°

O C E A N

ST. KILDA

ORKNEY IS.

HEBRIDES

N O R T H

TORY IS.

THE MINCHES

SCOTLAND

September
1952

S E A

DENMARK

ARAN IS.

ULSTER

Dublin

Liverpool

POLAND

E I R E

ENGLAND

April 1959

HOLLAND

E. GER.

BLASKETS

Celtic

London

BELG.

W. GERMANY

CZECH.

MAY
1959

Sea

Portsmouth

Falmouth

Two
Smuggling
Runs

ENGLISH CHANNEL

FRANCE

30°    Map by Lewis A. Armstrong    15°

# ICE!
## by Tristan Jones

S

SHERIDAN HOUSE

*Other books by Tristan Jones
published by Sheridan House:*

| | |
|---|---|
| Adrift | One Hand for Yourself, |
| Aka | One for the Ship |
| Dutch Treat | Outward Leg |
| Encounters of a | Saga of a Wayward Sailor |
| Wayward Sailor | Seagulls in My Soup |
| Heart of Oak | Somewheres East of Suez |
| The Improbable Voyage | A Steady Trade |
| The Incredible Voyage | To Venture Further |
| | Yarns |

---

First paperback edition
published 1995 by
Sheridan House Inc.
145 Palisade Street
Dobbs Ferry, NY  10522

Reprinted 1999

Reissued 2008

Copyright © 1978 by Tristan Jones

First published 1978 by Sheed Andrews and McMeel Inc.

*Library of Congress Cataloging-in-Publication Data*

Jones, Tristan, 1924-1995
    Ice!
        1. Creswell (Ketch) 2. Jones, Tristan, 1924-1995
        3. North Atlantic Ocean  4. Voyages and travels
        I. Title
        G470.C78J66   910'.09'1632   78-8455

Printed in the United States of America

ISBN 978-1-57409-273-8

# Contents

# Acknowledgments

For help, support and encouragement in making the voyage to the Arctic, thanks to the many good people of whom lack of space prevents mention. Some are dead, many are old, many may think they are forgotten; they are not. In this book they live. They, too, *made* the voyage. This saga is theirs.

For help, support, and encouragement in writing this book, thanks to:

Dimitra Nikolai, who typed it, as she does anything, courageously;

Frank Braynard, New York (of the Manhattan South Street Seaport and organizer of the Tall Ships events), for his hospitality to my boat *Sea Dart* during the spring and summer of 1977;

Russell Gurnee, New Jersey, past president of the Explorers Club, and his wife, Jeanne Gurnee, chairman of the Society of Women Geographers (U.S.A.), who were the first to recognize my message;

Professor H. Barraclough Fell, of Harvard University, author of *America B.C.*, who, interpreting ancient inscriptions in North America, has cast a bright light on old legends of Celtic trans-Atlantic voyages.

TRISTAN JONES
*Hope Bay*
*British Antarctic Territories*
*New Year's Day, 1978*

# PART I

---

## Vidi
*(I saw)*

*Oh, they say there's a troopship just leaving Bombay,*
*Bound for old Blighty's shores,*
*Heavily laden with time-expired men,*
*Bound for the land they adore,*
*There's many a soldier just finishing his time,*
*There's many a twirp signin' on,*
*You'll get no promotion this side of the ocean,*
*So cheer up my lads, bless 'em all!*
*Bless 'em all, bless 'em all,*
*The long and the short and the tall,*
*Bless all the sergeants and W.O. Ones,*
*Bless all the corporals and their bleedin' sons,*
*'Cos we're sayin' goodbye to them all,*
*As back to their billets they crawl,*
*They'll get no promotion, this side of the ocean,*
*So cheer up my lads, bless 'em all!*

Song of the British Army in India
(origin in 1920s).

# 1

## *August 1952*

In Aden Military Hospital everything was hot, dry, and sandy: the walls, the floors, the nurses, the sheets, even me. After six weeks of lying painfully on my stomach with a badly bruised spine, I had taken the first hobbling steps over to the shady veranda and had gazed with pained eyes across the dun-colored town to the arid escarpment of the Crater. Ships lay at anchor beyond the shimmering docks, waiting like mother-hens for the long, black, sinister-looking barges to be bustled alongside by tiny, tooting tugs.

The British army doctor's verdict had been quite definite—no more heavy work; certainly no more seagoing. I would be lucky ever to be able to walk properly again. Ever again, at twenty-eight years of age! Just arrived in full manhood and condemned to idle ashore for the rest of my life—never again to feel the lift of a ship's hull under my feet as she departed her haven and danced to the sea's welcome swell; never again to meet the first flying fish glittering in the midforenoon sunlight as the vessel drew the waiting tropics to her heaving forefoot; never again to sense the magic anticipation of a new, strange shore rising over the horizon ahead, or to hear the icebergs calving from their mother mountains in the low, long, bittersweet dawn of the Arctic; never again to know the utter comfort of a mug of cocoa more softly, gratefully sipped from a great china mug than any wine from any chalice, as the iced hull slipped through the hazy, freezing fog of the Denmark Strait.

I leaned on the balcony rail, mid-Victorian Gothic iron, beaten into shape by men in faraway England, an England pregnant with the power of Empire, a hundred years before, when my grandfather was a boy apprentice on a Black-ball line trooper to India; half a century and more before my father deserted sail in Capetown to join the Australian Horse and chase Christian de Wet and his Boer commandos across the Kalahari desert of South Africa.

Gazing across the shimmering midday heat to the great Crater of Aden, past the miles of mud hovels to the glistening hotels and stark minarets in the distance, I felt, for the first and only time in my life, self-pity. I grabbed the handrail tightly and looked down to the dusty courtyard below. It was crowded with the usual complement of beggars and local patients' families, some with cooking pots steaming over small fires, some just patiently waiting in the shade for the next call of the muezzin to prayer. It was a good fifty-foot drop. More than enough. It would be so easy. A painful heave over the rail when none of the eagle-eyed matrons of the Queen Alexandra's Royal Nursing Corps were around; two seconds' rush through space and it would all be over.

"Good morning, Jones. Still alive I see!"

"Good morning, Matron. Yes, but only just."

She smiled at me, her blue green Scottish eyes the color of the heather of Tiree itself.

"Och, come now," she rejoined, "a braw laddie like you talking like that; just imagine it! You've far to go yet. Let's see now, you're Welsh, are you not? And talking like that—just think of all the folk that you'll meet when you get home."

"What, Matron, in Greenwich Hospital for Naval Pensioners?"

"If you go on talking like that, then that's where you'll probably end up. But I think not, Mister Jones. If I've got you reckoned up, well, you'll be back on your feet in no time at all." She smiled again. "And mark wnat I've said, for all my family were well noted for the second sight. Now, my lad, no more fashin' yoursel'. Off you go for your meal—and this afternoon you can pack your kit."

"Matron?"

"Aye, pack your kit; you're off to England on this night's flight. I'll have a nurse around at five o'clock to help you. And mind, laddie, no flirting now, or I'll have you on Captain's Report."

"Aye, aye, Matron!"

At dusk the Royal Air Force Transport plane took off. I remember only a few details of the flight—that the plane crew was efficient, friendly, and kind; that we landed somewhere in Tripoli and again in Rome; and that the fields of England were startling in their greenness as we swooped down onto a base in Wiltshire. And that my mind was made up. No matter how much pain and suffering it would cost me, I would go back to sea. Somehow, only God knew how, I would find the strength and the means.

As we flew out of Aden into the lightened sky to the west, across the southern end of the Red Sea, I glimpsed for no more than a few seconds the Strait of the Bab el Mandeb, its rough white water far below looking like snow flakes in the dark sea of the narrow, rock-strewn channel. The Bab el Mandeb—the *Gate of Tears*! Despite the pain from twisting my head, I stared down at it. The Gate of Tears . . . the Sea of Sinbad . . . I *would* go back, even if it killed me. Nothing could keep me from the wide waters of the world!

I *would* see the flying fish and the dolphins, the porpoise and the whales; I *would* see the trade wind clouds and the albatross; I *would* hear the call of the calving ice and the hymn of the wind over Tierra del Fuego and trace the weft of green Sargasso weed as it drifts from Bermuda to the Azores. I *would* creep into the womblike fiords of Greenland and whistle on the wind to the coral reefs of the Arafura Sea and hear the wailing muezzin-call of the Com oros!

"Good luck," whispered the air force nurse as I was wheeled down the ramp onto the ground of England.

"It's not luck we need, love."

"No? What is it?" She leaned closer; her femaleness even in her starched uniform disturbed me. Uncomfortable, with a cracked pelvis.

"Bastardy, sweetheart. Bastardy, and a good pint of ale."

"Well, the Royal Navy's got plenty of that," she laughed.

The ambulance wafted smoothly through the English lanes and roads for a couple of hours, finally coming to a halt before the venerable hospital of Haslar, where men had been treated after all of England's past fifty or so wars. After two months in the care of the British army and air force, I was once again in the stern arms of My Lords Commissioners of the Admiralty. There would be no kidding and joshing here. *Fear God, Honor the Queen! Up Spirits! Pipe Down!* Everything to order, like an orchestration of clockwork precision. And yet, as with the Royal Navy rope, there was a "rogue's strand" running right through the middle of it all. A saving grace of toleration and humor which made, but only just, life bearable in the "Andrew" (the British sailor's name for the Royal Navy).

Gradually the days of English summer passed by, the trees in sweet blossom, warm worn brick, cottagelike walls, grey flagstones washed by the feet of thousands of broken men from the Nile, Copenhagen, Trafalgar, the African Coast slave-chasers, the Crimean War, Tel el Kebir, Jutland and the convoys, Gallipoli, the Falklands, North Cape and the convoys, the Mediterranean, the Pacific, the North Sea, and the Channel.

"Must have been a hard lot in the days of sail, eh, mate?" I commented to the sick berth "tiffy," an Irish lad who ran our ward.

"Yeah, and sure the bloody seas was rougher, too, auld son."

I laughed. He was right. They'd gone back to sea from here in the old days, with God only knows what limbs and other spare bits missing. They'd gone back to sea to sail the great, swiftly lumbering wooden walls of England, and by the living Jesus, so would I. And if I couldn't go in their navy, then I would go in my bloody own! The die was cast. I hobbled around, but faster now, with rising ambition and the star of *Cymru*—Wales—the brightest star that ever the sea shone under, racing in my blood, and the song of Madoc and Morgan in my mind, willing my body to repair itself all the faster.

But how? And then I remembered all the sailing lore I'd learned from my old master, Tansy Lee, and I thought of all the surplus war boats and materials lying rotting in Her Majesty's Dockyards, and I suddenly saw it all clearly. I sat down on the nearest bed and grinned: *I knew how*. I would shortly be discharged with a pension of ten dollars a week, and a paying-off gratuity of fifteen hundred dollars. I would somehow get hold of one of those craft and put all the knowledge and care I had left into her. I would lay hands on good galvanized wire and canvas, rope and fittings. I would cherish and put all I had into her. God would do the rest, and the Devil, who had done his bloody best to nobble me, could go and get stuffed. Once I was back at sea, nothing, *nothing* in the whole world, could touch me!

Sure it would take time, maybe years. It would also take a lot of patience, courage, and determination. I wasn't at all certain about the time, the patience, or the courage, but by Jesus, I knew I had the fourth attribute. The fifth—luck— was in God's hands, but I couldn't expect him to do much without a great deal of help from me.

I hit one fist into the other: I'd do it! The game was afoot!

*I don't want to join the army,*
*I don't want to go to war,*
*I'd rather sit around Piccadilly Underground,*
*Living off the earnings of a high-paid lady.*
*I don't want to join the army,*
*I don't want me bollocks shot away,*
*I'd rather be in London, lovely dear old London,*
*Fuckin' all me bleedin' life away!*

First World War British Army song. This was *not* an antiwar song, it was the soldier's sardonic comment on the shirkers and profiteers at home.

# 2

## Free!

The first place I made for after my discharge from the Royal Naval Hospital at Haslar was the Sussex Bar, right in the center of Portsmouth. This was the great gathering place of all the time-serving men. If there was anyone around who knew anything about what small craft were available, anyone in the Service, that is, this would be the place to find him. My new issue civilian suit, cheap and ill-fitting, felt strange, and after carrying my sea bag from the bus stop, my back was paining me.

The first two pints went down like a balloon in a spring Channel breeze. I looked around. Kiwi grinned back at me. I'd seen him last three years before, in New York.

"Hi, Tris. What're you doin' here, mate?"

"Wotcher, Kiwi. Just got my discharge. Having a quick look round."

"Heard you got clobbered. Singapore, wasn't it?"

"Aden, bloody hell hole."

"What were you doing there?"

"Official Secrets Act, old chum." I tried to look conspiratorial.

Kiwi, so called because he had been born in New Zealand, grinned. "Come on, Tris, what the bloody 'ell you been up to?"

"Catching butterflies."

"Yeah, well, what are you goin' to do now?"

"Looking for a job. Something to do with small boats, if I can."

Kiwi poured another pint of foaming ale down his lithe body, then turned to me. His gold stripes and anchor gleamed under the bright pub lights. "Why don't you stick around for a week, Tris?" he said. "I've got my discharge coming on Monday next. Look, I've been watching the papers for likely jobs, and for us blokes, me an able seaman, you a stoker, there ain't much around. But I see the White Star Line are taking on crew up in Liverpool for the South America run."

"What's the money like?"

"Pretty fair, fifty quid a month and all found."

"Blimey, that's not bad, is it? How long does a round trip take?"

"Well, Tris, it's September now. Supposin' we took off on the west coast of South America run, we could be back for Christmas, and you'd have another two hundred quid up your sleeve, if you took it easy. Better than hanging around here, spending money."

"Yes, Kiwi, but it's big ships again. And anyway, I don't know if they'll take me in my condition, buggered up like this. It's as much as I can do to carry that bloomin' sea bag."

"Well, listen, old son," he said, putting his hand on my shoulder, "give it a try anyway. Why don't you go up to London and stay at the Union Jack Club? It's only a week, and you've nothing to lose."

"O.K., Kiwi, I'll tell you what I'll do. I'll have one more pint of ale, then I'll catch the train up to the Smoke and book in at the Union Jack Club. It's only five bob a night and the beer's cheap and there's stacks of crumpet round Waterloo Station."

"Right, Tris, do that and I'll see you next Monday. We can have a night in the Smoke, a few pints of wallop, look up the birds round the Dilly, then take off early for Liverpool. We can be at the shipping offices by nine o'clock on Tuesday."

"O.K., Kiwi, but I'm not promising anything with the White Star, I've got my mind on something else."

"What?"

"My own boat. A sailboat."

"You must be joking, Tris. A bloody yachtsman? You? Christ, that costs a fortune."

"Not the way I'm going to do it."

"Well, anyway, Tris, hang on until Monday. See you then. By the way, mate, watch them birds up round Waterloo. Things have changed a bit since you was last up there; they're all bleeding rotten now. You've only got to look at 'em and you're away up the sick bay with a dose of clap that'd kill King Kong. The Yanks ain't there to clean 'em up, now."

"Right, thanks for the tip, Kiwi. See you next Monday!"

At Portsmouth Station I bought a couple of boating magazines to read on the journey up to London. As the train trundled through the autumn countryside, I glanced at the scenery only now and again, for my eyes were on the Craft for Sale advertisements. It was clear that any kind of production boat was well beyond my means.

None of the naval surplus craft were suitable, for they were all powered vessels which would require money for fuel and regular engine overhauls. Besides, they didn't have the range for what I wanted. From the very first I aimed at ocean passages. I would settle for nothing less than a five-thousand-mile range.

The scene in London was morbid. World War II had been over for years and the scars still showed, not only in the buildings, but on the faces of the people. They had taken a hammering, and the only bright thing in the air was the coronation of the new queen in June. This and the end of rationing of food and fuel, which they had suffered for the past twelve years. London was at the nadir of her fortunes, and though I have seen her several times since at times when things were supposed to be bleaker than ever, I have never seen the Londoners looking more grim than they did in the winter of 1952. That was the middle classes, of course, not the ordinary working man. He'd always had the rough end of the stick, and now he was as witty and cheerful as ever and would still stand a hearty sailor a pint in the pub, if he had a couple of shillings in his pocket.

At that time the Union Jack Club was run on the lines laid down by Florence Nightingale for the operation of British army field hospitals during the Crimean War. It was cheap, the bar was always crowded, the dining room spotless, the meals sustaining (in a very British way—boiled cabbage and steamed bacon, with rubbery fried eggs that could have decorated the walls of the Museum of Modern Art). The waitresses were dressed in a sort of pre-World War I outfit which Queen Victoria herself would have approved, and they slaved along with lowered glances, on low heels, under the eye of a female superintendent whose stern demeanor would have made the American bald eagle look like a bloody parakeet. The decor of the place was a cross between the foyer of a public bathhouse and the gentlemen's waiting room at the Winter Palace in St. Petersburg. I always thought, when entering the Union Jack Club with its mock Gothic ornamental pillars and decorative tiles à la Aubrey Beardsley, that if ever there had been a British Communist revolution led by sailors of the fleet, the first resolution of the Soldiers', Sailors', and Workers' Party of the London Soviet would have rung out from behind the potted plants of the Union Jack Club.

But British beer is too good to foment revolution, so we had to make do with concerts on a vintage piano and strings by equally vintage ladies (vintage vinegar). They all, with the exception of the violinist (who appeared to be still chained to the railings with the suffragettes), looked at us as if we had only just returned from chastising the dreadful Mr. Kruger and relieving Mafeking. The tunes they played as we sank our beer gave added strength to this impression—selections from *Bohemian Girl* and *The Witch of the Wood*. I could always tell the Welshmen in the audience;

they would stare at this trio of Saxon dragons as if they thought it would have been better to let the bloody Germans take over after all. Even Wagner would be more *musical*.

The Scotsmen were mainly recognizable by the glazed look in their eyes as they dreamed of bagpipes, haggis, and the Khyber Pass; the Irishmen, by their look of transfixion as they worshiped the three Mother Machrees on stage; the Englishmen, by the way they totally ignored the whole proceedings and played billiards as if all four other phenomena in the hall did not, could not, and never would exist.

The place was run like a prison, with the exception of the smell of urine and the porridge. The guardians of Law, Order, and Discipline carried out the letter of the *Queen's Rules and Admiralty Instructions*, making sure that while drunkenness and cleanliness went hand in hand, the least sign of affection between two of the returned heroes was clamped down on with the utmost severity. The slightest sign of liberation of any variety was pounced upon with the same horror as a cockroach caught in the kitchen. The hall porters, who looked like veterans of the Ashanti War; the kitchen staff, who appeared still to be resisting the Siege of Cawnpore; the library attendant, whose walrus mustache made him look like the bastard son of Lord Kitchener; the night-desk clerk, an ex-Indian army sergeant major, who, rumor had it, was actually Martin Bormann in disguise; plus the Holy of Holies, the Commanding Officer—all, *all,* would have descended on the offending demon like a ton of bricks. We lived in the shadow of a ghostly gibbet.

But it was somewhere for us, the Legion of the Lost Ones, to sleep and eat, so that's exactly what I did, spending the rest of the day in the friendly pubs around Kensington, or going down to Greenwich to see if I could find a boat.

On Monday Kiwi arrived, half-sozzled, wearing the most God-awful grey suit. It looked like the one Trevor Howard wore in Noel Coward's film *Brief Encounter*. But the face above it had had no brief encounter; it had had a bloody long one. And so had mine, so we went to Piccadilly, got drunk, performed a ten-shilling "short time" with the same straggly whore, then went off on the night train to Liverpool.

Back in those days, train journeys in England took much longer than they now do. The rail system was only just beginning to overcome the traumatic effect of six years of war and the nationalization which followed. From London to Liverpool, a distance of around two hundred miles, took eight hours. Since we were traveling second class on Admiralty warrants, our compartment was unheated, except by the fifty or so unwashed bodies crowded inside.

By dawn we were passing through the English northern midlands, the Black Country, as it is called. A hellish blight of smoke, soot, and grime in the green fields of England. Our legacy from a revolution which not only shook the world, but remade it. Among the great grey slag heaps, across swamps of stagnant brown water, long, dreary black rows of steelworkers' cottages oozed away over the exhausted hills into the sulphurous fog beyond. Above, in the molten steel sky of Staffordshire, towered black cumulus clouds.

Kiwi looked out of the window as the train pulled into Stoke-on-Trent. "Christ, they've got some smashing-looking women here," he murmured, eyeing the lasses on their way to the mills—those "dark, satanic mills" Blake raged against.

"Kiwi, you horny twit, is that all you can think of?" I said. "All this stinking bloody smoke around, all this hopelessness, all these people with their wasted lives, exhausted from fighting a bloody war for this? Look at them—they lost one generation on the Somme in 1916, and now they've lost half another in this last bloody lot. And look what they've got to show for it—a four-roomed house you couldn't swing a cat in for two quid a week, twelve quid for forty hours in one of those grimy supershithouses, and a few pints of beer on Saturday. No bloody wonder they vote Labour. And all you've got to say, you ignorant colonial bastard, is how pretty the women are. Of course they're bloody pretty; what else have they got?"

"Arr, you bloody Welsh are all the same, always stirring up political shit." He passed me a cigarette.

"Too bloody right, and wouldn't you? This is our country. Look what's been done to it!"

"Well, if you don't like it, what are you going to do about it?"

"Bloodywell fight to change it."

"Not a chance in hell, Tris."

"My way, there might just be!"

"What are you, the Lone Ranger?"

"No, and I ain't Oliver Twist either. And neither are a lot of those people out there."

"Labour'll ruin the country, bloody welfare state, nationalizing everything, chucking away the colonies——"

"Listen, mate, me and millions, not bloody thousands, *millions* like me never got one measly thing out of those goddamn factories, or private enterprise mines and railways, or the bleedin' Empire, but bloody starvation, misery, and flamin' war! To hell with the Empire! Give me Wales and England and Scotland for us, so we can own our own lands and make them once again what they should be!"

"Bolshevik Welsh bastard."

The train pulled into Crewe. A tall, red-faced military police monster eyed us, recognizing our Service issue suits and hating the thought we were out of his power. As we passed him Kiwi looked straight into his storm-trooper eyes.

"Thank Christ we've got a bloody navy!" he growled.

The monster, in puttees and kicking boots, glared at us.

"Go and fuck yourself," I said to his great beefy face. He staggered back in shock, then drew himself up to his full height and shouted down the platform to a policeman just emerging from the lavatory, "Constable, arrest those men!"

"On what charge, sergeant?" The bobby's voice was calm and low.

"Obscene language and insulting Her Majesty's uniform," replied the dragoon.

The constable, a fair-looking chap of around thirty, turned to us. "Is the charge correct, you two?" He looked at me.

"I never used no obscene language, mate. All I did was tell him to go and fuck himself."

"What about you?" said the copper, just barely able to stop himself from grinning.

"Well, officer," said Kiwi, "all I can say is, if that's Her Majesty's bloody uniform, I pity the bloke she's married to, 'cos he'll have a bloody hard time in bed! If that's her uniform she must be built like a brick shithouse!"

The policeman nodded at the stationmaster's office. "I think you two had better come along with me." He turned to the red-capped beetle-crusher. "I'll take these two along and question them. I'll see you for any evidence later, sergeant."

"Right," said the sergeant, huffing and glaring at us. He snapped his beady, piglike eyes around the platform, searching for other victims among the hundred or so uniformed men alighting from the train. The bobby walked along with us for twenty yards or so, then said in a low tone, "Andrew, eh?"

"Yeah."

"What depot?"

"Chatham."

"Chatty Chats. I was Portsmouth meself, destroyers, came out in '46."

"You did the right thing, mate," said I.

"Yes, I sometimes wonder, though. Now look, you two, sod off as soon as we turn the corner."

"How are we going to get to Liverpool?" I asked the grinning rozzer.

"Buggered if I know. Take the bus. I'm letting you go because that MP back there is a right bastard and I can't stand him. But if I see you again, it won't be Liverpool for you two, it'll be bloody Chester Prison."

"O.K., wings, thanks a lot. We'll have a pint for you when we get to the 'Pool."

"Right, Jack, right, mate, now piss off—"

"Christ, we got out of that one," I said.

"Only one snag, Tris—the bloody sea bags!"

"Oh, Jesus!"

Kiwi grinned. "Ah, well, it was good while it lasted. Right, there's a bus over there. Liverpool, here we come!"

We clambered onboard with all we had in the world on our backs. As we settled into our seats, Kiwi murmured, "Well, Tristan, me old mate, there's one thing."

"What's that?"

"It's either ship out or the bleeding Salvation Army."

"Don't talk to me about bloody armies!"

"Right, not if they've got bastards like that one back there in 'em.

The bus rolled off. "How d'ye feel now, Kiwi?" I said.

"I'm dying for a bloody pint, mate!"

I grinned; we were free at last. And my back didn't hurt anymore.

Now, gather round you sailor boys
And listen to my plea,
For when you've heard my tale you'll pity me,
I was a goddamn fool in the port of Liverpool
The first time that I came home from sea.

I was paid off with my share
Off a ship from God knows where,
Five pound ten a month was all my pay,
With a whisky and a gin I was very soon taken in,
By a little girl whose name was Maggie May.

How well do I remember when I first met Maggie May,
She was cruising up and down in Canning Place,
Her figure was divine, like a frigate of the Line,
And me bein' a sailor I gave chase.

Next morning I awoke, bleary-eyed and stony broke,
No shoes, no pants, no waistcoat could I find,
When I asked her where they were
She replied, "My dear young sir,
They're down in Paddy's market, number nine."

To the market I did go, no clothes there could I find,
So the bobbies came and took poor Mag away,
The judge then guilty found her,
For robbin' a homeward bounder,
An' little Maggie's down in Botany Bay!

Chorus: Oh Maggie, Maggie May, they have taken her away,
        And never more round Lime Street will she roam,
        She robbed so many sailors and captains of the whalers,
        Now poor old Maggie never will come home!

> Liverpool merchant seaman's song, origi-
> nally nineteenth century.
> A "pulley-hauley" shanty, sung when the
> longboat falls were heaved in.

# 3

## Entertaining the Ladies

Comparing London to Liverpool is like comparing Monte Carlo to Pittsburgh, Pennsylvania. Not that I'm for one or opposed to the other. It's just that one is for the eyes and nose, while the other is for the ears and the heart.

Liverpool is like a small New York, only much, much kinder. The biting wit of the people on the street is the same, with its dislike of pomposity and bullshit, and so is the attitude to government, except that, as far as I can see, corruption is better hidden in Liverpool. The friendliness, too, is a bit less offhanded than in New York. New Yorkers are better at hiding their personal feelings toward a stranger than are Liverpudlians, but not as good at masking their public feelings.

London reflects the outer Britain, the country which the prating pedlars of propaganda would have us believe is the United Kingdom. It is the city of Covent Garden Theatre and the Ballet Rambert and red-coated, black-busbied Guardsmen standing at the gates of "Buck House." The city of the military mustache and the bowler hat, the umbrella and the briefcase, Hampstead Heath and pale blue gentility.

Liverpool, on the other hand, is the real center of industrial Britain, where the heartstrings of England, Ireland, Scotland, and Wales all join together. If London is the capital of the Normans, then Liverpool is the capital of the

19

Celt and the Saxon. If the umbrella is the symbol of London, then that of Liverpool is the wheelbarrow. London has its nose in the air, Liverpool has its in a pint of beer.

Kiwi and I pulled in on the train. The terminal, down by the docks, under the shadow of the great brick-pile Liver Buildings, was abustle with seamen from all over the world, shoppers coming in from the country and from over the River Mersey, Irish and Welsh coming in from the west, Scots heading through from the north.

"Tris," said Kiwi, as we headed for the nearest pub, "do you think the Liver bird will shit today?" He looked up at the two carved stone birds perched atop the twin towers of the huge Dock Authority building. The legend in Liverpool is that every time a virgin passes, one of the birds shits.

"If the Irish boats come in, I wouldn't be at all surprised."

"Never had your end away in Ireland, then?"

"Yeah, but her wig fell off."

"How come?"

"She was too busy telling her rosary beads to hold it on."

We entered the pub. There was none of your London nonsense here, no red-plushed seats and cut-glass chandeliers, nor carpets. Just a plain wooden bar, two dartboards, and sawdust on the floor.

"What'll we do, Kiwi?" I asked, after the third pint.

"We'll have to hang about until tomorrow. The shipping office is closed in the afternoons, the recruiting side anyway. They don't want to take chances of getting a load of pissy-assed seamen in there when the pubs shut at three. The best thing we can do is get a night's lodging. We shouldn't go to the Seamen's Institute, though."

"Why not?"

"Jesus, it makes Portsmouth Barracks look like the Strand Palace Hotel."

"Where do we go, then?"

"We wait till the pubs shuts at three, then hop over to the Mersey Ferry. The bar on the boat is open all day, so we ride over and back a few times, have a couple of pints, then at opening time, nip ashore on the other side, find a good pub, and ask around."

"Sounds good to me. Game of darts?"

"Right, you're on."

And so it was, and by the time we did alight from the Mersey Ferry, we were three sheets in the wind, about ten pints each under our belts. It was a bit shaky, playing darts on the ferry. Every time a tug or a big steamer passed by, the boat would roll, and then we would demonstrate true skill, aiming for double-twenty at the top of each lurch and winding up with a treble six or even a bull's-eye.

As we landed on the Wallasey side, I said to Kiwi, "You know, my old man brought the first roller-skating rink ever landed in Britain, back in 1924. He brought it from Australia in his ship."

"What happened?"

"He did pretty well for a year or so, then the slump came and he went bust. No one could afford the three-pence-a-go any more."

"Where was that, Tris?"

"New Brighton, just along the road a few miles. Why don't we go there? It's a sort of seaside holiday resort."

"Won't be much there now. Season's over."

"Not in New Brighton. There's always a good crowd in the pubs, and plenty of crumpet at the New Brighton Palace Dance Hall. That's where my old man had the rink."

"O.K., you're on," he said, and we headed for the green double-decker bus.

By the time we'd had a few in the local pubs, it was time to find lodgings. I signaled to the landlord, a small, rotund, friendly fellow.

"Know anywhere we can doss for a few days, guv?"

"Seamen?" he asked, sizing us up.

"Sort of; R.N.——" The navy was very popular in Liverpool.

"Oh, right, Jack. Yeah, there's a place just around the corner, nice and clean, good meals. Tell Aggie I sent you."

"Ta, guv, see you later."

"You'd better hurry. Closing time at ten-thirty."

Aggie turned out to be an aged treasure, spotlessly pina-
fored, rosy cheeked, eyes asparkle. Before we knew it we
were signed up and settled in. "If you hurry, I can get you
in for the last sitting at supper, love," she said. We spruced
ourselves up as best the beer under our belts would allow,
turned our jerseys around to show the clean side, and
headed for the dining hall. Once there, we were in for a
surprise. The place was crammed with old ladies, none of
them looking a day under eighty. It was an old folks' home!
There were about twelve of them, all sitting around the
open fireplace, some knitting, some chatting in low, sweet
voices. As Kiwi and I scoffed down the tucker, well cooked
and plentiful, for which we were paying twelve shillings a
day (one dollar, at today's rate), a couple of the old ladies
eyed us, smiling.

"D'you play the piano, Tris?" Kiwi said to me. "You're a
Welshman. All Welshmen play the piano."

"Well, of course I learned. I was never very good at it and
that's years ago. Couldn't get much practice in bloody
destroyers, now could I?"

He turned and pointed his spoon. "Well, there's one over
there."

"O.K.," I said, standing up and walking over toward the
wall. "Do you ladies mind if I have a go at the piano?"

They all smiled sweetly. One, more lively than the rest,
said, "Oh, no, by all means do, we shall be delighted.
Ladies, I've had a word with Agnes and she tells me that
these two young men have just retired from our brave
navy."

The old dears sighed and twittered.

"But you must first introduce yourselves, and as we've
no one to do it for us, I'll introduce myself—Mrs. Rosina
Steele, widow of dear Captain Steele." Then she went on to
introduce all the rest, whose names, though not their faces,

escape me now, twenty-five years later.

The piano turned out to be a pianola, a sort of phony piano into which you insert a roll of paper, with holes punched, like a computer program. When you pump with your feet, the air from the bellows inside the machine blows through the holes and makes a sound resembling music. At the side of the pianola was a large basket crammed with paper rolls. I grabbed the nearest one, inserted it into the roller-holder, and started playing. As the notes came flowing out, Kiwi's face was a picture of startled desperation. It was "Selections from *Bohemian Girl*"—the same music we had escaped from in the Union Jack Club, back in London. Awful, terrible, sentimental, sloppy tripe.

Kiwi, standing at my shoulder, whispered, "Jesus H. Christ!" The little old ladies were sitting entranced, listening to the music of their youth, when they had been beautiful in a different way, listening to the music they had danced to with their sailor lovers just back from the sea. The dreams in their faces were tangible. Even a rough bastard like me didn't have the heart to stop, so I pedaled away while the paper-music slowly rolled itself out and the clock ticked away inexorably over the potted plants, towards pub-closing time. When the tune finally came to a grinding, wheezy halt, the clock stood at five minutes before pub-closing.

I jumped up and shut the lid. The ladies clapped and sighed. Kiwi edged for the door. "Thank you so much, Mr. Jones," said Mrs. Steele, grasping my hand. "You have made such a welcome change to our evening. We are so grateful indeed to you. Now may we offer you some tea and cake before you go to bed?"

"Highly honored, ma'am," I replied, "but we have to make a very urgent telephone call to London."

"Oh, really? It must be naval business, I'm sure."

"Yes, ma'am, an extremely urgent *intelligence* call."

"Something to do with those dreadful Russians, I

shouldn't wonder," said Mrs. Steele, addressing the company in general. All the ladies put on suitable expressions of alarm.

"No, ma'am, not this time." I leaned closer to her ear and whispered, "Albanians."

"Oh, dear, how very exciting. Well, off you go and do your duty, dear Mr. Jones, and don't forget, I want a word with you tomorrow."

"Thank you, ma'am, and good night, ladies."

"Good night, God bless you," they all echoed, as the aspidistra plants in the hall quivered at our hasty passing.

As I followed Kiwi through the cut-glass-windowed door, I distinctly heard Mrs. Steele say to the others, "Our dear, brave navy—they never sleep, you know!"

Outside, haring round the corner to the pub with just two minutes to go to closing time, Kiwi turned to me and murmured "Bloody *Bohemian Girl*, fucking Albanians—where in Christ's name do you get it from, Tris?"

"From the circumstances, Kiwi—two pints, best bitter, please!"

"Sorry, sir," said the blowsy barmaid, "we've just rung Time Gentlemen Please."

"Holy Shit!" whispered Kiwi.

"Well, Kiwi, you got the women and song, what more do you want?"

"Ahh, let's turn in," he said. "We've to be at the Seaman's Pool tomorrow, early!"

Sadly we turned our steps towards the door of the old ladies' home.

*Oh, the sun is on the harbor wall,*
*We must away to sea;*
*It's not the leavin' of Liverpool that grieves me,*
*But me darlin' when I think of thee.*

*So fare thee well, my own true love,*
*When I return united we shall be;*
*It's not the leavin' of Liverpool that grieves me,*
*But me darlin' when I think of thee.*

> Old capstan shanty, eighteenth century,
> early nineteenth—it also survives, changed
> somewhat, as an American folk song.

# 4

## *Faith, Hope, and—Luck!*

The scene in the Merchant Marine recruiting office next day was something like a proletarian United Nations meeting. There were about five hundred men all jammed into the assembly room, with its green paint peeling up to shoulder level, as if it had been blistered by the colorful appearance of all the men who had passed through in the last fifty years. There were Lascars from the West Coast of India who walked as if they were climbing a ship's ladder, small, black men, with violinists' faces and long (for those years) hair. There were blue black, lithe, and handsome Somalis from the desert coast of Northeast Africa, standing like painted ibis birds on the fringes of the floor. Arabs from the Yemen, good seamen, nothing like the people I had encountered in their poor, dry land. Laughing Chinese from Hong Kong and Macao, cooks and stewards to a man, who could make a living out of what even a Liverpool stoker would throw away. There were big, hefty, black tribesmen from the Gold Coast and Nigeria, their tribal scars cut on their cheeks in neat, curious patterns; small, fat, worried-looking Maltese, talking their strange mixture of Italian, Arab, and English; hungry-eyed Cypriots; big, jolly mulattoes from the West Indies; and seamen from the underdeveloped countries of the West—Irish, Scots, Welsh, and Norwegians, and a combination of all of these, the "Scousers," as the Liverpool sailors are called around the sea world. They all accepted the presence of the others with mutual respect and good humor. No prison-yard or dole-office scowls here. These were seamen. They had only one enemy—the sea.

As we went into the assembly room, we were handed cards with numbers and had to wait until our number was called before going into the signing-on office and passing the medical examination for tuberculosis and VD, plus sundry other ailments to which merchant seamen are prone, not the least being, in the case of non-Moslems, drunkenness.

After about an hour's wait Kiwi went in. Moments later he was back out again. "O.K., Tris, I'm in," he said.

The signing-on official sat at a desk, a burly, jovial man in the blue uniform of the Harbor Authority.

"Name?" he asked. I told him.

"Discharge papers?" I handed them over. He looked through them, scanning each line, grunting with approval. Coming to the third page, he looked up and said, "Mmm, looks alright. Can you be onboard tomorrow afternoon?"

"Sure, tomorrow morning if you like."

"Right." He turned the last page, then sighed and looked up at me again.

"Sorry about this, chum. We can't take you on. You've a medical discharge from the navy. Look, it says 'Discharged Physically Unfit for Sea-Duties.'"

"But I'm almost recovered now. I've even started running in the mornings."

"Sorry, my friend, it's impossible."

"Look, I'll even sign on as galley hand or steward."

"I know it's hard on you, old son, but we can't take the risk. The insurers wouldn't wear it, and we can't have uninsured crew onboard—it's against Seamen's Union regulations. Sorry, mate, there just isn't a damned thing I can do about it. During the war it was different—then we'd take anyone we could get—but now——"

"O.K., well, thanks anyway. Don't worry, I expect I can find a berth ashore somewhere." I tried to grin.

"I hope you do," he said, standing up. "And jolly good luck."

"Thanks." I left his office feeling as if the world had caved in. As I walked out Kiwi offered me a cigarette. "How'd it go, mate?"

"I've had it, Kiwi; they won't take naval DW's [Discharged Woundeds]."

"Oh, f'chrissake."

"Never you mind, mate, you carry on. I'll find something, don't fear. Anyway, I've still more of a hankering for small craft than those bloody lumbering tin factories."

"Let's go and get a pint." He looked at his watch. "Ten minutes to opening time."

And so we went and sank another five gallons of Tetley's finest ale in the pub and another on the ferryboat back across the Mersey. I found myself wondering if this was to be my last sea trip, but as I looked out of the ferry windows on the fifth trip across and saw beyond the river mouth the Irish Sea stretching away into the distance, I knew it wasn't going to be, not by a long chalk.

When we finally arrived back in the Old Ladies' Rest Home, we both had quite a load on, but nevertheless managed to sink a good meal and give the ladies a rendering of selections from *The Pirates of Penzance*.

After the performance, Mrs. Steele came over to me.

"Well done, Mr. Jones, but you have been naughty because I did ask you to come and see me today for a chat. But never mind, talk with me tomorrow. My son is coming over from Holland to visit me, and you must join us for tea. Your friend will be gone to his ship by then, and I don't want you sitting here alone amongst all the ladies."

"Thank you, Mrs. Steele. I'll be delighted to."

Off we went, first round to the pub for a last pair of pints, then up to bed.

In the morning we slept late, then, after lunch, Kiwi took off to buy some seagoing gear over in Scotland Road, near the docks, and I bought him a last pint around the corner before he left.

"Cheers, Tris. I know you'll make out. You always did. But if you find it hard going, hang on here and I'll fix you up when I get back."

"Oh, sod off, Kiwi—I'd rather dig bloody graves."

"Right, old son, well, so long, see you again!" (And I did see him again, seventeen years later. It was in Bermuda; he was chief bosun's mate, still with the White Star Line, and I was the skipper of *Barbara*, bound on a forty-thousand-mile voyage.)

But this was all in the future, and at the time he left me in New Brighton, I thought I'd still be there when his ship returned.

At teatime, spruced up in a new shirt and navy tie, I joined Mrs. Steele and her son in the dining room for tea.

"Mr. Jones, may I present my son, Duncan? Duncan, Mr. Tristan Jones."

It was to be the first of many, many fateful meetings with people, in all kinds of circumstances all over the face of the world. Meetings which at first did not seem to signify anything, but which, in retrospect, the presence of some guiding hand, call it God or what you will, was startlingly clear.

"Pleased to meet you, Duncan. Work round here?"

"No, actually." His tone was educated, clipped and precise, just like his mother's. "Actually, I work in Holland. I'm over there on an exchange of information on the steel building of small craft. You see I work for Cammel Lairds, the shipbuilders over here in Birkenhead. The Jerries pinched all the Dutch timber, and you know they've lost, or are rapidly losing, the Dutch East Indies——"

"Yes, new country. What do they call it . . . Indonesia?"

"That's right. Well, the Dutch have taken to building small craft—work boats, harbor ferries in steel; even yachts."

"Yachts?" I was all ears.

"Yes, and they're getting quite good at it, too. Once you get down below on most of them, you'd never dream they were built of steel, all paneled out with Nigerian mahogany. Their galleys are a wonder, too."

"Where do they sell them, in Holland?"

"A lot, yes, but many go abroad, to the West Indies and the States and quite a few to South America." He puffed at his pipe.

I was getting more and more curious. Small craft! "And how do they get them out to South America?"

"Some are shipped out, but others are sailed out. You see the Rio businessman looks upon it as a great status symbol if he has a yacht which has crossed the Atlantic."

"How big are these yachts?"

"Oh, anything up to eighty feet long."

"Sail or power?"

"Both, but of course the ones which cross over under their own steam, so to speak, those are all sail."

"Really—and who takes them over?"

"Delivery crews. They join the yacht in Holland, sail her over, then either fly back or bring back another yacht, say from the States or the West Indies. The only snag is finding crews. The big cargo ships pay much better, and of course the usual sailing yachtsman simply hasn't the time to go off on a trip that long."

"Mr. Steele, if I come over to Holland, will you help me get in touch with these yacht builders?"

"Why, d'you want to buy one?" he smiled.

"No, I want to sail one, or two, or three."

I then went on to tell him my story about how I had studied navigation in the navy on my off-watch periods, and seamanship; about how I had been involved in Medfoba, which was the original name given to what is now the Outward Bound organization, formed to get young, big-ship seamen interested in sailing small craft just for the fun of it; and about how I was hoping to buy my own craft one day and make my own voyages. Both he and Mrs. Steele listened intently. When I finished, Mrs. Steele spoke up.

"Now, Duncan, you must help this man. You know your father went to sea in sailing ships from 1875 on, until those dreadful Germans started their silly war. Before he died he told me, dear old thing, that the Age of Sail is not dead. And we need this man, and others like him, others who may follow him, to bring back sail and sailors to Liverpool and all those other ports that your dear father took me to so long ago."

"Yes, I will, by Jove, of course I will. When you come over, look me up in Leiden and I will make sure my Dutch friends fix you up. Here's my address; I'll be there in two weeks' time. Do you need anything for fares? You can pay me back when you're working."

"No, thank you very much, I can manage fine. Yes, by gum, I'll see you as soon as I get over there, which will be right after you are!"

"Now, my dear Mr. Jones, look, your tea is cold. Let me pour you some more, then perhaps you'd like to play Duncan and me a little tune on the pianola?" Mrs. Steele gently touched my arm.

"Certainly, ma'am." *A little tune?* I'd have played them the bloody *Hallelujah Chorus* and the *1812 Overture* together, the way I was feeling!

And that is how I made my first real contact with the yachting world, with the builders and the sailors. That is how I was able to learn a mine of knowledge about sailing craft and the way to run them, during eight transatlantic voyages, a complete circumnavigation of South America and a circumnavigation of the world.

By 1958 I had saved enough money, together with my still untouched naval discharge money and pension over the five years, to look for a vessel suitable for carrying out a voyage I had long had in mind. To take a sailing-boat nearer to the North Pole than anyone else had ever done! Even to try to cross right over the Arctic Ocean!

Now I had sufficient money to find and fit out a hull, plus the experience to do the fitting out properly, and the determination to tackle the voyage. And this I would have to do completely alone.

Mrs. Steele died while I was at sea, in October 1954.

To the memory of her and of her husband, and to her son, this book is dedicated, for it shows how I managed to live long enough to see their dream start to come true.

*Now you take the paint brush*
*And I'll take the paint pot;*
*And we'll paint the Ship's Side together;*
*When Jimmy comes along, we will sing our little song;*
*Thank Christ we didn't join forever!*

Royal Navy traditional song,
"Jimmy" is slang
for a first lieutenant.

# 5

## Master and Mate: 1958

In August 1958, I left the yacht *Slot van Kappel* in Lisbon, after a hard and fast passage of almost two years around the world. The two co-owners were set on a leisurely cruise up along the Spanish and French coasts before returning to England and selling the boat. I had no time to waste, because on passing Antigua I had had an extrasensory message, as well as a dream, that my old skipper, Tansy Lee, was fast sinking. It was not surprising, as he had been born in 1860. He had been steadily at sea since 1872, under sail the whole time, except for a spell during World War II when he'd gone to sea in an armed trawler at the age of eighty, as he said, "to 'ave anovver go at them bloody 'Uns."

I had joined him in 1938, at the age of fourteen, in his old boomie sailing ketch *Second Apprentice*, knocking around the North Sea and the English Channel in coastal and Continental trade—coal to Cherbourg, fodder to Ramsgate, scrap iron to Germany, ballast to Hull. Rates were low, pay was a pittance, hours were long and arduous, but the food and the ways of sail were abundant, tasty, and well digested. Tansy was the skipper; I was his crew.

Tansy himself had gone to sea first at the age of twelve, with his father in "the Trade," as cross-channel smuggling was then known. But when he reached the ripe age of fifteen, his family "caught religion," and so Tansy was put into the Royal Navy. That would have been around 1875.

His first ship was a revenue cutter patrolling the rough Channel, flushing out Tansy's recent colleagues in all weathers. His tales were fascinating. They had worn tarred straw hats and cutlasses; once a week the crew had assembled to witness floggings. Indeed, some of the men that Tansy sailed with in the Revenue Service had themselves served their apprenticeships with men who had fought with Admiral Nelson at the Battle of Trafalgar in 1805. Tansy had gone on to sail with the navy all over the world: in the Ashanti Wars, in the antislave service on the east coast of Africa, and in the Boer War. During World War I, he was recalled into the Royal Navy for service on Q-boats, old sailing vessels fitted with six-inch guns hidden in the hold. After surfacing, a German sub would order the Q-boat crew to abandon ship. The crew would fake a panic over the side, then, when the gunner had the U-boat's range weighed off, down would fall the bulwarks, bang would go the guns, and glug-glug would go Jerry.

After his discharge from the navy, Tansy took over the family boat, an eighty-five-foot boomie ketch. When his brothers passed away, he continued to ply cargo while sail faded away and died in ignominy the world over. By 1938 there were only a dozen sailing vessels at work around the British Isles. The art was kept alive by a few elderly hardnuts like Tansy Lee and Bob Roberts, who persisted in the Trade until the late 1960s.

I had always been conscious that I was a direct link between the past centuries of sail-in-trade and the future, when sail will come into its own again. I can't wait for the oil wells to run dry, for the last gob of black, sticky muck to come oozing out of some remote well. Then the glory of sail will return. It may be unrecognizable, compared to the clouds of canvas which used to scud the seas, but sail it will be, computerized or not. Again we will use the winds of God and bend them to man's will. Again the needs of sail will dictate a grace and beauty to the hulls which has not been seen in ship design for almost a century, and we shall look back on the ugly slabs of hacked power which now so arrogantly force the seas and thank the Lord himself that the last one is headed for the breaker's yard. Merchant seamen will eye their vessels with love and pride, as they once did, instead of thinking of them as mobile factories. I hope I live long enough to see that day.

But on the train down from London to Sandwich, back in 1958, I had little inkling of all this. All I knew was that I must make my voyage. Sail it would be because it never occurred to me to do it any other way. The Arctic it would be because most of my heroes had left their marks there: Davis, Hudson, Cook, Bering, Shannon, Amundsen, Norden, Peary, Nansen . . . Nansen! *Nansen* and the *Fram*! I would try to do as well as the *Fram*. I would never be able to do as well as Nansen, because with my education I would never be able to write about it, or to get the flavor of adventure, pure and simple, through anyone else's skull, through their bloodstream and bones, into the fibers of their being, as Nansen had done. I would never be able to learn, as he had done, that true humanity, true charity, can only come to a man through real effort and endeavor against the impossible.

Physically by this time, at the age of thirty-four, I was in excellent condition after six years under sail in all conditions of weather and welfare. Mentally, I was shaping up. I was extremely pragmatic, almost to the point of short-sightedness; very curious about every and all things, though not yet very observant about people and their nature, as I would become later. If I had great faults, they were that I thought I knew more than I did and that I didn't suffer fools gladly. I was still impetuous in most things, where later I would find that one should be choosy about what one is impetuous about. I was, to use the sailor's phrase, "full of piss and vinegar."

As the train chugged through the apple orchards of Kent, my mind was intent on finding a suitable vessel. If possible, she would be somewhere near one of the Royal Dockyards.

There, through the grapevine of ex-sailors, I would be able to get hold of good cheap gear. I had now fourteen hundred pounds (three thousand dollars) saved up. That should be enough to find a craft, furbish her for a five-year cruise, and victual me without too much strain.

I took the one and only taxi in town to Tansy's cottage, about a two-mile hike in the glorious English autumn—apples on the trees and sweet wildflowers by the lane's edges—through a countryside so rich that even the cows looked as if they owned the land they grazed upon. The ancient taxi wheezed out of the neat, tidy, spoon-fed Borough of Sandwich, once one of the ancient Cinque Ports of medieval times, but now stranded some miles inland through centuries of silt deposits. Through villages and hamlets as old as man's delight in the taste of a pint of ale, through the weft and warp of England, the taxi trundled. Past gnarled oak trees forged by the forceful Channel breezes as they blew eternally eastward from the Celtic Sea, bringing their lilting chant to the green-topped cliffs and gently rolling downs; past the swinging rings of creaking inn-signs, worn away through untold lives—the Iron Duke, the Royal Oak, the Sailor's Return . . . .

Tansy's cottage was like Tansy. It managed to glower and grin at the same time. Low, with a steep thatched-straw roof and whitewashed walls, the bedroom curtains drawn at the shady orchard end, it looked, as he so often did, as if it were blind yet all-seeing. The weatherworn brick path from the green wicker gate was so eggshell delicate it seemed it would crack under the weight of a sailor's sea bag. An empty swing dangled expectantly. The old wooden door had a rope's-end served into a back-splice, with a Turk's-head knotted into it so shipshape you would think it had grown that way. That was the knocker. So I knocked.

Tansy's niece, Daisy, opened the door, but not in the cheerful way she had done on my previous visits. Her rosy smile was a sorrowful frown. She grabbed my arm.

"'Lo, Daisy, what's up?"

"Oh, Tristan, he's gone——" She burst into tears. I put my arm around her shoulder.

"Come on, love, where's Bogey?" This was her husband.

"Out fishing, but he'll be in any moment." She sniffed, then said with a gallant attempt at a smile, "But come in, Tris, I'll make a pot of tea. And there's some cake if you'd like. You must be famished."

"Thanks, Daisy. Yes, I am a bit, but let me do it for you."

"No, don't be silly, I'm all right." She walked into the kitchen, just beyond the tiny, cluttered living room, with its flowery wallpaper, shiny piano, and best-china-bedecked dresser in the corner. A stern photograph of King Edward VII glared down imperiously from one side of the chimney, while Queen Alexandra did her royal best not to look frightened from the other. A coronation mug, where Tansy had kept shillings for the gas meter, stood at one end of the mantel shelf, with a Peek Frean's biscuit tin, where he kept his half-crowns for his daily outing down to the pub, in the middle. At the far end was a small china statue of a little lad eating a bunch of grapes, only his arm and the grapes had been knocked off years ago.

As Daisy tinkered with the tea tray in the kitchen, I studied the pictures on the walls. Tansy's dad, looking like the wrath of Jehovah in the center of a group of lifeboat-men, stood next to the Ramsgate rescue craft. They all looked stolidly intrepid, except for one, a rather small, mustachioed chap in the front row, to starboard, who looked half-crocked. The caption said, "Ramsgate Lifeboat Crew 1872—ready, aye, ready."

On another wall was a picture of Tansy as an able seaman on the West Coast of Africa during the Ashanti wars. Tansy and his mate wore pith helmets and white neckerchiefs, like the Foreign Legion used to, bandoliers across their shoulders, Lee-Enfield 303 rifles, with cutlasses slung from their belts. The Ashanti tribesmen in the picture looked fierce.

Just as Daisy trotted in with the tea, there was a rustling under the table. Tansy's old Labrador dog, Nelson, looked at me through his one good eye. He hopped over on three legs and nuzzled my leg. By now he was at least twelve years old and wise in the ways of the world. His tail wagged, but it looked like the black feathers on a funeral horse. I patted him. Nelson sighed.

"When did he go, Daisy?"

"Last week. We put him away three days ago."

"Where?"

"The Baptist Chapel. He couldn't stand parsons. He wanted to be buried behind the Royal Oak pub, but you know how folks are, so we settled for the Baptists. I mean, they're not the same, are they?"

"No, I suppose not. A bit more easygoing, like, I'd say, Dais."

"Anyway, all his old chums came for the funeral. You should have seen it, Tristan. Some of the old boys could hardly walk. At least not until they got the darts out in the pub. Tansy had left twenty pounds for beer money. Well, they got through that within an hour of opening time. Old Shiner Wright, the landlord, reckoned it was the best day's business he'd done in years."

"Bully for him. Was there free booze?"

"Yes, three free pints all around. The old boys, by the time they'd got that lot down, as well as the twenty quid's worth, couldn't think what it was all about. I swear some of them thought it was Coronation Day."

"Tansy would have loved that, Daisy. Right up his street."

Daisy poured another cup of tea and cut another slice of Dundee cake.

"What will you and Bogey do now, Dais? Will you keep this place running, or what?"

"I don't know yet. There's an editor fellow down from London wants to buy it."

"What's he like?"

"Funny little cove, effeminate-like. Bogey says he sits down when he goes for a pee." She giggled.

"Ah, well, lass, that's the way it goes!"

"Yes, and Tansy said he wanted you to have Nelson."

"Nelson? What am I going to do with him? Look, girl, I'm going to be knocking around looking for a boat, and then I want to do some serious cruising. Hell, it's going to be hard enough for me, without some lame old mutt traipsing around after me."

Nelson knew we were talking about him. He looked at me with an eye so pitiful it would have melted the heart of Attila the Hun.

"Can't you take him?" I asked her.

"We've already got two, and with the baby on the way. . . ." Nelson stood looking at her, his tail brushing my foot.

"Oh, Jesus Christ, Daisy. Well, all right then, but I can't see me taking a bloomin' cripple to sea. One's bad enough, but with two——" I fondled Nelson's head and he fairly jumped for joy, putting his one front paw on my lap.

"Now cut that out, yer black bugger, behave yourself!" He dropped to the floor, all ears, wet nose, and attention.

Just then Bogey came in, bobble cap, ginger hair, eyes like the summer sky, seaboots and sweater, and a great sack of flounder under his arm. We sat by the fire yarning and drinking tea, eyeing the grandfather clock for pub-opening time. Just before dusk, off we went to the Royal Oak, Daisy, Bogey, Nelson, and me, to talk of times with Tansy at an ancient wooden table in the garden, while the sweet, quiet English evening folded itself into a parcel of dreams, leaving light caught in the leaves of trees and streaming with cheery sounds through the backdoor of the Royal Oak. And though we laughed at tales of Tansy, we silently wept in our hearts for the passing of a good man.

*My father was the keeper of the Eddystone Light*
*And he loved a mermaid one fine night,*
*The result of the union were offspring three,*
*A dolphin and a porpoise and the other was me!*
Oh, Ho! *the wind blows free,*
*Oh, for a life on the* rolling *sea*!

From a traditional English Channel song.

# 6

## *God Helps Those What Helps Themselves!*

I stayed with Daisy and Bogey Knight for the next two days, Monday and Tuesday. Bogey, like most Channel fishermen, did not go out on Mondays and Fridays because of old superstitions. He and I sat around in his living room in the morning until opening time, then, with Daisy's blessing, for she was pleased to have Bogey's great frame out of the way while she prepared lunch, we adjourned to the Royal Oak. Two pints of ale and a game of darts, then back to the cottage for cold cuts from Sunday's dinner, with applesauce, for it had been pork this week, all washed down with a great jeroboam of "scrumpy," as rough cider is called in those parts.

Old Tansy had never installed running water. As we ate I could see beyond the kitchen door, with its rusty horseshoe. There was a whitewashed wall streaming with sunlight, and on it the shadow cast by Tansy's well-water-bucket yoke, and there were deep grooves worn by the bucket chains as he, and his father before him, and *his* father before *him*, had restowed the yoke. There was a small window above the stone sink, and I could see the tips of mint leaves growing outside, nourished by the sink drain, which emptied straight into the garden soil.

"What will you do now, Tristan, old son?" said Bogey.

"I'm looking for a boat. I want to have a shot at making a different cruise."

"Not much round here, all fishin' boats. No sail left, except for a few old yachts, an' like I was sayin', most of them are survivors from Dunkirk." He warmed his under-shirt by the open fire.

"I thought I'd have a look around Sheerness, Bogey. There's this advertisement for an ex-R.N.L.I. [Royal National Lifeboat Institution] hull up there, and I think I'll go and see if I can do anything with her. The price is reasonable enough—four hundred quid [a thousand dollars in those days]—and it'll leave me with a tidy sum to fit her out, if she's any good."

"When was she built?"

"It says 1908."

"Should be good then. Is she one of those beach-launched boats?"

"I think she must be, Bogey. It says thirty-four feet. Must be a Watson design."

"Should make a good conversion, 'cos in those days they were building hulls like bloody cathedrals with the finest wood ever brought into U.K."

"It's not a cathedral I want, Bogey, just the flamin' parsonage'll do."

And so it was that next day Nelson, my sea bag, and I caught the early morning train to Tunbridge and Sheerness, with me wearily wondering how much wandering I was in for before I found a boat. Nelson got stroppy with every male dog coming in sight and handsomely gallant with every bitch, making all the old ladies on their way to Tunbridge market nervous and sharp. As soon as the compartment was clear, I gave him a belt over the ear. "Pipe down, you randy old bastard."

By late afternoon we were in Sheerness, for distances in England are only great in time and memories, not in miles. Shortly, we were at the back of a boatyard looking at a hull, all thirty-four abandoned feet of her. I often wondered afterwards if we looked at her or if she looked at us. She seemed an even sorrier sight than Nelson with his one eye and three legs or me after three days of knocking back the bevvys with Bogey. The dirty grey paint on her sides was peeling off, and she was covered by an even dirtier tarpaulin, tattered and oily, which had been played upon by every wind in southeast England for the past decade. Grabbing a ladder, I propped it against the boat's side and lifted the rotting canvas cover. Inside the bottom of the boat was a two-foot-deep pool of black, stagnant rainwater, with a botanical display around the edges that would do justice to Kew Gardens. Minnows jumped, frogs croaked, and a rat rustled into safer hiding.

I hopped inside the hull. Out with the knife; quick poke around into the double-diagonal planking underwater. Vicious shove into half a dozen frames. "Mahogany . . . oak . . . mmm."

I sloshed my way aft, poking and prodding. Back out, I shinned down the ladder and checked the garboard and the deadwood aft. All sound. I stood back to study her. She had the classic lines of a lifeboat, with a whaleback cuddy fore and aft. Her original short stubby masts and oarlocks were still in her. She was narrow in the beam, only seven feet, but she was built like a tank. Her keel was as straight as a die, and under the filthy paint her West African mahogany was as good as a Steinway grand piano—a good inch and a half thick!

Her rounded hull was fitted with two long but shallow galvanized-steel bilge keels. She would need ballasting internally and even then she would not be able to carry much sail. But in the strong Arctic winds she wouldn't need much sail. The watertight bulkheads fore and aft were still sound, and there was room for a good twelve-foot cabin amidships and eight feet to spare for the cockpit—nice and roomy.

Nelson emerged from sniffing the keel. I looked at him. "Nelson, old son, I think we've got ourselves a boat." He looked at me, then at the boat, moving his tail as if to say,

"Well, I hope to Christ you know what you're doing."

Then the owner arrived, a worker at the Royal Dockyard, which was, at that time, in the process of closing down. After introducing himself, he said, "Make a good fishin' boat. She'll take any amount of power in that hull."

"Yeah, but all I want is a boat for messing around in. Like on weekends, you know, trips up the Thames and all that, take the bird out for a jaunt. I like the hull, but the price is a bit steep for me."

"Well, seeing as how it looks like she'll go to a good home, how about 350 nikker?"

"Three hundred?"

"I'll tell you what, you being ex-R.N. and all, I'll let her go for 325."

"Right, you're on." I shook the slight little man's hand and the deal was concluded.

Next day I went into Chatham and bought a surplus Army tent, pumped out and cleaned the inside of the boat, set up the tent inside the hull, and there we were, in residence. Paying rent revolts the Celtic soul.

The five months of hard work which followed, from blooming August until snowy January, lie outside of the realm of this tale. If you are a boatman, you will know what effort was expended, what problems were solved, what limits of exasperation were reached, what resigned patience was nurtured, what poking around in heaps of scrap to find good but cheap materials, what marvels of expediency were arrived at, and how many tears were almost shed when nothing at all seemed to be going right.

Finally the day came when *Cresswell* (her original Lifeboat Institute name) started to take shape, to become a vessel instead of a hulk. I sat patiently in a snowbound shed cutting sheets of quarter-inch pure lead, recently "salvaged" off a blitzed London church, into "kentledge," as we call the shaped ballast cut to fit very closely between the frames of the hull in the bilge of the boat. I studied every surplus war material leaflet which came my way, and soon I had installed my engine. This was a twin-cylinder, horizontally-opposed diesel engine which had formerly been mounted on a trailer. The trailer had been towed around London behind a truck, and served as an auxiliary fire pump during the great German aerial bombardments. With the pump end detached and a shaft and propeller buttoned on, it worked admirably, with its ten horsepower, to shift *Cresswell* along at five knots or so. And it used only half a pint of fuel an hour! I started it by ramming lubricating oil down into two brass cups which fed the oil into the cylinders. Then I swung like hell on the handle, there was a loud explosion of noise and fumes, and off she went. I stopped the thing by simply shutting off the fuel. There was no throttle or astern gear.

The deck and doghouse I built also out of West African mahogany, which was expensive, but I wanted to carry the scantlings of the boat (i.e., the material specifications) right through the additions. Between the mahogany strakes I laid oiled canvas, just as it was in the hull, and over the deck and doghouse roof I laid and painted canvas so fine that even after I played water on deck for hours not one drop got through. I laid out the entire compartment, with access from above through a close-fitting hatch with hasps like you'd find in the Bank of England.

The amount of good, solid, hefty material which I collected on my nightly forays in a borrowed dinghy under muffled oars to the abandoned Royal Dockyard on the other side of the river and the muted conversations on the misty jetties and foggy foreshores, keeping a wary eye out for H.M. Dockyard Police, plus the number of pints stood for in the Admiral Jellicoe pub would be a wonder to anyone except those who have fitted out a long-distance cruiser with such meager resources as I had. I had no qualms of conscience about it, for I thought My Lords Commissioners of the Admiralty owed me something a bit more than a measly ten dollars per week.

The sails, the standing rigging, the running rigging, the diesel fuel tank (of finest copper), the zinc water tanks, the fuel piping, the stove, the one good sleeping berth in the cabin, the steering cables, the huge hand bilge pump, and the great brass fog siren, all came out of Her Majesty's custody and into mine, and so into the furbishing of the gallant ketch *Cresswell*. With the aid of half a dozen boat-loving cronies employed in the Dockyard, we fitted her out as good as Captain Watts (the *gentleman's* boat outfitter) could have done for two thousand guineas and more. Practically everything except the engine, that is. We'd have had one of those, too, for there were a dozen old fleet tenders lying rotting and woebegone at their moorings, but their engines were all too big. So we made do with the London Fire Brigade pump engine. The engine trade name was Vixen, and if ever a collection of nuts and bolts had a will of its own, that one did. But once running she'd run forever, and I got hold of some insulation out of H.M. Dockyard in which I sheathed the engine compartment. What with that and the rigid-resilient mountings (which I got out of the old Dockyard printing shop), she was at least smooth and steady, once the initial purgatory of starting her had been suffered.

I had concentrated first on the cabin, so that Nelson, the sea bag, and I would have somewhere reasonably warm and dry to live during the coming winter months. By mid-October, we were cozily battened against the weather and the curiosity of the local constabulary.

By Christmas (which we celebrated by making the church roof sheet-lead deal with some of "the boys" in the Elephant and Castle district of London), the masts—beautiful, hollow British Columbia pine—the rigging—courtesy of Sheerness dockyard and a week of fog—and the engine were all in place. By the end of January I had hand sewn a total of fourteen hundred square feet of heavy canvas sails, as well as received delivery of eight hundred square feet of heavy Dacron sails from Jeckells', up in East Anglia. By the time the ice had cleared out of the River Medway at the end of February, she was ready for launching, with one of the most lovingly applied paint jobs seen in the Thames Estuary since Queen Victoria was a lass. The outside of the hull was white gloss, picked out with French blue on the rubbing strake and Admiralty varnish (*fourteen* coats) on the "brightwork." Down below, all was Royal Navy grey, for one of our nocturnal outings had rewarded us with a great thirty-gallon drum of the stuff. It wasn't very chic-looking, but then, neither were Nelson nor I, and it served its purpose. Anyway, it was the light grey used in warships on tropical stations, so it would remind us of starry, balmy nights in the West Indies and the South Pacific during the long, dark, cold, Arctic nights to come.

Down below, I had a bit of brasswork—two gun tampons, the great bronze badges which they used to wedge into the muzzles of a destroyer's guns when they were not in use. A brass fiddle rail ran around the table and there were brass portholes set into the doghouse sides. Then there were pictures of Shackleton, Nansen, and Scott, all cut out of old "London Illustrated News" magazines, and one of the queen at the forward end of the cabin.

The coke-and-wood-burning stove was an admirable little contraption I had located in the old captain of police's office in the dockyard. As my need was much greater than his possible successor's, I borrowed the stove on a permanent basis.

In March 1959 I was ready to get in the navigational gear. The sextant I already had, an old Dutch model from the 1880s which had a micrometer reading so fine and brass-polish-worn that no one but I could read it. The chronometer I bought in a Petticoat Lane flea market for seven shillings (about a dollar). It was a fine London job from around 1860, brass, set on all-round gimbals, in a beautifully made walnut case with a green baize cushion inside. It was accurate to less than a second a day. A taffrail log, for telling the distance run, snaffled from Her Majesty's stores, cost three pints of ale.

I scoured the secondhand bookshops of London for read-

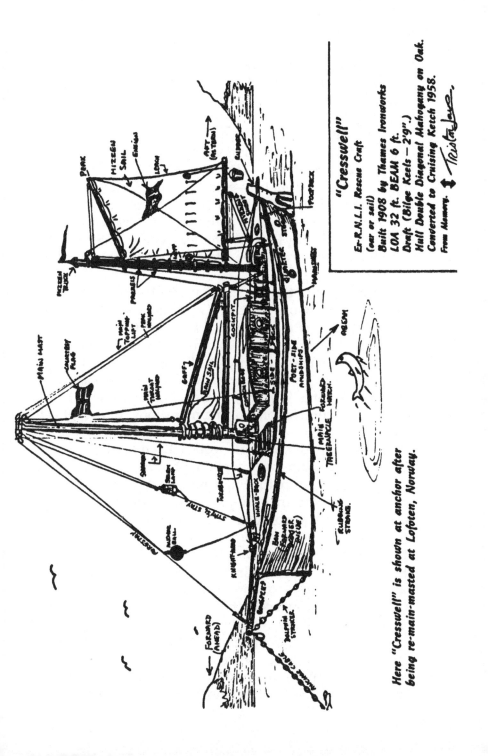

# "Cresswell"

Ex-R.N.L.I. Rescue Craft
(oar or sail)
Built 1908 by Thames Ironworks
LOA 32 ft. BEAM 6 ft.
Draft (Bilge Keels – 2'9".)
Hull Double Diagonal Mahogany on Oak.
Converted to Cruising Ketch 1958.
From Memory. ↕ Tristalane.

Here "Cresswell" is shown at anchor after
being re-main-masted at Lofoten, Norway.

PEAK

MIZZEN SAIL

ENSIGN

AFT
(PO TRIM)

MIZZEN PEAK

PINK

BRACES

MIZZEN MAST

SUPPORT

FOREDECK

MAIN TOPPING LIFT

PEAK HALYARD

JIB STAY

MAIN MAST

COUNTRY FLAG

PEAK HALYARD

VANGS

MAIN THROAT HALYARD

GAFF

MAIN SAIL

COCKPIT

PORT SIDE
AMIDSHIPS

ABEAM

SLIDE

SHROUDS

THROAT LINE

CABIN TOP

GUARD HATCH

MAIN
TABERNACLE HATCH

SHROUDS

STAY GUY STAY

WHALE BACK

BOW
FENDER
ROPE
(SALLIE)

FORE-HATCH

RUBBING
STRAKE

KNIGHTHEAD

FORGASTAY

ANCHOR
BALL

FORWARD
(AHEAD)

DOLPHIN STRIKER

BOWSPRIT

ANCHOR CABLE

ing material. Some of the bargains I found were a complete works of Shakespeare, Gibbon's *Decline and Fall of the Roman Empire*, a full set of Mark Twain's works, Marx's *Das Kapital*, plus definitive editions of Kipling, Byron, Wordsworth, and Keats, together with the works of W. B. Yeats and Wilde. I also managed to scrounge several of Joseph Conrad's books—*The Nigger of the Narcissus, The Heart of Darkness, Lord Jim*—and many of the Maigret books by Simenon, which I think much of. I also secured a copy of one of the greatest sailing fiction books ever written, *The Riddle of the Sands* by Erskine Childers, who was later shot as a traitor by the Irish Free State troops during the Irish Troubles.

I found later in the voyage that I had a treasure indeed onboard in the books by Alain Gerbault *In Search of the Sun* and *The Voyage of the Firecrest*. I also had Cervantes's *Don Quixote* and several scruffy volumes by Balzac and Dumas.

These, together with my *Reed's Nautical Almanac*, the *Admiralty Pilot for the Arctic Ocean East of Greenland*, and Charles Darwin's *Voyage of H.M.S. Beagle*, were to be my appreciated companions during many long, dark nights to come.

So much for the modern works. Even more important than all these, with the exception, of course, of the navigational volumes, were the English translations of *De mensure orbis terrae* by the Irish monk Dicuil, written around A.D. 825, and the Venerable Bede's accounts of Celtic settlement in Iceland up to the century before the Norsemen arrived there, *De Ratione Temporum*. I had notes on the account of the voyage made by the Greek geographer Pytheas of Massalia from Britain to Iceland (or Thule, as he called it) in 330 B.C. There was also a collection of translations of the works of Strabo and Pliny, written around the birth of Christ, which gave accounts of sailing directions from Britain to Thule. There were also scraps of written Celtic lore of the voyages of Saint Brendan to the islands of the North, and translations of the great Icelandic sagas. Snorri Sturluson's

*Prose Edda* and a history of Iceland entitled *Islendingabók* by
Ari the Learned; also, the *Sturlunga saga* and the *Fornaldar-
sögur*, the Sagas of the Old Times, Icelandic translations of
the Celtic and Romance legends of Tristan and Yseult, or
Erec and Blanchfleur, together with the classic *Islendin-
gasögur*, the Saga of the Icelanders. These tales, woven of
fact and fantasy, of calamitous cowardice and cold courage,
are living proof of the leavening influence of the Celt on the
savage Viking soul, for in no other Scandinavian culture
was such a standard of heroic prose and poetry reached.
Nowhere else did the blood gush from the word so wetly
and redly, nor the sun rise in such paeans of splendor;
nowhere else was man so human, nor yet so godly, except
in the old (much older than the Sagas) legends of the Gaels.

By the end of March I had spent approximately $2,700.00
on lead, charts, engine, navigational tables, tools, and
other items which, for one reason or the other (usually the
other), were impossible to obtain from Royal Navy stores.
Also on food and beer and a brand-new bowsprit.

By the time I had laid in my two years' supply of canned
food and other bits and piece of necessary gear, such as
sleeping bag and warm clothing, I had about a hundred
dollars left. With this I launched *Cresswell*, stood a pint of
beer all round at the Admiral Jellicoe, bought a compass,
a small radio receiver, and a bundle of mutton cloths from
the local butcher to serve as extra blankets and insulation
for the cabin, and I was off, in foggy weather, flat calm sea,
down the Medway, out of the Dickens-haunted Thames
Estuary, and into the North Sea. Destination Whitstable.

As *Cresswell* lifted her thirty-six feet to the first sea swells,
I was elated. Nelson stood up forward in the bows, sniffing
the wind, standing as steady as a rock on his three legs,
content that there was a full bag of bones for him in the
engine compartment and that he was at sea again.

In the afternoon the fog lifted. The low green hills of
north Kent and, beyond them, the North Foreland's chalky
white cliffs, rose out of the murky North Sea waters. Soon

Whitstable was in view and I had completed my first solo voyage in my own craft. It was only a matter of thirty-five miles or so, and there was no wind, but the old Fire Brigade pump worked as good as a homing Trojan, and there was plenty of daylight to spare as I guided *Cresswell* into the open roadstead, to anchor in front of the town of Whitstable on that faraway April evening.

It was good that we called at Whitstable, for here I found out more of the history of *Cresswell* than I ever imagined I would. In Sheerness, where I had fitted out in the shadow of the dockyard walls, she was something of a mystery, of uncertain age and lineage. But as soon as she stepped her forefoot into the salty North Sea swell, I knew by the very movement of her hull that here was a vessel which had known men and the sea. She was no shy virgin.

If you wake at midnight, and hear a horse's feet,
Don't go drawing back the blind, or looking in the street,
Them that asks no questions isn't told a lie.
Watch the wall, my darling, while the Gentlemen go by!
   Five and twenty ponies
   Trotting through the dark——
   Brandy for the Parson,
   'Baccy for the Clerk;
   Laces for a Lady, letters for a spy,
And watch the wall, my darling, while the Gentlemen go by!

If you do as you've been told, 'likely there's a chance,
You'll be give a dainty doll, all the way from France,
With a cap of Valenciennes, and a velvet hood——
A present from the Gentlemen, along o' being good!
   Five and twenty ponies
   Trotting through the dark——
   Brandy for the Parson,
   'Baccy for the Clerk,
Them that asks no questions isn't told a lie——
Watch the wall, my darling, while the Gentlemen go by!

                    Rudyard Kipling, "A Smuggler's Song."

# 7

## *Watch the Wall, My Darling!*

Two good things about not having much money: your pockets don't get holes in them and you meet a lot of interesting people whom otherwise you might miss.

The boatman who ferried me ashore in Whitstable was obviously not one of the Brethren, though he was a cheerful enough chap, well fed, rotund under his blue jersey, with sparkling grey blue Saxon eyes over a smoothly shaven jaw. But he didn't have the lean and hungry look, and his oar strokes were a mite too gentle for me to confide in him what was on my mind.

"You come far?" he asked me, as we headed for the town jetty.

"Only from Sheerness. I motored all the way; no wind."

"That's usual this time of year. Where're you bound?"

"Oh, just knocking around. You know, Ramsgate, maybe Broadstairs. Depends on the weather." I tried to sound uncaring.

"Yeah, I s'pose so." He'd got the message alright, and charged me a shilling, twice the going rate. "Well, it'll help him buy a new peaked cap," I thought, as I handed him one-thousandth of all my worldly wealth.

I headed for the shops, to buy some safety pins and envelopes and exchange surreptitious niceties with the lasses behind the counters. Then, as it was but half past four and still thirty minutes to go before pub-opening time,

I sipped a slow cup of tea and chewed a sticky bun, surrounded by most of the genteel, elderly ladies of the resort.
I was waited on by a chirpy little London cockney girl who
managed to look sedate and ladylike in front of the dowa-
gers and at the same time wiggle her hips every time she
squeezed past my table.

It was raining when I eventually made my way to the
Standard after fixing a date with the waitress for ten
o'clock. Business picked up and soon the public bar was
filled with fishermen and longshoremen. After a while one
of the crowd, a cheerful-looking, lanky, red-haired fellow,
dressed like most of the others in jersey and bobble-cap,
approached me.

"Saw you come in with the old *Mary Eleanor*."

"Not me, mate, that's the boat *Cresswell*, ex-R.N.L.I.," I
replied.

"Not on your nellie. I know that boat. By the way, my
name's Bill Travers, ex-Australian navy. I took my pension
over here."

"Tristan Jones, ex-R.N." I finished off my pint. He
bought another.

"Like I was saying," Bill went on, "I had to look twice at
that hull, but no mistake. You've done a bloody good job of
the conversion, but she's still the *Mary E.* I knew her, in fact
I sailed in her, once or twice, about ten years ago. She
belonged to a bloke called Rattler Morgan. He used to be in
and out of Ramsgate running stuff over to France. He got
her from the joker who took her over to Dunkirk in 1940 for
the evacuation."

"What? I never knew she was in that lot."

"Yes, and that bloody patch on the starboard bow is
where a Jerry plane put a forty-millimeter shell right
through her and killed four Tommies and a Frenchman."
He swigged his beer again. "How long have you had her,
mate?"

"Oh, a few months. Found her derelict in Sheerness."

"I'm not surprised, 'cos Rattler drew five years in the nick when they eventually caught up with him. They reckoned he'd moonlighted more flamin' booze into Froggyland than Johnnie Walker had sent legally."

I pushed over another three bob for two more pints.

"Where you bound, mate?" He was studying me closely.

I eyed him. "Well, speaking sort of general-like, I'm heading down Channel. What I'd like to do, if I can, is get over to Ireland for the summer. I heard living is much cheaper over there."

"On the blink, then?"

"Oh, I've got a few bob, but I wouldn't mind a few more."

"Yeah? Well, I might be able to put you onto something."

The conversation drifted into the usual realms of boats and people, the age-old exercise of sailor-strangers meeting in a bar, finding out if they have friends in common and if one knows any of the vessels the other knows, then a joke or two, a game of darts, hints on what pubs are good—the same scuttlebutt the world over.

Towards the end of our seventh pint, Bill leaned over close to my ear.

"If you're stuck, Tris, I can put you in with a setup which is genuine, and you'll earn more than a few bob in just a couple of runs over the other side."

"What are they running?"

"Scotch."

"What's in it?"

Bill lowered his voice. "Two hundred quid a time. A hundred on sailing and a hundred when the stuff's landed."

"Where?"

"I can get you to the blokes at this end, but I can't tell you about the other end. They'll put you right on that score when you sail."

"What's in it for you?"

"I sail with you. I get a hundred nikker for the trip."

"Where's *your* boat?" I was wary.

"Piled her up off Portland back in November. No insurance."

"How do I know you're O.K.?"

"Ask him." Bill nodded towards the landlord of the Standard.

I had already spoken to the landlord, who had known old Tansy Lee when he used to frequent the pub, and I'd weighed him off as a straight-shooter. He had probably taken his share of the "bent" booze.

"Right," I said. "Hang on a minute and I'll have a word with him. If he okays it, Bill, you're on."

A few minutes later I got the landlord to one side and he confirmed that he had known Aussie Bill for some years, that he always paid his due, and that he was trusted by all and sundry in the town. I returned to Bill. "Right, cobber, you're on. When do we sail?"

"When can you be ready?"

"Where are we bound?"

"The Nab."

"The Nab? Well, let's see, that's about . . . 140 miles. If we get an easterly, say thirty-six hours; a westerly, say three days. How soon can your mates meet me there?"

"I'll ring 'em up to confirm, but off the bat I'd say yes in three days. It'll be ideal. Not much moon."

"O.K., you talk to them and if it's O.K., we'll sail tomorrow at dawn and be off the Nab for sure in three nights from now."

"Good on you, blue. Have another pint. Then I'll get on the blower and find out the score."

"Right. Hey, Bill, you married?"

"You must be jokin'!"

"Got a bird?"

"Yeah, all over the place." He grimaced. "Why?"

"Well, I've got a date with this tart in the caff down the road and I can nip down and see if she can bring one of her mates, if you like. They both look like goers."

"Sounds fair enough. What time?"

"See you back here at ten. How're you fixed?"

"Not too good, but I can buy a couple of gin and bitter lemons."

"That'll do."

He disappeared into the saloon bar where the telephone was located, at the posh end of the pub. At ten o'clock I reappeared with my girl and her friend. Being *gentlemen* that night, we took them into the saloon bar with its black leather sofa-seats and soft, pink lights, where the bank and bookmakers' clerks sat with their wives brushed and combed and not five bob between the lot of them. We soon had the lasses titteringly teased over Booth's Dry Gin so that by the time "Gentlemen Please" was called they would have willingly sailed with us for the Nab. Instead we hauled them around to the fairground and whooshed and whizzed our way into their eyes and thighs to the tune of the organola.

Merry with beer and gin, we made our satiated way back to the girls' rooming house. At twelve, as the clouds broke, the battle-ax who shepherded their morals locked tight the door as they wafted their way to wherever girls go when a door is locked. Bill and I wended stumbling weary steps through the winklestalls of Whitstable in the wet-streaming, windstormy night.

The old ferryboat man, the same one who had taken me ashore that afternoon, nine pints and two orgasms ago, said not a word. He took one look at Aussie Bill, then a fleeting glance at me. As we came alongside *Cresswell*, old Nelson wagged his tail, all the while staring at Bill through his eye.

"I know that bugger," said Bill, reaching up and patting him. "That's ol' Tansy Lee's dog!"

"Did you know Tansy, mate?"

"Know him? Course I did. I've had more pints with Tansy than you've had hot breakfasts!"

"Blimey, I used to sail with him. He was my first skipper!"

"Yeah? Where is he now then?"

"He kicked the bucket last August."

"Aboard?"

"No, he was ashore, sort of semiretired the month before."

"Christ, he wouldn't have liked that, Tris."

"Too bloody right, but he had a good send-off. They had practically every old salt on the coast at the wake."

"I'll bet that was a sight for sore eyes."

"So they say, Bill. Want a nightcap? There's some Black Label here."

"Good on you, mate, splash it out. We'll bloody soon replace that!"

And so, for an hour into the windy night, as the boat rocked away on the tide's changing, tales of Tansy were exchanged, while Nelson made a fuss of Bill, whom, of course, he remembered from five years back.

Bright as the bottom of a soldier's sock, we were up at dawn, with the anchor weighed and the mainsail filling to a good easterly. The wind and rogue's luck were with us, and we bowled down the Channel, after clawing our way around the North Foreland.

It was a magnificent, swift sail, that first run down the English Channel, and *Cresswell* made the Light on Selsey Bill in just forty-eight hours out of Whitstable. As we had a day to spare, I stood off about six miles and we whiled away the hours hove to, fishing. We caught two bream.

On the morning after, that is the day of the night of our rendezvous with "the Brethren," the wind swung around to the west, so we slowly started beating in to Spithead, the channel between the Isle of Wight and England. By dusk we had the old Nab Tower (an artificial island with a great round fortress, built during the Napoleonic Wars to guard the naval port of Portsmouth from French intrusions) in sight, and by ten in the evening we were hove to in the lee of the fort, showing two dim lights from the forestay.

At eleven we heard the noise of an engine close by, and

soon we were tied up alongside a motor fishing vessel, around eighty feet in length, with her engine softly keeping us head to sea in position while the soft-spoken Hebridean Scottish crew quietly and quickly transferred 150 cases of whisky onboard. These they distributed into *Cresswell* with an eye to her trim. They were obviously good seamen, but we knew no more about them, for they spoke only of the job. Their skipper, a chubby man of around sixty, with an Oxford accent and a peaked cap, shook my hand as the last cases were loaded and pressed an envelope into my pocket. "There's half there. Your destination is written down. Don't open it until you're half-way across the Channel. Head due south until you know the destination. You'll get the other half when the cases are ashore. Good luck!" The lines were cast off, and as we hoisted the mainsail, the fishing craft became a dark shadow, disappearing towards the east. *Cresswell*, with the extra weight of the booze, was well down in the water.

"Let's get away from here fast, Tris. She's probably got another rendezvous and won't want us around."

"Right. Hoist the jib and mizzen. We've got a good run out to Selsey Bill, then a smashing broad reach due south. Where d'you think the destination is?" I fingered the envelope, itching to open it.

"I don't know for sure, but if it's where I think it is, you've got no worries. I've been there a hundred times."

By two in the morning we had dropped Selsey Bill light astern and were leaping over the short Channel seas with every sail drawing. We showed no lights, and when there was no shipping around, it was an eerie feeling. The night was pitch black overcast, and *Cresswell* became a ghost ship on a sea of spirits.

By dawn I reckoned by the log we were half-way over the Channel, and I opened the envelope eagerly.

"What is it, Tris, Omonville?"

"Yeah, Omonville, how did you know?"

"I didn't, but the Major knows me, and I thought that's

where he'd send us. He knows I know that bay like the back of my hand."

"Good. How much water?"

"No problem, you can drive her straight onto the beach under mizzen and jib. It's soft sand. Chuck out the stern anchor as you go in. We'll be there at half tide up. In half an hour she'll be afloat again and we can kedge out."

"Pity we've no chart."

"Don't worry; I've got one in my head. I was there only a month ago last time. It's a cinch."

I thought, "By God, it has better be a cinch, or no voyage for me!" More like five years in a bloody French jail!

That evening we sighted the fishing boats off Cherbourg, and as dusk fell handed the sails and motored in among the fleet. The idea was that if a radar sight of us had been gained by the French customs or navy, they would think we were a fishing boat. We waited hove to, in the middle of about a hundred fishing craft, all with nets out, until around midnight, then slowly made our way out of the western end of the fleet. Anyone who has not done it cannot imagine the difficulties of such navigation; there is always the risk of getting the nets or lines wrapped around the propeller. Not only is this risky, as the propeller shaft might be bent by the nylon lines piling up as the propeller revolves, forcing the shaft out from the hull, but it also meant being seen and reported by the French fishermen. The only way out of that predicament would have been to ditch all the booze before the fast French police launches arrived on the scene. But we were lucky and careful, and so emerged unscathed, though the night was very dark and a fresh breeze, around twenty-five knots, was blowing from the west.

By two in the morning we were off the bay of Omonville. Down main, and, guided by Bill, who certainly did know the waters, for the entry was tricky, I eased her in, no lights, and as quiet as a wary witch. I soon spied the dull, silver beach right ahead, and when I judged we were fifty yards off, softly lowered the kedge anchor and slowly sailed the boat under mizzen and jib right onto the beach. She touched with a slight judder, then slid up over the silky sand and came to a halt. The moment she bumped, a car's headlamp blazed right in front of us for half a second, and we were soon boarded by six men led by another whom Bill knew. The cases were offloaded in less than ten minutes, while not one word was spoken except a few muttered exchanges between Bill and their chief. As the cases were offloaded, the boat was lightened and her stern lifted out of the sand, then her bow. Ten minutes after the Frenchmen had disappeared back into their wagon, we were hauling *Cresswell* out again to the kedge anchor. With the westerly wind blowing offshore, on the eastern side of the Cotentin peninsula, we were soon out in deep water with the main, mizzen, stays'l and jib pulling like dray horses, headed back for the French fishing fleet. As we came up to the outer craft of the immense fleet, we handed all sail, started the engine, and again chugged our way slowly through them. Then, after an hour of this, we broke through the northerly line of nets and were away, with all sail and the engine pushing, the wind fair for England.

"Good job!" said Bill, handing me an envelope with my other half of the earnings inside. *Cresswell* seemed to be quite at home, Nelson normal. They'd both done all this before.

"Yeah, two hundred quid will see me O.K. for two years."

"Fancy another run?"

"Not really, Bill. Too risky."

"We can ask for another destination."

"Where?"

"I know a good 'un, don't worry."

"When?"

"Before the moon grows."

"Next week?"

"If you like." He grinned. "Head for Weymouth, north-

northeast by north; drop me off there and I'll fix it up."

"Right. You're on, but mind you, Bill, this is the last one."

I then explained to him what my true intentions were, and after a first grimace of astonishment, he saw that I was serious.

"O.K., Tris, just this one. That'll at least give me enough to put down a deposit on my own boat. Once I've got that, I'll be right."

And that's how, when I set sail from Falmouth for Ireland, I had onboard two years' supply of canned and dried food, a new rubber dinghy, three years' supply of boat's stores, and three hundred pounds sterling.

After all these years, I do not regret having done this. It helped keep some otherwise impoverished Hebridean island going for a few more months; it brought the delights of good Scotch whisky to many a benighted Frenchman; it helped Aussie Bill (whose name I have changed because he is now a prominent figure in the worldwide charter boat scene) recoup his loss and find his feet; and it taught me that *Cresswell* was an extraordinary vessel.

After a few days in Falmouth, I got out the charts for the south and west of Ireland. Saint Brendan's land! Falmouth parish church bells rang as *Cresswell* cleared for Erin. "Oh God, our help in ages past. . . ." In the offing, Nelson sniffed the Atlantic breezes for traces of Chihuahuas away across the ocean in Mexico, from whence blew the wind. I sang my own song, for we were free with all the world before us.

# PART II

---

# Veni

## *(I came)*

*Foolish men overlook and disregard their present blessings, because their thoughts are always intent on the future, but the wise keep the past clearly in mind through memory. To foolish people the present, which allows us but the briefest instant to touch it and then slips from our grasp, does not seem to be ours or to belong to us at all. . . . With most people, a stupid and ungrateful forgetfulness has possession of them, and wipes from their minds every past accomplishment . . . breaking the* unity of life, which comes from the *weaving of the past into the* present. *For by separating yesterday from today, as if it were something different, and tomorrow, likewise, as if it were not the same as today, it soon makes what is now happening into what has never taken place, by not recalling it. . . . So those who do not keep or store in memory things that are past, but let them float away, actually leave themselves vacant and empty daily, while they cling to tomorrow, as if what happened last year or day before yesterday or even yesterday mattered nothing to them, or had not happened to them at all.*

*This habit, then, is one* interference with peace of mind. (Emphasis added)

Plutarch, "On Peace of Mind," *Essays*.

*Oh some they came from Boston*
*And some came from New York,*
*Some came from the County Down*
*And some from the County Cork,*
*Some they came from Kerry*
*And some came from Kildare;*
*But the boys who bate the Black 'n Tans*
*Were the boys from the County Clare!"*

Irish Republican Song. The Black and Tans
were British-recruited auxiliaries, a bad lot.
The words' order changes according to the
locale. I have arranged it for Corghain. Sung
to the tune of "Wearing of the Green."

# 8

## *The Irish Islands*

From Falmouth, my sail plan was to cross the St. George's Channel, as the English call the Celtic Sea, and make for a landfall in southwest Eire. The most likely haven to make for was Bantry Bay, about 250 miles' straight sailing. In this long, wide bay, on its northern shore, was the port of Castletown. But if the weather held good, I would hold on course for Knights Town, in the lee of Valentia Island, at the southern end of Dingle Bay. The first landfall, in both cases, would be the Fastnet Rock, a lonely pinnacle, surmounted by a lighthouse, twenty miles south of the southern shore of County Cork. I would be heading west-northwest-by-northwest, and as the prevailing winds which sweep into the British Isles are southwesterly, it meant I would be on a close reach, that is, with the wind coming from about sixty degrees off the bow. This was important, because *Cresswell* was an old-fashioned gaff-rigged ketch, and unlike the modern Marconi-rigged ocean-goers, she could not sail very efficiently with the wind anywhere ahead of fifty degrees off the bow.

Bear in mind also that these were the days before the self-steering wind-vane gear, as now shipped aboard ocean-cruising boats, was developed to its present efficiency. In *Cresswell* it was all hand-steering with the wind anywhere abaft (behind) the beam (right angles to the boat), except when she was closehauled or on a close reach (that is, sailing with the wind ahead of the beam). Then, the sails could be trimmed and she would sail herself for long periods, holding the course with only minor adjustments to the helm. So in those conditions I always tried to shape a course where the wind would be slightly ahead of a direction at right angles to the boat's intended course.

If that sounds complicated in practice, imagine what a job it was to work out the courses. It was for this reason, among others, that my course for Iceland was laid out to pass outside the western periphery of the British Isles. To have gone directly up the east coast of England and Scotland would have been a thousand miles shorter, but in the North Sea the winds are both strong in force and fickle in direction. On the Celtic fringe they are strong, but mostly steady in direction. For this reason, the old sailing directions of Pliny had given this route. For this reason, too, the isolated Christian missions, the last remaining refuges of the light of Western civilization, had been able to communicate with each other during the centuries of savage destruction, blood, and ignorance which in Europe we call the Dark Ages. Now, replete with 184 twelve-ounce cans of corned beef, 100 pounds of porridge, 500 pounds of rice, 300-weight of potatoes, 200-weight of flour, 5 pounds of yeast, 50 pounds of tea, and 70 of sugar, 240 pounds of peanuts, 20 pounds of lemon powder, besides new fish-trolling gear, I was ready to take off.

In Plymouth, on a swift trip up by train from Falmouth, I had been able to obtain all the charts I would need of the Irish and Scottish Islands, the Faroes, Iceland, Eastern Greenland, Jan Mayen Island, and Svalbard. This had cost a tidy sum, but it was essential to have them.

On 7 May I worked *Cresswell* out of Falmouth, having cleared with the customs for Eire, and worked my way out against the wind, until, early on the morning of the eighth, my thirty-fifth birthday, I dropped the light of Lizard Head, Cornwall, astern. This was the last sight I would have of England for more than four years. As I made a kettle of tea I glanced out of the hatchway at the lightening dawn in the east over the ray of the Lizard Light. I threw Nelson a bone. "Well, old son, that's that. Ireland, here we come!"

The passage over the Celtic Sea took three days, because of a slight shift of the wind to due west on the second day. The weather was fair, with not much cloud or rain, so I was able to get good sights, which put Fastnet right on the starboard bow early in the false dawn. Beyond it I could see, as the sun rose slowly in the east behind me, the faraway, seemingly low hills and mountains of Ireland, rising, first black, then lightening to grey, purple, blue, and finally green, Irish green, emerald green indeed. The sea itself was blue green, topped with fresh frisking white horses, driven by the Gulf Stream wind, charging along to the rim of Ireland and beyond, to the roaring coasts of Cornwall and the singing shores of Wales.

On the port bow there was nothing between *Cresswell*, Nelson, and me but salt water all the way to Battery Point in New York. It sometimes happens, presumably due to abnormal activity of sunspots (as the gigantic hydrogen explosions spearing out millions of miles from the surface of the sun are called), that there is freak radio reception, and local radio broadcasts are bounced back to earth thousands of miles from the transmitter. On the night before my sight of the Skelligs, the holy sanctuaries of the Christian monks in the sixth century, ten miles or so off the coast of Kerry, I hove the boat to (that is, dropped the headsails and stopped her) while I made supper. The pressure cooker was steaming away merrily, with the spuds, corned beef, and Oxo gravy bubbling away inside, and I was fiddling with the dial of my small transistor radio receiver trying to find the shipping forecast from Niton radio station in the Isle of Wight. Suddenly I heard a conversation, loud and clear, between a *New York taxi driver* and his radio control office. There was no doubt about it, because he was heading for La Guardia Airport! The reception lasted quite clearly for several minutes, then static took over and I was back with Saint

Brendan in the sixth century, sailing in the moonless dark, off one of the oldest coasts in the world.

On the morning of the third day out, I sighted the two conical peaks of the Skelligs, the remains of two mountains lost to the ocean in some dim and distant past. I worked my way into the lee of the larger islet, which rises two hundred feet sheer out of the sea, and as the landing stage hove into clear view, let go the sheets, dropped the anchor over the bow, and looked around. There was no one in sight. I lowered the sails and waited a few minutes to make sure the anchor was biting properly, for the seabed around the islands is littered with rocks; then, admonishing Nelson to keep a good lookout, I went below to snatch some sleep. This having been my first solo voyage of any length in *Cresswell*, I had not slept much in three days, no more than ten minutes or so every few hours. I was crossing a heavily used shipping lane, and I did not yet know all of my craft's idiosyncrasies when she sailed herself; so, until I was sure of her steadiness, I was forced to keep watch on her. The weather was fine and springlike, with the wind blowing gently from behind the island and flat calm water in the roadstead.

It must have been mid-forenoon when I was awakened by Nelson barking and growling at the hatchway. "Pipe down, you son of a bitch," I growled in return, but he persisted and so I turned out of my bunk, donned my jersey, and made for the companionway.

"Halloo, there, halloo the boat riding there at anchor this fine day!"

I poked my head up over the hatch and gazed towards the shore. There, standing on the tiny landing stage, was a man in a peaked cap wearing pajamas and carpet slippers, holding a bicycle.

"Hello!" I shouted. He was about fifty yards away, but voices carry well over water, even against the breeze.

"Where are you hailing from in that fine, upstanding boat of yours?"

"England. Falmouth, England!" I shouted back.

"Arr, ye poor fellow, the shame of it! Come ashore and have a drink!"

"I'll be right with you!"

I had been towing my brand-new Avon rubber dinghy, and in three shakes of a gnat's ass I had the oars onboard and was paddling away for the jetty. The man in pajamas caught the painterline as I came alongside and tied it to a ring set in the stone.

"*Céad Míle Fáilte*," he said softly in Erse. "A thousand welcomes."

"*Ddwy Da*," replied I in Welsh. "A good day to you."

"Is it Saxon you are?"

"Welsh."

"Corrigan's the name." He spoke now in English. "I'm the keeper here, and sure it's not a soul I've seen for the three weeks past of my life. Is there no one with you?" He was a large, hefty man, about fifty, with Viking blue eyes.

"Just the dog."

"Bejasus, he earns a fine keep for himself. He'd guard a tinker."

"He's been at sea most of his life. He's used to it and knows what to do." I climbed onto the jetty and took his proffered hand.

"Did you ever see the like of such? Now, it's up the brew we'll be climbin' an' you can tell me of the news. Are there wars still burning down the world?" His eyes saddened.

"Nothing big."

"There's the pity of it. A fine thing, wars. Sure they bring good pensions to half the widows of Ireland!"

"Have you no radio?" I asked him as we puffed our way up the finely paved but narrow concrete path to the lighthouse perched a hundred feet above the sea.

"Sure, Flaherty's thinkin' of installin' one but it's me against it, what with all the strange things comin' out of the blue sky and the gulls screamin' their heads off in pain at all the human misery, what with all the riots and strikes and wars goin' on."

"I thought you said wars were a fine thing?"

"Sure, and so they are, as long as the birds do be left in peace."

"That's a thought," I said. Arguing with a Gaelic Celt is always an exercise in convoluted geometry fit to make the Sermon on the Mount sound like the concept of relativity.

Once in the lighthouse cottage, low, lime-washed walls and slated roof, with kettle singing on the peat-burning, black-polished stove and mugs of tea to hand (for the Western Irish and Scots are tremendous tea drinkers), I addressed myself to Corghain, as Corrigan was known in his native tongue.

"How is this island called Skellig Michael? Who was Michael?"

"Begab, it's terrible pagans you must be in the wild land of Wales, if you don't know that the chief of all the angels and everythin' so high it would touch the foot of Almighty God"—he crossed himself swiftly—"is Michael himself with his flamin' sword and terrible eyes."

I crossed over to the open door, the one on the side away from the wind, and looked down onto the sea, a hundred feet below. *Cresswell* was sitting down there in the green water over the black shadows of rock patches, like a toy boat. I saw Nelson, a mere dot, padding his way round and round the deck. In the near distance, a mile or so away, rested the perfect cone of Little Skellig, grey and blue, with the green grey Atlantic breakers heaving mightily against its symmetric shore.

At eye level and above me, in the blue sky tempered by fat cumulus clouds spawned by the Azores High a thousand miles to the southwest, wheeled hundreds of fulmar petrels, surely, with the albatross, the most beautifully moving creatures in the whole natural world. With the faintest movement of their wings, they glided onto the ocean airstreams and soared up, up, a thousand feet or more to hover like a song of joy and love. Then their wings sagged and down they went, right down to the neck bristles of the Atlantic seas heaving far below. It was a sight of holy wonder.

"What are the round huts up there on the cliff face?" I asked Corghain. They were shaped like beehives.

"The cells that the monks lived in in the old times. Sure, when all hell was loose upon the world it's to here they came, and wasn't King Olaf of Norway himself christened here on this very island?"

"When was that?"

"Long, long ago, before the English came,"—he spoke as if it were yesterday that Gilbert, Raleigh and Cromwell had brought bloody murder to Erin—"when the wild Norsemen changed their ways and became themselves a blessin' to God."

We climbed on up the steep narrow path cut into the face of the sheer cliff and came at last to two pinnacles on the peak, steep, needlelike crags, one with a hole about three feet diameter passing straight through it horizontally. Corghain told me to pass myself through the hole and lean over the crevice between them to kiss the rock on the other side. "It'll leave you never short of a word in your head," said he.

Once my head passed through the hole I found myself looking straight down a *two-hundred-foot drop*, to where great Atlantic rollers crashed into a split cutting almost right through the island. The sight was enough to make me dizzy, but I persevered and leaned right over the four-foot gap, seemingly hanging between heaven and earth, and brushed the hard, cold rock on the other side with my lips. As I wriggled back to Corghain and safety, he said, "Sure, and it's the storyteller you are now even though it was myself that was thinkin' you were before you stepped your foot on this shore!" I was sweating, for I'd been swinging out there in space supported only to the thighs, with Corghain sitting on my feet.

Shaken, I trod down the hill with Corghain still telling me

tales, for he was a man of the long memory.

"Do you get a lot of fog around here?" I asked him.

"Aye, we do, and in the winter it's a fog so thick you could poke your finger in it and leave a hole. Sure and all, before the German war, Flaherty, whose younger brother's in America and who has great, grand ideas that would turn a hare into a fine racehorse, installed the new electric fog signal house."

"Look." He pointed down, far below, to a small concrete hut perched over the great tumbled rocks of the shore where the ocean breakers broke in white spume under the soughing wind. "Look, you see, that's the place. In the old days we'd go down there in a fog, feelin' our way with nothin' but suspended vapor before our eyes and little else but faith in the Lord behind them, and set off the maroons [explosive fog signals—like big fireworks] by hand. Three hundred of the wild explosive cartridges we have in there. Well, Flaherty, whose older brother is no less than an inspector on the trams of Dublin City itself, said that this was too slow and dangerous, so he brought this little spalpeen of a fellow with his suit and tie, lookin' like he dug money out of the sands of Kerry, and his gossoon to carry all the wires and paraphernalia, batteries and such like. Sure you would have thought it was Thomas Edison himself come for a holiday! Then they set up the wires down the holy cliff of Archangel Michael, so we could set off the maroons one at a time from the cottage. Flaherty to me he said that this would preserve our lives until the Second Comin', with no more perilous scramblin' down the cliff, or risk of blowin' ourselves directly into the presence of the good Lord himself."

"That was a good idea."

"Sure, and it was, and would you not expect it to be, Flaherty's brother bein' in Boston and all and the Dublin tramways behind him?" He puffed on his short pipe as the cottage came into view below us. "But they got a sort shirk-it, they called it."

"A what?"

"A sort shirk-it."

"And what happened?"

"Well, I put my finger to the pressin' thing on the box and Holy Mother of God," he crossed himself, "if the whole three hundred maroons didn't blow up all at the same time with an explosion so mighty it almost lifted the island right out of the sea!" His eyebrows shot up above his sparkling blue eyes.

"What did the Dublin men do then, Corghain?"

"Ten Hail Marys, two mugs of tea, and off to the mainland they went. Flaherty brought over another three hundred maroons, which we still set off in God's way without fancy wires and boxes. But never a sight I had again of the spalpeen, nor his gossoon, and that was all of twenty years' past."

We sat for a while in the whitewashed living room of his cottage, with the box-bed set in the wall by the fireplace and the picture of Patrick Pearse, the poet who gave labor to Irish independence, gazing with the look of crucified Christ from the wall and a calendar from Boston over the door.

"And where is it you go from here, Tristan?"

"I'm thinking of Waterville Spunkane, in Ballinskelligs Bay, for I must see the police and enter Ireland legally."

"Ahh, they'll not miss a paper or two from a good man like yourself. Look, why don't you head for the Blaskets. I've good friends there, and Tom Keanan's king of it all. He'll look after you as I look after the light."

"Well, Corghain, the weather looks promising enough, and it's only fifty miles, so that's what I'll do. We'll write down the names of your friends, and it's them I'll see when I fetch the Blaskets."

Corghain walked down the hill with me to the jetty, still puffing on his pipe. "A fine craft you have there, and God go with you and calm the waters" were his last words as I pulled away from the jetty. Nelson was pleased to see me safe back onboard. We would sail that evening after tea and make a night passage to the Blasket Islands, the next parish to America!

*They have considerable knowledge of the stars, and their motions, and the dimensions of the earth, and the Universe around. Also of science in general, and of the powers and spheres of influence of the immortal gods. These subjects they debate, and also teach to their young students.*

Julius Caesar, *De bello Gallico* VI. 14—
"Description of the Celtic Druids."

# 9

## The Old Times

The radio weather forecast from Niton was good, and in the western approaches to the British Isles this is more the exception than the rule. "Sea areas Shannon, Fastnet, Land's End, winds moderate to fresh, increasing to gale force in twenty-four hours." It was time to strike while the iron was cold—the cruel cold blasts of Atlantic iron, which in the waters of that world are enough to daunt Finn McCool himself. Like a long, steady procession of Inquisition torture-masters, the sweeping black clouds of the low-pressure, anticyclonic gales roll in from the southwest, winter and summer, to breed a race of seamen and to sound a bass dirge to the rising descant of Celtic song, and draw a curtain of blinding energy and mighty force across the drift of Gaelic dreams.

Hauling a sixty-pound anchor with its arresting chain is always a chore, but soon it was lashed down on the foredeck, the jewel green moss of Saint Michael's seabed clinging to it. Up jib, up staysail, and away, waving to Corghain as he slowly clambered the track to his eyrie and the portrait of Patrick Pearse, with the fulmar petrels hovering on the bellied edges of the clouds high above. On the fishing line I had left hanging over the stern was a fine shiny pollock, about eight pounds, which, before you could say "Holy Mother of God," was in the pressure cooker and sizzling away on the stove for supper. I grabbed the wheel and headed out to the offing, to pass well clear of the Dursey Islands and the Bull Rock, where many a fine mariner over the centuries has taken leave of this world, for this is the weather-edge of Europe, the receiving end of all the Atlantic furies. It was not for nothing that Shannon Airport was built on the western end of Ireland. The tail winds of the Atlantic all push home here.

The night descended with stars steady and bright peeping through the scudding black clouds and a half-moon rising astern. As I was off a lee shore, I stayed on deck to fondle the kicking wheel and listen to the wind softly wailing in the shrouds, and to glimpse, now and then, lonely calling lights, signals of innocent intent, low on the distant black shore of Ireland. And I recalled what I had learned of the Old Times, before history had been trimmed to suit the ambitions of Rome and her heirs.

Around three thousand years ago and more a people had lived in the west of Europe, the people who built the accurate Stonehenge solstice computer. Dark, with prominent noses, lithe, intelligent, worshiping the life force itself. Their descendants, clearly recognizable from other strains around them, still endure in the wild places on the edge of the continent—the mountain fastnesses of Northern Scotland, Wales, the Irish Islands, parts of Cornwall and Brittany. These people were called, in Ireland, the Goidels, or Gaels; in Britain, the Brythonics.

About twenty-five hundred years ago, into their midst came a great wave of wandering fair-haired, blue-eyed nomads from northern Persia and Afghanistan—the Gaulish-Celts. When the Gaulish-Celts reached what is now Rumania, they split off into three main branches. One turned southeast down through Turkey and the Middle East, to mix with the Semites and become the Phoenicians. Others pushed on into North Africa to leave behind a racial strain known as Berbers, before crossing north over the Strait of Gibraltar into Spain (Iberia) to form the blood base of the nations of Portugal, Aragon, and Castile. Some of these Celto-Iberians, about 800 B.C., under one of the first known ocean navigators, Mabo, pushed on across the western ocean to the West Indies and America, there to establish Punic colonies and become the ancestors (at least by language) of the Pima Indians of New Mexico. The second stream of Gaulish-Celts turned directly south into the Greek peninsula and founded the great civilization of which the modern western world is the inheritor. The third stream pushed on due west across the plains and mountains of Europe, leaving behind pockets in Austria and Switzerland, to become the Gauls of France. From France other Gaulish-Celts passed on into the British Isles and, mixing with the Brythonic Goidel tribes, became the Cymru of Wales and Picts and Scots of Northern Ireland and Scotland. The Goidel Celts pushed out of England and Wales became the Erse of Ireland.

With Gaulish-Celtic intelligence overlaid onto the dreaming imagination of the Goidel-Brythonics of Western Europe, a great culture with widespread communications was developed, a loose confederation of states, in the ancient Greek style, with high priests, called *vates*, in charge of religion, kings, princes, and druids in secular command. To imagine that when Julius Caesar invaded Gaul he was fighting blue-painted savages is foolish. He in fact managed to overcome, and only by the skin of his teeth, a highly organized alliance of more-or-less democratic states peopled by a race in a state of civilization not far short of Rome itself, with a system of communications by land and sea, as good as, if not superior to, that of the Mediterranean folk. The Celts were sailing as far afield as present-day Morocco in the south, Germany in the east, America in the west, and the then much warmer Iceland in the north.

When an invading army subdues a country, the majority of the inhabitants of that country remain as they were before the conquest. So with Britain during the so-called Roman times. Ninety-five percent of the population were Brito-Celt during the Roman occupation; ninety percent after the Norman Conquest; and probably eighty percent now, even after all the successive inroads by continentals and Scandinavians. But in four areas the population always was, and still is, ninety-nine percent Celtic—North Wales, the Irish Islands, the remote fastnesses of the Scottish Highlands, and Brittany.

As early as 330 B.C., Pytheas of Massalia (now Marseille) sailed westward through the Mediterranean to the great Phoenician port of Gades (the modern Cádiz). There he transferred to a Gaelic curragh, a great ocean-worthy vessel over a hundred feet long, built of hides stretched over a wooden frame, even more sea-fit than the oar-and-sail-propelled galleys of the eastern Mediterranean. From Gades the ocean venturers of the western edge of the world sailed northwards, calling at the Celtic port of Vigo and the island of Oléron, on the west coast of Gaul, near the present-day port of La Rochelle. In those far-off days, before the might of Rome was hurled across the Rubicon, Oléron was a center of a maritime activity as important as Venice and Genoa were to become fifteen hundred years later, after the tide of barbaric ignorance had at last subsided in Europe.

Here, at Oléron, the first internationally respected laws of the sea were drawn up between maritime merchants from as far afield as the Baltic, Iceland, Morocco, the northeast coast of America, and Phoenician Lebanon. Through Oléron passed southward-bound around the Gibraltar Strait, or overland across Gaul to the Mediterranean Phoenician port of Massalia, wool, tin and gold, ambergris and walrus tusks and sweet-scented pine needles from the far-flung lands of the Northern and Western Celtic people in Iceland and America. From as far north as the Faroes and Scotland came the wools and ambergris, also from the Baltic; while from Cornwall, Ireland, and Wales, as well as England, came hundreds of cargo vessels every year in the spring and summer, bearing gold, tin, and woad dyes, much prized in Lebanon and Persia. In the great long

warehouses of Oléron and Gades, these goods were exchanged for the fine woven silks, the aromatic scents, the
wine and spices from the Mediterranean and the East, by
Greek and Phoenician sailors, some of whom, calloused
and wise in the ways of the sea, had ranged as far afield to
the east as Arabia, Ceylon, Mozambique, and Borneo, and
who told fantastic tales of sandy deserts, coal black people,
and yellow men with slanted eyes living in unimaginable
splendor, and of a land of gold and silver far to the east of
Borneo. The Celts, in their turn, told of a country way to the
north where hot water spewed out of the ground and
islands were born out of the sea, only to die again in clouds
of steam. They told stories of Lugh, the god of light, born on
the island of Tory, off the kingdom of Terganaill (Donegal),
who made far-ranging journeys into Europe with his
mighty spear which he could hurl fifteen miles, who was
the grandson of Balor, king of the Formorians, and who
founded the cities of London (Londinium), Leyden
(Lugudunum) in modern-day Holland, and Lyons, far
away in eastern Gaul. They told tales of Dedaanan, the king
of the Firbolgs, and his enemy, the magical man with three
legs called Manaanan who ranged as far as the Isle of Man
and Etrusca in Italy, where his sign, the triskelion (three
legs), is still in use, and who, long, long before, with his
great army, "rode the white horses" across the sea from
Man to Ireland to defeat the Firbolgs at the battle of Moy-
tura. And to this day, when the Atlantic winds sough
across the blue green waters of the ocean, sailing men speak
of the driven seas as "white horses."
    It was with these storytelling sailors that Pytheas set off
northward on his voyage to Thule, the end of the world,
calling first at the busy Eirean port where now stands the
city of Limerick. They sailed north through the Faroes, six
days' hard sailing, ever to the north, until they sighted the
spouting volcanoes and devil-torn rocks of Thule—Iceland.
There they picked up a cargo of ambergris and walrus
tusks, gathered by Celts temporarily settled in that lonely

outpost of the world, and then returned south again. It is perfectly obvious from Pytheas's account that this was no voyage of exploration, but a merchant-venture along an old established trade route.

In the night watches, as the curragh ploughed north, the Gaelic sailors from the Irish Islands and the rocky coast of Wales told Pytheas tales of *Iarghal*, "the land beyond the sunset" (later known in low Latin, even to the Irish and Welsh fighting to stay outside the Roman Empire, as Hy-Brasil), the enchanted land westward across the ocean, the Land of the Dead, to which the spirits of the Gaels sailed across the watery wastes of the Atlantic. Tales were told by men who had actually seen this land; who, after many weeks of hard voyaging, had sighted the land in the west far, far away; who had landed and seen the *Iarghaltes*, "the Sundowners," *red men of the redland,* and who had stayed with them and traded with them for tusks and furs. They had made their way back across the ocean to Erin and to Cymru (Wales), and, as old men, told the tales over the tribal fires of peat on the cold winter nights when the sea was too wild for the curraghs to sail. And so Pytheas learned of the Celtic colonies of North America, the land of *Iarghal,* that is, if he did not already know about them.

So the stories passed back to Phoenicia, where, along with all other knowledge of distant parts of the world, they were locked away until Phoenician power shifted, a millenium and a half later, to Venice and Genoa. In tattered scraps, these stories were handed down among families anciently rooted in Lebanon, like that of Christopher Columbus. (Columbus found an Irish sailor, living in Galway, who had seen the "redland" far to the west. This Irish-Gael sailed west with Columbus in the Santa Maria, and I have seen the stone slab on which his memory is kept in the church of Saint Nicholas in Galway town. He had seen the "red men" in the land of the sunset, *Iarghal,* in 1478!)

When Caesar entered Gaul with his army to seize the land now known as France and to cross the Channel to tackle the heart-islands of the Celts, the old sea passages were still maintained, for the Mediterranean sailors of Rome were no match for the Atlantic-hardened mariners of the West. Caesar's invasion force sailing for Britain in early 55 B.C., in fact, encountered a British fleet of 220 seagoing vessels in the Channel. A sudden calm in the wind enabled the Roman galleys, commanded by Brutus, with slaves at the oars, to drive alongside the great curraghs and board them with overwhelming hordes of foot soldiers. A far cry from the usual story of the "civilized" Romans landing unchallenged on an island populated by primitive, blue-painted savages! What better camouflage is there for a night attack than blue woad dye?

Rome's power extended as far as the eye could see from the land, and as far as the foothills of the mountains of Wales and Scotland. There, on the high ocean seas and the remote broken rises, the tide of the Roman Empire beat itself for 450 years, but made few inroads. The Celtic sea trade, from Iceland and Germany, though drastically diminished, continued. With Rome astride the ocean road to Cádiz, the American trade died, delaying, for good or ill, the arrival of Christianity on that continent for fifteen hundred years. The far-flung, lonely Celtic outposts of *larghal* were cut off from Europe, their folk to mix with the Amerindian *larghaltes*, and to become part of the Algonquin tribes. From then on, legends record only isolated voyages across the Atlantic, such as the Irish Saint Brendan's in the sixth century and the Welsh Prince Madoc in the twelfth century.

About 290 years after the birth of Christ, the Roman governor of England, Carausius, sent a mighty fleet to sail completely around the British Isles, and then to Iceland, carrying a legion to raid Gaelic settlements in that remote land, as well as the coasts of the wild Picts in Northern Scotland and the Erse of Ireland. The only relics ever found of this expedition, apart from the written accounts, are two Roman coins recovered from the seabed at Bragoarvellir and one at Hvalnes, both sites on the southeast coast of Iceland.

As is well known, when an invading army subdues a country, the effect on the culture and racial composition of the people is mainly felt only among the high and mighty. The common people, the vast majority, are not changed one whit. This is especially so among the seafaring folk of the conquered country. They are brought up on local sea lore and traditions. Once the conqueror is onboard their craft, in their sea, he is present on the sufferance of the native, unless the conqueror is himself a seaman from a hard-weather land. This the Romans were not. The sailors of Carausius's fleet must have been Celts. Their sailing masters knew very well the coasts and the passages as far as the shores of Iceland.

As the military power of Rome waned in Western Europe during the violent incursions of the Goths and the Teutons, so the assault of the Roman Christian church on the militarily unconquered Celtic lands of Wales and Ireland increased. Finally, Saint Patrick, a Welsh Christian, entered Ireland and captured the romantic Irish soul.

With the coming of the Saxons, Angles, and Jutes into England in the fifth century from the fog-bound marshes of North Germany, the Celts were again cut off from land communication with the Mediterranean, the center of world power. But the old sea trade went on and still the curraghs ploughed the deep seas, finding their way by the sun, moon, and stars, while back at home, in Wales, Ireland, and Scotland, the Teutons were resisted. But when the Goths reached Cádiz, the sea roads to Rome were cut, and Christian Ireland and Wales were separated from the main body of their new religious and cultural sources in the Mediterranean. But sea travel still continued between Brittany, Ireland, Wales, and Iceland.

In those days, the northern latitudes were a good deal warmer than they are now. It is estimated up to five degrees Fahrenheit on the average. Certainly, from all accounts, the ocean weather was kinder, and no tales of icefloes or bergs are found in the old Celtic stories and very few in the Norse sagas, even of Greenland and Labrador.

While a wary "detente" had been reached between the Celt and the Saxon during the seventh century, far away across the North Sea, in Norway, the gradual immigration of people across the mountains from Sweden, together with a tremendous increase in the birthrate, had caused the peaceful farmers in the *vikke,* as the remote, tiny homesteads at the inner ends of the deep fiords were called, to turn to fishing the sea for food, and then to raiding each other's miserable plots. In the course of this warring, a type of craft was developed, the *karfi,* which made full use of the excellent timber readily available and of the bitter experiences gained over the years from the rough seas of that country. The *karfi* was a vessel about forty feet long, double-ended, with excellent coastal characteristics. It could deal with the steep heavy seas in rough weather, it could sail fast in the calm waters behind the long coastal island leads, and it could be beached easily for a raid or upon returning home with loot.

From the *karfi,* the next step forward was the *hafskip,* or, as it was more commonly known, the *knarr.* This was the much longer, wider, oceangoing "longship." It was, in contrast to the Celtic curragh, like comparing a Maserati to a Model T. It was fast, and it was big enough to carry thirty men with all their battle gear and provisions; it was shallow and could be sailed up rivers deep into enemy territory. The average knarr was eighty feet long, nineteen feet beam (providing excellent stability), and about four-and-a-half feet draft amidships. From the bottom of the keel to the top of the gunwale, the hull was about seven feet high.

Tents were erected when the knarr hove-to at night. The Vikings (as the vikke farmers were known) had no rudders or compass; steering was by a large sweep oar over the starboard (steer-board) quarter, and navigation was by the stars and sun for latitude. The longitude was mainly guessed at. From Norway, it was "sail into the setting sun for five days, then turn left for Britain and Europe, right for Iceland." It was as crude as that. Though we hear of all the successful Viking voyages, we have no idea how many were lost in the ocean. The number must have been great. With the bad weather in their area, I would hazard a guess of probably thirty percent losses.

Once the Norsemen had the knarr, they let loose upon all of northern Europe, and indeed as far round the continent as the shores of Morocco, a sea invasion of burning, looting, murder, and rapine unique in mankind's long history of warfare. In the process, they cut the Celtic sea roads and invaded most of the Gaelic lands. They ravaged England, France, Scotland, and Ireland. Only in three places were they successfully resisted—North Wales, Brittany, and a few of the Irish and Scottish Islands. These became small isolated centers of the old Celtic culture, overlaid with remnants of Greek and Roman civilization and ancient knowledge—a light kept flickering fitfully, but faithfully, by the Christian monks and anchorites hidden away in almost inaccessible fastnesses and islands, from the volcanic desert of the Vatnajökull of Iceland in the north, to the rocky, steep inlets of Brittany, protected by the terrible tides of that shore. For the darkest three hundred years in Western man's history, the tiny lamps flickered; some extinguished only to be lit again on yet another storm-tossed rock, like Tory, Iona, and Barra; some to die forever. During three dark centuries these selfless, faithful Celts held the sum total of Western man's culture in their hands.

As *Cresswell* heaved and sloughed her way through the kindly night, with St. Finan's Bay and Puffin Island under the lee, I thought of these tales of the sea empire of the Gaels. Here I was passing through one of the crossroads of the ancient world, a world of light and magic and beauty, a world of delightful dreams as well as terrifying nightmares, on the track of a race of people, *my people*, who worshiped the life force not only in living things such as the oak tree and the elder, the ash and the thorn, but in the rocks of the world and the sigh of the wind and the thunderous crashes of the mighty ocean on the shores of their homes. And I thought of the curtain of lies cast upon the world in the cause of goodness by the Christian missionaries, who drummed into the ears of the magical folk for centuries the incessant untruth that nothing before the Son of God was good. That all before Jesus was sin and ignorance and savagery, that all was evil, that the living spirit of the wind and the oceans, of the waving heather on the soul-hills was evil. How the memory of the Celtic ways, of their stories and art, full of love and terror, was cast into the first door-way of hell so that men's minds could be chained to the cross. And how the resulting cleavage of the Celtic mind is still, to this very day, shown in rivers of terror and violence in the back streets of bloody Belfast.

Ever since the Norman conquest of England, and especially after the loss of the Plantagenet domains in France, the aim of the English Power has been to dominate Europe, and especially Northwest Europe. The method has at all times been to secure a position from which the balance of power could be held, making sure that no one country on the continent became powerful enough, militarily or economically, to dominate any two other European countries.

With the shift of economic power from the Mediterranean shores to Northwest Europe after the great sea explorations of the fifteenth and sixteenth centuries, the geographical situation of Britain dictated an enormous increase in her political power, for she sits fair and square across the sea routes of the most powerful nations of the continent, and at that time, of the world. From the north of Scotland you can gaze out to sea, north and eastward, and know that you are looking at Iceland and Norway. Move south and in turn you look towards Denmark, Germany, Holland, Belgium, France, and Spain. Over very short lines of communication, the English could reach out and throttle the ocean throats of all these countries.

There was, however, only one Achilles' heel—Ireland. *Whoever controls the west coast of Ireland controls the sea approaches to Northwest Europe.* Cromwell knew this full well; he was the originator of modern sea power. The Spanish, the Dutch, the French, the Italians, the Germans also knew it, and for centuries their aim was to foment revolt among the Irish Catholics to keep England looking over her shoulder and thus divert her attention.

Nowadays the world runs on oil. Oil is moved in supertankers which are deep-draught vessels. The seas around Northwest Europe are shallow. The supertankers cannot enter the narrow seas. Western Ireland has fine, extensive, natural, deep-water ports. In the next decade or two, a great percentage of European industry will be drinking oil coming through the Irish gullet. Whoever controls Ireland will, to a large extent, control North-European industry; thus the shipment of arms to the IRA and the Protestant extremists of Ulster from *Libya*, of all places!

But to the English, God is an Englishman, and so he revealed to them the extensive oil deposits under the North Sea. And once again the Irish threat is neutralized, while Irishmen kill and maim each other for foreign causes of which they know nothing and care less. Pawns in a power game. The Celt can see and touch the stars, but when he looks at his feet he is lost unless he tries to understand himself.

As the light on Bray Head, Valentia Island, dropped down over the horizon over *Cresswell*'s bucking starboard quarter, and as the shimmer of the loom of Great Blasket light shivered under the stars ahead, I recalled the stories of long ago. Now I was sailing one of the oldest trade routes in the world, where every rock, every blade of grass, every tiny islet had its own legend of wonder, delight, bloody death, heroic blunders, and magic. The magic of the youth of the world! The magic of innocence, as it was before the veil was ripped asunder and the blanket of sin was flung over the worship of life!

*On the eighteenth day of December,*
*In nineteen-twenty-two,*
*The Tans in their big Crossley tender*
*Outside of the town of Macroom,*
*But the boys of the village were waiting,*
*With hand grenades primed on the spot,*
*And the Irish Republican Army—*
*Put paid to the whole fuckin' lot!*

Irish song (I suspect, because of the last line,
it originates in Dublin or Liverpool—I never
heard an Irishman, outside Dublin and
Belfast, use so-called obscenity in Ireland).

# 10

## *The Next Parish to America*

The sight around me, as the dawn shone over Dingle Bay, was astonishingly beautiful. Away to the east, across silver-shining water (though fairly rough, for the Irish Atlantic is not Long Island Sound, and every view is well earned the hard way), rose a line of piled mountains, Macgillycuddy's Reeks, lifting black, shattered elbows into the heartbroken sky. The shores were misty with Gaelic modesty and the Reeks seemed to be borne in the air by some mighty unknown force.

To the north lay my destination, the Blasket Islands, sprawling low out into the ocean in gallant defiance of all the laws of gravity. There is an optical illusion here which makes the horizon seem to run downhill to the west. It looked as if the Blaskets were trying to escape from Erin. The island furthest to the west, Inishtooskert, was uninhabited. It lay slinking on the surface of the sea, blue green below its grey, scaly skin, with the sun shining on it betimes as the clouds passed over on their way to take rain to England. On the inshore side of Inishtooskert lay the main island of the Blaskets, Slievedonagh; and behind it, seeming to claw the ocean like the talons of a great eagle, the headland of Sybil Head and the Three Sisters, which are as far as Ireland flings herself after the setting sun.

As I had no detailed chart of the islands, and as navigation among the reefs and rocks is tricky, I clambered forward on the heaving deck and handed the jib and staysail. This was always hazardous in *Cresswell*, because her bow had a whaleback deck, rounded, to shudder off the heavy seas breaking over her. Consequently, the actual treadway of the foredeck was tiny in area, no more than a triangle of about six square feet. But I had rigged good, hefty guard-rails all around the boat, and while on the bow they were only a foot or so above the gunwale to allow the headsails to pass over them when the boat was beating to windward, if I kept low, on my knees, I could manage well enough. Not being able to swim since my spine was damaged in Aden, I had always to be careful on any boat in motion. I could, and still can, float all right, but I cannot manage the kicking motion of swimming; and if I fell over the side, the chances were that the boat would, with her sails balanced to govern her course, carry on away from me.

With the headsails dropped down on deck and lashed to the hand rails, *Cresswell* rode head to wind and sea under her mainsail and mizzen, and even in those lively eight-foot waves off Dingle Bay she was steady enough for me to make a breakfast of fried corned beef and eggs. This is a very simple, easy meal, and Nelson loved it. Some of the pollock from the night before was left, and so as there would not be much time for lunch (there never is when you enter a haven in mid-forenoon), we scoffed that as well, and I washed the lot down with a pint mug of hot tea.

After breakfast I swilled down the decks and squared up all the gear above and below. I am very reluctant to enter any port with an untidy-looking craft. It's impolite to on-lookers, if there are any, and if there are not, it's still unseamanlike. Besides, while carrying out these cleaning chores, there's time to think about the passage in, and whether all the gear is in place.

After I had a good swill and scrub around the decks and a sweep-out below (it's surprising how scruffy a boat be-comes, especially if she's coastal-passage-making, with the company landing ashore often), I drank another mug of tea, smoked a cigarette, and thought for half an hour. I could plainly see the roadstead between Slievedonagh and In- ishtooskert, where, in 1588, one of the largest ships of the Spanish Armada, *Nuestra Señora del Rosario*, "Our Lady of the Rosary," a great lumbering galleon of one thousand tons, with the bastard son of King Philip of Spain on board, went to anchor in the calm water of Blasket Sound. During the night a great storm rose out of the southwest, leaving the galleon completely open to the weather. Her anchors dragged in that terrible sea, and she beat herself to death on the fierce fangs of the Three Sisters. King Philip's bastard son is buried in the graveyard at Vicarstown. The intention, when the Armada sailed in pomp and glory from Cádiz, was that he would become the king of Spain's viceroy in Northern England. Instead he got six feet by three of Irish sod in the rocks of Kerry.

A lot of people wonder why it was that so many of the ships of the Spanish Armada were wrecked on the West Coast of Ireland. If we look at maps of Ireland for the period, the reason is soon obvious. On all of the maps at the time of the Armada, the West Coast is shown as a straight line running north to south, with just one inlet, the great bay of Galway, whereas in reality it is a very jagged coastline, a continuous series of rocky headlands flung out far to the west of the general trend of the coast. The Spanish fleet sighted Ireland, and from the first northern headland they came to, sailed due south, straight into the rocks. The survivors of the Armada in Ireland were very few indeed. The word was out that they must be slaughtered to a man, and slaughtered they were, not only by the English but by the Irish too. Great was the amount of loot taken from the ships of His Most Catholic Majesty. Eight years before the Armada sailed, two Spanish ships had sailed for Smerwick Harbor in County Kerry, to foster revolt among the Irish. Well informed by the Irish, the English lord deputy for Ireland, Lord Grey, along with his friend and ally, Sir Walter Raleigh, intercepted the ships, took six hundred

Spanish and Italian prisoners, and on the heights of Sybil Head, had them all massacred and cast from the dizzy cliffs into the raging seas a thousand feet below. Meanwhile, back in the courts of the Estoril and Hampton Court Palace, the spinets tinkled and bejeweled feet twinkled.

There is the impression that very dark-featured folk from the West of Ireland, Wales, and Scotland are the descendants of survivors of the Armada. I very much doubt it. They are much more likely remnants of the old pre-Celtic folk who inhabited the lands five thousand years ago. Their general characteristics are wiriness, occasional frenetic energy, imagination to the extremes, and they are mostly long-headed with prominent noses. This type is very common in the Irish Islands, Cornwall, Wales, and some of the Hebrides. Others may be descendants of Iberian merchants who established themselves on the coast of Ireland in the sixteenth and seventeenth centuries, but this would be in the large towns and ports of the mainland, certainly not on the islands or in Wales.

All the while I was thinking of these things, I was also thanking the gods for the easy and safe passage across the Celtic Sea, which had brought me beyond the ken of the French Customs. They'd have a job to catch me now. *Cresswell* had a good run to the nor'rard ahead of her, southwesterly winds on the port quarter, and after I departed the Blaskets she made good time. That was important, for I wanted to be off Iceland early in the summer in order to sight as much as I could before the winter set in with its raging gales.

By mid-forenoon, carefully looking out for rocks and shoals, I had worked my way inside the Blasket Sound until I was within sight of the harbor of Slievedonagh. There, as I didn't know the depths, and there were no large craft lying inside the tiny creek, I hove to again. The wind was freshening, girding its loins for the gale due that night, so I started the engine and handed all sail. Very shortly, a small curragh came alongside, with two men in it. The boat was of

tarred canvas stretched over bent wood frames. She was
about fifteen feet long and had a cuddy fore and aft. She
looked very seaworthy indeed, and the men in her knew
how to handle their oars, though they had hardly any
blades. They rowed out to *Cresswell* at a good speed with
the curragh slicing the waters, yet the blades seemed to
glide gently and slowly. One of the men was large-boned,
but not heavy, while the other was slight and very dark,
almost like an East Indian or a gypsy.

"*Céad Míle Fáilte,*" they both said in low, gentle tones.

"A very good day to you," I replied. Nelson was fascinated. They had fish in the curragh.

"A fine craft ye have there. Is it Belfast ye're from?" asked
the larger man.

"The boat's from London, but I'm from Wales."

"Then you have the Erse?"

"Something like it."

"Keanan Blinder's the name, and this is my second
cousin Keanan Black."

"Tristan Jones, and it's Mr. Keanan the Postman I'm
looking for."

"Well, that's very convenient, for it's him you're looking
at," he laughed.

I said, hopping below, "I've a message from Corghain on
Skellig Michael." I got the postcard up from the bookshelf.

"Is it still alive he is, the auld blatherer?" said Keanan the
Postman.

"He is, and still setting off the maroons one by one."

They roared with laughter.

"Come aboard," I said. "I've a touch of the hard stuff
here."

"Is it English territory you're on?"

"Aye."

"Then I'll not put me foot onboard. No offense to you, for
it's a fine man you are as we both can very well see, but I
was arrested in Liverpool one fine day in the darkness of
the Troubles, and when they let me go and I was onboard

that mighty ferrycraft to Dublin, I swore by the merciful Mother of God that it's never again I'd set foot nor shoulder onto anything English as long as I live. But sure, there would be no harm in sliding a drop down here as I sit in my boat now, would there, and we'll drink to your fine and timely arrival, for it will be blowing the trousers off the devil himself in very short order." Keanan looked up at the black clouds moving across the water-heavy sky, racing for the Reeks in the east.

"That's for sure, and we do be better to enter the harbor straight," said Keanan Black. He was a quiet man, with weathered eyes and hard hands.

"Then we'll wait until you're safely alongside before your health is tokened," said Keanan the Postman. "Come now, we'll guide you in. What draft is it you have?"

"Two feet and a half," I replied.

"Oh, bejasus, that's no more than a cup in a spilt saucer."

"How's the entrance?"

"Like a dog's hind leg, but sure to a fine sailor like yourself it's no more than the daisies in the mouth of a bull."

"Lead on, Mr. Keanan."

And so the welcome to the Blaskets was made, and in ten minutes *Cresswell* was cozily secured in one of the tiniest harbors in Europe, if not the world.

The two Keanans, after a dram or two to the health of Corghain on Skellig Michael and the catching of the fine pollock the night before, then escorted me to the post office, which was Keanan Blinder's cottage. This was an old cottage with a thatched roof. Unlike the ones in Wales, the rush thatch rested on the inner edge of the stone walls, so that all around, where the eaves would have been, there was a platform, the top of the wall, which a man could walk around to repair the roof after the wild Atlantic storms had done their worst. On many of the cottages this ledge around the thatch was planted with flowers—a very refreshing sight to see after a week of nothing but the green seas, the fulmar petrels, Nelson, and Corghain's pajamas.

The cottage was one story, and the main part consisted of one large living room, into which the fireplace projected about four feet. This again was unusual, and Keanan said it was to make the room warmer. To one side of the massive chimney was a box-bed on a stone shelf. As in most of the cottages I saw on the Irish Islands, there were two doors, one on either side of the living room. The door facing away from the wind was always left open in the daytime. The walls were whitened with lime-wash, and the only decorations were a picture of Christ holding in one hand his bleeding heart, a photo of Patrick Pearse taken long before he was shot by the British army after the 1916 Easter Rebellion, and a calendar from Nestlé's Milk Company in Philadelphia, U.S.A.!

I remarked on the calendar, and Keanan told me that everyone on the Blaskets had relatives in the United States, mostly around New York and Boston, and that, in fact, about three-quarters of the income of the fifteen hundred or so islanders was in the form of remittances from these exiles. The emigration from this part of Eire was still going on in dribs and drabs, but until World War II it had been massive. In 1959, expatriation was mainly to England, where the men were hired by the big construction contractors. Some went on contract as far afield as Nigeria and Australia, building dams and electricity-generating stations. This had been going on for years, and it was always a shock to meet some old man speaking Gaelic, dressed in the simple way of the islanders, with his short, stubby pipe, once-a-week shave, and the sparkling, expressive eyes and gentle voice, and to hear him speak of the time he was building Sydney harbor bridge or the Mersey Tunnel. Their sojourns in faraway distant lands did not seem to affect them one iota, except that they could converse on any subject under the sun.

I remember sitting on a garden wall, looking across to the West, as the sun set over Inishtooskert, listening to one

ancient man of about eighty tell me of his days with the
British army in India (he had served two years on the
Khyber Pass), and how he had been recruited into the
Australian police while he was still in India, and how a
group of Irishmen and Scots had sailed from Calcutta for
Sydney with twenty camels intended for use in the Australian desert! I can hear him now, intoning the tale with every
embellishment that a Gaelic Celt can muster, yet with tiny
details remembered from sixty years before. He even recalled the colors of the loincloths of the ghilly-ghilly men on
the Suez Canal bum-boats and how, as a lad in Liverpool,
he and the other Irish recruits had spat on the king's shilling. The sergeant major had lost his temper at them, thinking it was an insult, until an officer ("Sure, a fine, tall, jewel
of a gentleman he was, for had he not a hundred acres in
West Meath itself with keepers and partridges running
around like fishwives on a Friday?") informed the sergeant
major that the Irish Islanders seal a bargain by spitting on a
coin, which signifies that the promise will be kept regardless of the financial result.

That night the gale blew, and with it came sheets of rain
and lightning. As Keanan Blinder walked back through the
rain with me, I could see the vague ghosts of people walking around their cottages. Keanan explained that when
there is lightning and thunder, they sprinkle holy water on
the ground around the walls.

I stayed in Slievedonagh harbor the next day, for the
Atlantic furies were loose and screaming vengeance for the
bastard son of the king of Spain. After the morning chores,
when the sky had cleared up a touch, I went, at Keanan's
invitation, to lunch with him. It was a fine nutritious meal
of fish and potatoes, goat's butter and porter ale. I asked
him about a small flower which was growing wild all over
the village. It seemed vaguely familiar.

"Sure, there was a fine fellow over here before the German War (the last one, for we call the first one the English
War), and he came over here all the way from London. We

had a few flowers growing here, but he said he would send us some better seeds. One fine day after he'd gone (and wouldn't all the days be fine after that, for he was a devil of a man for knowing everything), he sent us six packets of seeds. Well, when the little flowers showed themselves they were growing wild, for we'd thrown the seeds away. London Pride, they're called."

"How was life in the old days, Keanan?"

"Not much harder than now, Tristan, but of course we'd no radios to hear the fine experts of Dublin sorting out all the cares of the world. I remember when I saw my first radio and this Dublin man turned on the music. Keanan Buffer—a fine woman she was, such a command of the tongue!—when she heard that, she says to the Dublin man, 'Holy Mary Mother of God, did you ever see the like? Blinder, get the paper and pen out, sure we've to write to America and tell our brother of this miracle!' "

"When was that?"

"Let me see . . . the shark washed ashore the same year as King Edward condemned himself to eternal damnation by casting off himself the crown of England and marrying a divorced woman and leaving us nothing to fight but thin air. That was . . ."

"1936," I prompted.

" 'Tis right you are, then it was 1935."

"But radio was invented in 1910."

"Sure it was and all, and who invented it?"

"Marconi, and he was an Italian."

"Right, and was he not a good Catholic son of the Holy Church herself?"

"What have you heard about television?"

"Ach, we'll never have it here. Father O'Rafferty says it's the work of a Scotch Calvinist. What's his name?"

"John Logie Baird."

"Right you are, indeed. 'Tis the work of the devil himself!"

As I walked back to *Cresswell* that evening, I noticed the

crosses stuck in the thatch. Saint Bridget's crosses, they are called. I would not see them again until I reached Taquila, on Lake Titicaca, high up in the Andes. There are many surprising similarities between the Andes Quechua Indian and the islanders of Ireland. This is but one of them. Another one is the clothes they wear, even the brightly colored woven belts and the long stockings, and the leather sandals.

When I took my leave of Keanan the following morning, as he stood on the jetty, I asked him how I was to get the boat and myself officially entered into Ireland.

"Aah, sure, a fine man like yourself, what would we be wanting to do that for? You're here, are you not? We'll let God do the entering of you, and the devil take the office spalpeens in Dublin City."

"Well, fare you well, Mr. Keanan, and thank you for everything. One day I will be back this way."

"Sure, with a double-ended boat like that you might be back sooner than you think, for it's a holy wonder to me you know which way you are going, forward or backward. But God save you and keep the seas kind. Is it to England you are bound now?"

"Scotland."

"Good whisky they have, in the Catholic parts, anyway." His eyes twinkled with humor.

*Cresswell* edged her way out of the tiny creek, with most of the folk on the island standing on the mole head to see me off. I could hear the women saying, "Holy Mary, Joseph, and Jesus, what kind of a mother can the great man that he is have, who'd send him to sea alone like that and such a ruin of a dog? Do ye never catch pneumonia?" they called out thinly in the keening wind.

"He does not, he catches eight-pound pollock," retorted Keanan.

" 'Tis a fine craft he has there."

"Aye, bigger than the curraghs of Aran, and him a fine man, to be sure, but no bigger than Keanan Darcy's boy who's short in the head." As I left them out of earshot, I stored in my memory the sights and the sounds of the island next to New York, an island where there is not one tree and where fat people are greatly admired. As it was in the ancient tribes of Israel, where waxing fat women were worshiped for their beauty, so it is still in the Blaskets, where life has always been too hard and strenuous for anyone to put on too much weight. But if I ever did get beyond my normal 150 pounds and sought a mate, it's to the Blaskets I would go, for the people are handsome, with a grace and carriage which would do justice to a ballet dancer.

*Cresswell* was soon floundering away in the rough seas left by the recent storm. There was not much wind, and I wished to preserve my ten gallons of diesel fuel. The distance from the Blaskets to the Aran Islands is about one hundred miles between ports, and it took two days to cover. But on the second day the wind piped up and *Cresswell* danced again, while I sang the Eriskay love-lilt in the starboard shrouds as the green waters flashed by, and Nelson gnawed a fresh sheep bone.

Wales England wed; so I was bred. 'Twas merry London gave me breath.

I dreamt of love, and fame: I strove. But Ireland taught me love was best:

And Irish eyes, and London cries, and streams of Wales may tell the rest.

What more than these I ask'd of Life I am content to have from Death.

Ernest Rhys, "An Autobiography."

# 11

## On the Track of Columcille

The morning of the second day out of the Blasket Islands, the wind shifted round from southwest to the west. *Cresswell* had been running directly before it for a glorious twenty-four hours; now she was on a broad reach. That means that the wind was blowing from a direction at right angles to the boat, which is the fastest point of sailing, especially in a gaff-rigged ketch, for all the sails get their fair share and more of the wind, and all pull together.

The wind increased to around thirty-five knots by mid-forenoon, and it was plain, although there had been no warning on the radio, that we were in for a spot of lively weather. I dowsed the jib at eleven and the mizzen at noon. The sky was still fairly clear, and from a noon sextant sight between the scurrying clouds, forerunners of a high wind, I obtained a latitude which put me about twenty miles due west of the mouth of the River Shannon.

If I had had charts for the Shannon entrance, I would have worn in there for safe haven, to wait out the gale; but as I had not, I decided to weather out the blow. Duly I stood the boat out to the west, to put as much sea room as possible between *Cresswell* and the broken-toothed coast of Ireland. By mid-afternoon I had made a further ten miles out into the ocean offing, and the wind had increased to gale force. The main was reefed down four hands, and I settled down to hand steer her due north for the night. This course would keep me well clear of coastal hazards. During the morning I had made a large pot of burgoo—layers of porridge and corned beef, porridge and bacon, porridge and anything else to hand, each layer laced with a dram of whisky.

All that night it blew, and by midnight, after crawling around on the heaving deck with seas crashing right over, I had the sails down to mizzen and storm jib only. This kept the boat moving through the water, but not fast. Now she was only rearing, bucking, and dropping fifteen feet, instead of twenty, every four seconds, while the strain on the wire rigging and the masts was minimized. Of course, any double-diagonal–built vessel, after working in heavy seas like that for hours on end, will start to take water through the garboard (where the hull joins the keel), and *Cresswell* was no exception. This meant that I had to pump her out once an hour or so, to keep the water inside the boat as low as possible. Pumping out was heavy work, and I soon found myself wishing I could change places with Nelson, who, as usual in rough weather, was comfortably wedged in between the bulkhead and the table forward in the fairly dry cabin.

The night was thunderous and black, with slashing rain cutting visibility down to a few yards. No lights, no moon, no stars, nothing but the roaring wind and the flailing ocean raging fiercely in the wan light of the small kerosene lamp hanging in the mizzen shrouds. By two in the morning I'd had enough of fighting the kicking wheel, so I struggled forward onto the foredeck and dropped the storm-sail—an endeavor something like trying to subdue a berserk mountain bear in the dark while riding on a giant fairground switchback with someone throwing three tons of icy cold water at you every five seconds.

As soon as the spitfire jib was down and lashed, the boat came head-up to wind and sea, weather-cocked with her reefed mizzen, and there we were, in comparative peace and security. I lashed an extra line around the rubber dinghy, which was stowed upside down atop the cabin roof, then went below. The contrast between the noise outside the boat, with every wet, wintry spirit in the Atlantic screaming in the rigging, and down below was amazing. Even though the cabin was heaving up and down like an elevator gone wild, it was a haven of comfort. I managed precariously to make tea, half filled the pint mug, leaves and all, then dropped into wary, one-eyed slumber. Nelson crawled topside to keep watch.

The sky at dawn would have brought tears to the eyes of a bloody undertaker. Greys and blacks low on the western horizon, while slashed across the east was a blood-gutter streak of flaming red across the length of Ireland. It was enough to make Columcille, the holy Saint Columba, throw away his crozier. But I knew I was near enough to the Aran Islands to try to get into their lee before all hell and damnation was let loose on the world from the watery west. Clouds like the eyebrows of John L. Lewis himself. I decided to make a course west of the outermost of the Aran Islands, though I was strongly tempted to run for the nearest shelter, which was the passage between Inisheer Island and the coast of Clare. But I knew that if I did that, I would have the devil's own job to beat to windward, westward, again, to reach the port of Kilronan, on the main island of Inishmore.

By mid-afternoon, in terrific seas, I had worn around the westernmost of the Aran rocks, and was running free, under mizzen and working jib, at a great rate. As I reached the shelter of Inishmore Island, I looked to the north. The seas were moving mountains. I rounded up in the bay of Kilronan about six o'clock, dowsed sail, and motored up to the jetty. *Cresswell* was in good order; nothing had broken or been washed away. Everything had held tight and seamanlike. When I tied the mooring lines, for there was no one around in the lashing rain, I stood back and looked at her. There was an indefinable *something* about her, something I'd not noticed before, an air, an ambiance. I stood there and stared at her. How many gales and storms had she tackled from 1908 onwards? How many hard, strong, hefty men had shoved her out into seas raging beyond belief to rescue the helpless? How much strong emotion had been broadcast in her hull over the years in innumerable dramas of courage and bravery, patience and perseverance; how many sacrifices had been made on her heaving deck? She looked absolutely content; and then I realized with a shock, as I stood there, wet through under my oilskins in the pouring rain out of the black sky of Inishmore, that the old girl had enjoyed herself! She had reveled in it. The bloody old bitch was a storm-finder who'd sulk like a child in calm, balmy weather and refuse to hardly move; but, by God, when it blew she loved it.

I hit the side of the companionway as I climbed down the ladder. Nelson wagged his tail in anticipation of supper. "Old son," I said, "the old girl is as happy as a pig in shit out there. She's a cow in breezes or light winds, but, Jesus, she'll wear out the hammers of hell in a blow."

I fried up some of the already prepared burgoo, while Nelson wagged his tail even faster, sniffing the aroma of the sizzling bacon, well laced with Johnnie Walker. "I bloody well knew it, mate," I murmured, as I patted him, "I sensed it. She's got a mind of her own most of the time, but, by Christ, when the odds get heavy, she's with us all the way." Nelson hopped up topsides to piss over the side, which he always did before meals. Must have learned that from Tansy.

When the rain cleared, the first locals arrived on the jetty. They were mostly men, a crowd of about a dozen or so, all dark, with the long heads and prominent noses of the pre-Celts, all speaking Gaelic. The older men were wearing homemade tweed jackets and pants with slits up the legs about to the knee, so they could roll the pants up when they pushed their curraghs out. They also wore "pampooties," as they called the leather sandals worn rough side out and laced with cord.

The brightly colored woven wool belts they wore were

made in startling colors. These they called "criss," and years later I saw very similar belts among the Quechua of the high Andes, the fishermen of Lake Titicaca.

Among the crowd were two or three small boys, wearing a kind of skirt, something like that worn by the Evzone soldiers of the palace guard in Greece, or like a plain Scottish kilt, only not pleated. When I remarked on this later, I was told that "the little people" always had a fancy to steal boy-children, though they never bothered with the girls. So until they were nine years old, the boys were dressed in skirts to disguise them and to keep the leprechauns from stealing them.

Contrary to what the Freudians might think, the custom seemed to have absolutely no effect on the sex habits of the males of Aran. Still, they stay unmarried and continent until well on in life, the late thirties or early forties, and apart from husbands and wives joined in holy wedlock by the church, the sexes were separated rigidly from the cradle to (literally) the grave. On some of the islands, husbands and wives are buried in plots apart.

The skirted lads grow up to be fine, hefty fishermen, though the losses through heavy weather and fog have always been grievous. The islanders, as do all true sailormen, dread fog much more than storms. Over the centuries they have lost many of their menfolk by exposure in the open curraghs in thick fog, lasting for a week or more.

Two things struck me about the Aranmen: the difference in their faces and features compared to those of the mainland Irish, and the almost clinical cleanliness of their cottages. Here again, as in the Blaskets, many islanders live in exile in England and America. They spoke with familiarity of Manhattan and Fifth Avenue, yet knew nothing of Dublin.

All the fields in the Aran Islands are hand built—a painstaking task undertaken by men and women alike. When the Aranmen speak English, they call the fields "gardens." The soil is built up with sand and seaweed set down in alternate layers, all carried up from the beaches in baskets by asses, along the small, rocky lanes which in Ireland are known as "boreens." The islanders, besides being among the most devout people I ever came across anywhere, and besides being extraordinarily good boatmen, are also expert horse-riders. There was only one wheeled cart on the island, and that was used to carry the porter ale up to the pub from the jetty. All other transport was by a kind of sled about eight feet long, with runners of iron made from metal salvaged from the wrecks of that savage shore. The only other place I ever saw this was in Funchal, in the Madeira Islands, where they have been used ever since the first settlers arrived there in the thirteenth century. I have since often wondered, when I've sat drinking Bual wine on the main square of Funchal, if an Aranman had been among the Portuguese who found the Atlantic Islands, and if he thought that he had indeed arrived at Saint Brendan's "Isles of the Blest." There must be a connection. As far as I know, sleds are not used in mainland Portugal, or at least I have never seen any.

The cottages on Aran are interesting. Like those on the Blaskets, they have no eaves, but the fireplaces in Aran do not stick out into the room; they are flush with the wall. Alongside the fireplace there is a little alcove where the broody hens are put. As there is no real soil on the island and peat brought from the mainland runs out often, the main fuel used was cow dung, which, as it had been dried, did not have a very offensive smell.

Some of the cottages are extended when the family grows, but the fishermen told me that they never add on to a dwelling towards the west, "for he that builds towards the west is stronger than God." In quite a few cases I noticed that additions had been made to the little homes by actually cutting into solid rock to the east of the houses, rather than to the west.

I stayed with the Aran Islanders for two days, listening to their tales of fishing. They were frightened of the basking sharks, which grow to about thirty feet in length and which, they said, sometimes chased their curraghs. They had every reason to be scared of these monsters, because, although, like the whale, the basking shark is not a man-eater, feeding only on small plankton and tiny organisms of the ocean, it could easily upset one of the twenty-foot-long, canvas-covered curraghs.

At a gathering on the night before I sailed for Inishbofin, two of the older men and a couple of the younger ones performed what they called the "salmon-leap." They lay face up on the stone floor, with their arms held close to their sides and their feet close together, then, with a mighty lurch of the shoulders they threw themselves up into a standing position without using their hands in any way. An extraordinary performance. I have never seen this any-where else, before or since. They seemed to do it better with a couple of porter ales under their belts, and there was much merriment, especially from the girls and women, on their side of the room.

The eternal separation of the sexes does not include divi-sion of labor. In all the Irish Islands the only clear-cut male job was fishing, and the only definite female tasks were washing, cooking, and wool spinning, at which the older women seemed to be engaged from waking to sleeping. This, again, was similar to the custom of some of the Andes Indians. Every other task—spreading the sand and sea-weed, carrying great balks of driftwood miles from the beach, digging potatoes, even repairing the wind-torn thatch of the roofs—seemed to be shared alike by both sexes. Again, as with mountain Indians of South America, the females seemed to have much the heavier load of work. It was not unusual to see the women of a family hard at it in the fields while the men sat drinking porter and telling stories. The famous poteen, an illegal and highly danger-ous brew distilled from potatoes, is not made on the inhab-ited islands, nor, I was told, on any of the outlying islands. It is made on uninhabited islets close inshore and in the inland regions or desolate bogs and fastnesses of the rocky mountains. (Later, on the voyage north to Tory Island, passing close to the shores of Connaught beyond Achill Head, I did indeed sight several times the brown smoke of the poteen-men on islets close inshore.)

"Sure, now, in the old days before the Republic," said one of the Aranmen, "the Royal Irish Constabulary, they were fine men, with particular principles, and if it was a still they sighted with the smoke rising to heaven, why, they'd stand back for a pipe or two of good, strong tobacco, to give the poteen-men time to pack up and be off. But these Civic Guards of De Valera, why the fellows are so enthusiastic for the Republic they'd be down on you like a falling haystack, with no time at all for you to know they were there. Great men they are for lawful enthusiasm, but terrible men for patience. Aye, in the R.I.C., they were true Irishmen, and if they could help it, never brought the injustice of English laws onto our heads." All the other older men agreed with him.

The next sail, from the Aran Islands, was to Inishbofin, eighty miles north, the westernmost part of county Galway. I left Inishmore to the farewells of the fisher-folk, late in the afternoon, for the weather was kindly. By the following dawn I was off Slyne Head, with the quartzite Twelve Pins of Connemara gleaming away under the morning sun beyond the misty, blue grey hills of Connemara. The ocean was still bumpy, but the wind was fresh enough to drive *Cresswell* through the cross-seas without too much discomfort.

I was safe in the lee of Inishbofin by two in the afternoon, watching the lobsterboats being offloaded onto a French coaster. This is the main source of all the lobster and crayfish eaten in Paris, and they were sending out six or seven thousand lobsters weekly. The operation was run by a couple of Frenchmen who lived on the mainland. Each lobster had the sinews in its claw cut to prevent it from fighting with, and possibly damaging, the other lobsters.

They are kept alive all the way to Paris, and even after, until they are ready for the customer's table. What a contrast, the tiny island of Inishbofin, on the wild, stormy, rain-lashed shores of Connemara, under weeping grey skies, with the Champs-Elysées!

I went ashore in the afternoon to stretch my legs and, entering the pub for a pint of porter, met several of the local men. (No woman would be caught dead in a hotel bar in most parts of Ireland.) They were, as is usual among those folk, most courteous and accommodating to strangers, and especially to sailor-strangers.

One old chap told me how the island got its name—"White Cow." He said that long, long, ago, even before the days of Lugh, the god of light, two Fomorgian sailormen were wrecked on the island. Sitting on the beach, they were approached by an old woman driving a white cow. When they tried to milk the cow, the old woman struck the cow and the men with her stick, and they all turned into white rocks. "And, sure, they are still there, the big white rock and the two smaller ones, for all to see and to bear witness of the truth of this tale." To this day, no Inishbofin boatman will carry a white stone in his vessel. He will even pick out white pebbles from the loose stone ballast he might take on as cargo from the mainland.

There's more to it than the old man's tale, though. The symbol of the dead in Celtic times and before, to the ancien' Britons, was the white stone. In some parts of North Wales you will see people cross themselves when passing a white milestone on the road. In Spain, too.

In 1959 there were about eight hundred people on the island, and a friendlier lot I've never met. When I explained that I was going for a walk across the island, three of the younger fishermen came along, and we spent the time naming all the birds we came across in English, Erse, and Welsh, laughing all the while under the lightening sky, with cumulus rearing up thousands of feet as the wind dropped. I never saw a place with such a variety of birds—wheatears, starlings, larks, wrens, stonechats, ravens, choughs, house sparrows, looking exhausted, as if they'd just arrived on a windward beat all the way from Trafalgar Square; swallows, wood pigeons, crows, herons, oyster-catchers, ringed plovers, curlews, terns, blackheaded and herring gulls by the hundreds, and guillemots and the lovely fulmar petrels by the thousands. Down on the lee side of the island, the cormorants were busy at work fishing, while on the beach lay a hundred seals or more. The place was a living zoo.

On the way back to the pub, along a rocky boreen, the fishermen, who to a man are great storytellers, told me of the Spanish pirate Bosco, who built the castle in the harbor and stretched a great chain across its entrance to prevent enemies taking him by surprise. A cruel despot indeed. He used to fling his prisoners, men and women alike, over the high cliffs to their deaths below on the rocks. And they told me of Grace O'Malley, the great woman pirate *Grannuille*, who was queen of all the islands in the days of Good Queen Bess, and how she levied toll on all ships that sailed the Western Irish waters, French, Spanish, and English alike. Queen Elizabeth offered to make her a countess. But *Grannuille* sent a letter to Her Majesty declining the invitation, because, she wrote, she held herself inferior to no woman, and especially an *Englishwoman*! When she did eventually visit London, it was with such pomp and show of power that even the court of the Virgin Queen was astonished.

I spent one night in Inishbofin, refreshed by the walk across the island, the stories, and the porter ale. For the night I was invited to moor *Cresswell* alongside the French coaster, to avoid the worry of the anchor dragging; but after an hour or two of listening to the scrunching and screaming of thousands of lobsters and crayfish crawling over piles of mussels, scratching, with their sinewless claws, against the iron sides of her hold, I moved out again to quiet anchorage.

From Inishbofin to Tory Island, off the coast of Donegal,

is about 180 miles, and I covered this in four days of fine
weather, dry, and with a good breeze from the southwest.
For one whole day I was completely becalmed and sat it out
in the ocean swell, fishing, but catching nothing. I spent
two days in the shelter of the high cliffs of that desolate, yet
interesting, island, with its tall tors, or rock pillars (whence
the name). This was the home, in the legendary days, of the
one-eyed god Balor, the grandfather of Lugh, the god of
light, who killed the fierce old god of darkness with his
sword of lightning, and after whom London and the cities
of Leyden and Lyons, faraway in central Europe, are
named. Saint Columba, who founded the great Christian
refuge in Iona in 563, also lived here. The first Irish follower
of Saint Columba was named Dhugan, and his descendants, the Doogans, are still there.

Because Saint Columba, or Columcille as he was
called, banished rats from Tory Island when he landed
there in 555, no rat can ever live there, and even the ones
that survive shipwreck die only minutes after crawling up
the beach or over the rocks. The elder Dhugan is always the
guardian of the clay which is the specific, holy and anointed
by Columcille himself, against rats. Under no circumstances, not if he was offered a million pounds for a
spoonful, will he sell it. He will only give it, and the recip-
ient must be worthy of the gift. I was honored indeed
when Dhugan gave me a great handful of this magic clay to
take onboard.

I'd had a rat onboard *Cresswell* ever since mooring
alongside in Falmouth, and it was misery to hear the thing
scratching away where neither Nelson nor I could get at
him. I had tried everything—traps, poison, even smoking
him out. Five minutes after Columcille's clay was placed
onboard, in a paper bag on the lower galley shelves, he was
out on deck and Nelson had him in his teeth. Don't ask me
how or why, I can only tell that it was so.

Close by the landing jetty of Tory there is a Christian
cross, but unlike any other in Ireland it is in the shape of a *T*.

This is very ancient and most strange, for the only other place I ever saw it was in Ethiopia, where it is in common use by the Coptic church. It is the cross of Saint Anthony, who is held in great esteem in the Abyssinian church. Could it be that the same Saint Anthony who took Christianity into East Africa in the second century was also here in Tory Island? By what route could he have come except with Celtic mariners from Marseille or Cádiz?

One of the fishermen I talked to showed me his curragh, which was different from those in the islands further south, because the canvas was fastened to the gunwale after being stretched over the oak frame. In the Blaskets and in the Aran Islands the tarred canvas is fastened to the actual frames themselves.

Again, the number of birds in the sky above the island was limitless, as were the seals in the surrounding waters. In the evening, I retired to the old fisherman's house, for there is no pub on the island, and, over tea, listened to the tales of the Viking raids and how the monks used to hand-ring the bells in the tops of the ancient round-towers so that the islanders could take refuge from the bloody swords of the Northern sea-savages. Again, he spoke as if it had all happened last week.

This was the last of the Irish Islands, and from here I would plough into the plunging, plundering green seas of the Minches, the North West Approaches, 140 miles to the northward, to the Hebrides, over one of the roughest stretches of water in all the seas of the world!

*From the lone shieling on the misty island,*
*Mountains divide us, and a waste of seas,*
*Yet still the blood is strong, the heart is Highland,*
*And we, in dreams, behold the Hebrides.*

"The Canadian Boat Song,"
Anonymous - c. 1845.

# 12

## *Behold, the Hebrides!*

I took my leave of Dhugan the Elder, of Tory Island, on the last day in May. The weather forecast was about normal for the next part of the world in that time of the year. "Winds southwesterly, force five, sea areas Shannon, Rockall, Hebrides." As I was anxious to reach Iceland before midsummer, so that I would have at least two months of reasonable weather before the equinoctial gales of September set in, I pushed off without delay, northward direct to the southernmost islands of the Outer Hebrides, and the first port in the group, Castlebay, on the island of Barra.

As the anchor came aboard, I reflected that I had passed right along the coast of Ireland, from south to north, calling at five havens, without having officially entered the country, without having to show one piece of paper. Now I was leaving Irish waters with no official clearance and nothing to show for my sojourn but memories of good people, fascinating storytellers, kindness and courtesy, humor and hospitality, a bottle of poteen and a pound or two of Dhugan's rat specific.

I took on a few gallons of sweet streamwater from Tory Island and some diesel fuel from a fishing boat resting in the bay. Then, after a lunch of lobscouse, I hoisted sail and was away on the wind.

Lobscouse is a very old method of cooking several meals at once in one pot. Thinly sliced potatoes go on the bottom,

117

in a layer about two inches thick, then sliced carrots or turnips or other roots, followed by cut cabbage (and on Tory Island, dandelion leaves) and sliced onions, a one-inch layer, then on top of it all, fish cut into small chunks, just the flesh. Water is added until it just covers the food, a cube or two of beef bouillon (these days), and the lot is brought to a boil, then left simmering for a couple of hours, until the fish falls to pieces and mixes with the rest. A pressure cooker three-quarters full of this lobscouse provides about four meals. All you have to do is dish it out of the pan after it's warmed up. When the pot got low, I used to make a curry paste and add that to liven it up. It's good and sustaining, and very little trouble. It can be concocted before sailing, while the boat is steady at anchor. This obviates having to mess around too much at preparing food while the boat is lurching around in heavy seas such as are the case usually in the North West Approaches of Britain. Then, when sea legs are found, which usually takes a couple of days, another two-day stock can be prepared. In *Cresswell* I used to place the pot, after the food was cooked, in a "haybox," that is, a box packed with hay for insulation. This kept the pot hot for up to twenty-four hours, thus saving precious kerosene.

Lobscouse was once the staple food on the ocean-sailing ships out of Liverpool to America and the Far East. Liverpool sailors were nicknamed "scousers" for that reason.

The run from Tory Island was a rough 220 miles, with hard winds, which meant shortening sail. I rigged the "dodgers" (canvas cloths) around the cockpit, which was not self-draining. With the frequent rain showers, I spent the whole three days of the passage in oilskins. I had black oilskins, because yellow is supposed to be unlucky in a boat, at least in those waters, and I would take no chances, even though I am not particularly superstitious.

There are many superstitions among fishermen and sailing men. Such as never mentioning the word "rabbit" onboard and not sailing if you see one of these animals on the way to the boat. Never having a priest onboard and always referring to them as "the men in black." Never sailing out with a menstruating woman onboard. Never sailing on a Friday the thirteenth, or any Friday if it was avoidable. Never whistling onboard a sailing craft (it was supposed to anger the wind, but I suspect that it was just that it got on other crewmen's nerves; it was once a flogging offense in the Royal Navy, but that was because signals were passed between plotters at the Spithead mutiny of 1792 and at the Nore by that means). Again, it is very unlucky indeed to coil a rope "widdershins," or counterclockwise, or to stir a cooking pot in that fashion, for it is against the direction in which the sun travels. In ancient days, if a man found his wife stirring the pot "widdershins," he had the right to kill her, for it was thought she was putting a curse on his voyage.

As the light of Tory Island fell into the sea astern at dusk, Nelson and I could see the lights of many steamers out on the north horizon. The North West Approaches to Britain is one of the busiest shipping areas in the world, with trade coming from around the globe to Glasgow and Liverpool. This meant that I had to stay topsides all night, despite having the sails neatly balanced so the boat steered herself. Having a good stock of batteries for the radio, I indulged in the luxury of listening to music until the transmitters closed down around midnight. Then I switched to the trawler band and listened to conversations from as far away as south Iceland and the Norwegian Sea.

During the first night out from Tory Island, an overeager cod hooked himself on one of the two lines I had streamed astern. I made some batter and fried him up for a midnight special, which was a comfort from the rain and wind while bouncing and bashing over the seas.

The next day, early in the first light, I hove to and slept for an hour, then plodded on and at mid-forenoon sighted, far away on the starboard bow, low and misty, the rocks of Skerryvore and, beyond them, like Afghans in ambush, the turbans of the grey hilltops of Tiree, the island from where the matron at the Aden hospital hailed. Tiree and its neighboring island of Coll have the highest sunshine average in the British Isles, and I remembered the matron's eyes. I wondered if she was at home and was tempted to haul over to the isles to see, but June was upon us and the north was waiting, so I held course steady for Barra. I picked up the light of Bernerey, the southernmost of the Outer Hebrides, at dusk, and by midnight I was quietly hove-to in the Barra Passage, awaiting the dawn to show the way into Castletown. Again I was forced to stay topsides all night, for there were many ships and fishing craft in the passage. The wind had dropped to a breeze, and the sky was clear and starlit. I rigged up the bright Tilly oil lamp, hung it over the side, and tried my luck for a fish, but they were too crafty, and in the dawn the deck bucket was forlornly empty. At seven in the morning Nelson took over the watch and I turned in for two hours, until the light improved for entering the port. By eleven there we were, safe and secure, anchored in a lovely bay with a wide, white, sandy beach.

The harbor master was soon out in his launch, uniform and all.

"Where're you from?"

"Falmouth." I didn't tell him about Ireland.

"That's a lang run, laddie."

"Aye."

"Weel, mon, ye're lucky." A big man, he was standing in his blue motor launch, grabbing my gunwale with his great hamfists.

"Why's that?"

"There's a weddin' on, and it's you that's invited."

"What time?"

"As soon as ye're ready, the hard stuff's already oot."

"Where?"

"At the church up yonder." He pointed up the hill to the

grey tower. He didn't say "kirk," for this was a Catholic island.

"I've no suit."

"Och, lad, dinna fash ye'sel. Come as ye are. This is no' London."

So it wasn't, as I soon found out, with the fiddles playing and the lads and lasses dancing reels and jigs and even some modern dances. Whisky there was by the crate and beer by the hogshead. I had put two anchors down, and for the first time since leaving England, I took Nelson ashore with me. (He was getting randy and the island had a fair chorus of bitches yapping at him from the beach). In short, we had a whale of a time; so much so that it took me a week to find out who got married! I slept in a different cottage every night, and it was like home away from home, only better.

There was still no electricity on Barra in 1959. The population (around twelve hundred) gained their living fishing or crofting, working a small plot of land with potatoes and sheep for wool. They lived in what they call "black houses," oblong thatched cottages about fifty feet long and twelve feet wide, the narrow gable end facing the prevailing wind, like a boat at anchor. The cottages were built of stones, not hewn, but picked from the rocky ground and packed with moss. The walls were surprisingly thick, four to six feet, and the insides were lime washed, just as they had been on the Irish Islands. The insides of the black houses consisted of one long living room where everything was done. If the family grew, an addition was built on, but not, as in Eire, only to the east.

Crime is virtually unknown on the islands, and often the innkeeper left the bar while the customers paid their money into the till!

From the heights overlooking the dazzling white beaches, probably the prettiest beaches in the United Kingdom, I gazed down bewitched at the patches of purple and green where large rafts of seaweed had washed up, and the brown streaks where the peat streams ran their meandering way to the sea. Overhead, gulls and petrels screamed welcomes to the fishing craft entering the bay.

The island airfield, which in fact was the main beach, could only be used at low tide. It is the only one I've ever seen where the flight schedules were dictated by the state of the moon. A lady was in charge, who was thought to be the only female airport manager in Europe, if not the world.

The Outer Hebrides had been described by Pytheas 330 years before the birth of Christ. Agricola's fleet had called there in the first century A.D.; Ptolemy had shown them on his map of the world, drawn in the second century A.D. (the same map which had shown Peru). On it he gives the island of Skye the name of *Scitis Insular* and modern-day Lewis, the biggest of all the Hebrides, is called *Dumma*. But, before Ptolemy, Pliny had listed thirty islands in the Hebrides. In fact, he misnamed them, for their Celtic name was *Hebudes*, but to the ancient Gaels they were *Tir Nan Og*, "The Land of the Ever Young."

Columcille arrived in the Hebrides in A.D. 563 and by the time of his death, in 597, not only the islands, but the whole of Scotland was under Christian tutelage.

The centuries of peace lasted until around A.D. 800, when the dreaming islands were rudely awakened by the arrival of the Vikings, who drove their knirrer-longships south from the Faroes and the Orkneys. The latter they called the "Nordereys," while the Hebrides became the "Sudereys." Thus the oldest rocks in Europe became part of the kingdom of Norway for three hundred years until Scotland, under King Alexander III, defeated the Vikings in 1263. The Norse people of the islands were slowly absorbed into Scottish culture, yet kept their own identity.

The Celts always held on in the southern islands. The difference between the Norse-descended folk of the northern islands and the Gaels of the south was further widened during the religious reformation of the sixteenth century.

The dark, gloomy spirit of Calvinism appealed to the Norse blood, while in the south the Gael was faithful, as always, to the teachings of Rome, Saint Patrick, and above all, Saint Columcille. For five hundred years after the Scots defeated the Vikings, sporadic warfare flamed among the Lords of the Isles—the McLeods, the McLeans, the McNeils, the MacPhees, until the strength of the clans was broken, finally, at Culloden. The Lords of the Isles became lords of empty lands, as the clansmen flew in droves, like wild geese before a storm, to America and Canada. The lonely islands dreamed on, sad, bereft, and beautiful.

Time was pressing. There were only two months left of reasonable sailing weather. I sat down in the cabin with the charts and worked out a route. I had intended to pass up through the Outer Hebrides, in their lee, out of the way of the great Atlantic rollers, then sail north for the Faroes on the way to Iceland—the old "steppingstone" way of the ancient traders. But I had wasted a week in merrymaking. I traced the track to Iceland on the chart. I would sail direct. But first, there was a tiny dot on the chart, well to the west of the Hebrides, sixty miles out, all alone and remote in the deep Atlantic—St. Kilda—where I wanted to call and look around.

In 1942 I was in a destroyer which picked up two Norwegian seamen from St. Kilda. They had been torpedoed and, after surviving a lifeboat trip of two weeks, had washed ashore on the remote islands. There they had survived on birds' eggs for some weeks before being rescued. I recalled, vaguely, seeing the abandoned village from the decks of the warship. But we had not been allowed to go ashore because the skipper was anxious to get in and out fast in case of a U-boat attack.

Now I was in my own ship. Now there were no U-boats. Now I could see for myself. I cleared Barra for Reykjavík, Iceland, hauled up the anchor, hoisted the main, mizzen, and jib, and was off with a good forecast and a stiff breeze, through the Barra Sound, between that island and the lovely islet of Eriskay, flung like a green garment over the blue waters. Eriskay, where in 1745 Prince Charles Edward Stuart, "Bonnie Prince Charlie," landed from France with Gallic gold to rally the clans and cry rebellion against the House of Hanover. A rebellion that was later smashed on the bloody field of Culloden. Ever since the bagpipes have mourned the defeat of the clans.

Eriskay, where in 1941 the S.S. *Politician*, badly damaged by German torpedoes, drifted ashore carrying twenty thousand cases of whisky. *Uisque-bach Gu-leor!* Whisky galore! As soon as she touched the rocks, the news spread faster through the islands than the fiery crosses lit for the 1745 rebellion! In three days there was not one case of booze left onboard the pounding *Politician*.

Eriskay, where the musical poem of the Gaelic love-lilt was born! I settled down to a close reach for two days and nights in search of the three small dots of St. Kilda in the immense, eternal, infinite, heaving ocean.

To sail to St. Kilda was rough. With the seas piling up on the continental shelf after their passage across the Atlantic, it could not be otherwise, especially as *Cresswell* was sailing on a course only fifty degrees off the wind. But I had rested well in Barra and was fit as a fiddle. The days of empty sea and the nights under starlit skies, with the west wind moaning low in the shrouds and around the houndsbands, passed by. The daytime summer skies were clear enough to give me good sextant sights, and on the third morning out I spied the mighty capsized cliff of Boreray, the most remote part of the British Isles, dead ahead. I hove to, had breakfast and an hour's sleep, then worked into Village Bay, where there had once been a settlement.

As *Cresswell* sailed up to the root of the bay, I lowered the mainsail. The gaff hoist slipped out of my hand, and the heavy, twelve-foot-long spar clattered down on deck with a sharp crack. At this a million, a *million*, birds lifted up from the cliffs, which rise over fourteen hundred feet straight from the ocean, and darkened the noon sky. There were so many birds, sea birds of all kinds, that they turned day into night, and there was such a noise with their screaming that I can still hear it now. I had never seen anything like it before, nor have I since. It was so violent, that rise of life from the white cliffs of Dun and Boreray, that I was genuinely frightened in case they should attack the boat. Even Nelson cowered under the cabin table.

I dropped the hook and looked around. The granite cliffs were snow white with bird-shit. There was a tremendous feeling of sadness about the place, intensified by the wheeling and screaming of the birds. It was a sadness so real that I could reach out and touch it. Overhead, the sky was dark with rainclouds, which swept low over the lonely peaks of grey Hirta, the main island. The heavens themselves seemed to be weeping as the first raindrops pattered on deck. Then, as the birds descended to their nesting ledges, all was quiet again, except for the soughing of the wind as it swept down the valley and over the ruined cottages of the village which had once, only a short time ago, known the cry of mothers and the laughter of children. Despite my fatigue I stayed on deck for an hour, taking in this melancholy scene; then, with a shudder, I stepped below into the warm and cozy cabin, gave Nelson a shove with my foot so he would go topsides, and turned in to sleep until the rain ceased. I fell into darkness trying to sort out the pad of Nelson's paws on deck from the patter of the great, dolloping raindrops.

When I woke it was around two in the afternoon and the rain had stopped. After a quick meal of lobscouse, I made ready to go ashore. I took some rope, an ax, and my knife. And Nelson. From the deck, I had seen some sheep climbing the steep cliff faces, looking like goats.

I looked around the old village. Here, people had lived from the Iron Age on, right up until 1930. In ancient times they were the most isolated people in the Western world. Their life was very tough indeed. They could not fish from boats because there was no wood for boat building, so they

fished from the rocks, where the great Atlantic seas rushed
and gushed at these lonely specks of land under the grey
skies. Their main food was birds' eggs and bird-meat. They
made their clothes out of bird-skins and feathers. Then
sheep, which they plucked, not sheared, were introduced,
and for a while life improved.

Through all these centuries there were only three families
on the islands. The only visitors, from the mid-eighteen-
hundreds on, were stray trawlers coming to rest and the
twice-annual boat from the mainland. In 1912 influenza
arrived on the island and killed off many. These folks were
converted Calvinists. What the effects of that stern, gloomy
philosophy, together with the results of hundreds of years
of inbreeding were on these simple people, I can hardly
imagine. The sum result was that in 1930, the British government, under strong public pressure, decided to
evacuate the island.

All 36 of the surviving islanders (the population in 1850
had been 110) were taken to Ardtornish, in Argyll. And
what do you think the British government did to these
people who had never before seen a tree? They set them to
work for the Royal Forestry Commission! Of course, they
were totally unfit for this kind of labor, and eventually they
all drifted off to disappear in the slums of Glasgow. *Sic
transit miseria!*

I searched through the old cottages. All the thatched
roofs had blown away. Inside there was only tough grass
growing. But the spirit-presences were so strong they were
almost physical. I looked into the manse, the old preacher's
house, the biggest house in the village, with its tin roof
clattering away in the wind, and found old *Encyclopedia
Brittanicas* from 1840. The dining table had collapsed, and
the glassless windows swung in the breeze. There was an
air of complete and utter hopelessness about the place—as
the French say, *"une tristesse absolue."* I could not understand why this should affect me so. I had visited many
ruined places—the Coliseum, the scattered ruins of South

Turkey, and old, abandoned castles in Spain. Far from feeling sad, I had been curious, then interested, and even proud that men could leave such works behind them. As I knocked a timid sheep over the head with my ax and roasted it over a fire of wood chopped from one of the manse shelves, I thought and thought about it. Then it dawned on me. The reason I felt so sad here, in this tearful, remote place, was because there were relics and ruins of people of *our time* and of *our age*. This is what the world would be like if a nuclear holocaust came about.

I looked around me. *People who had lived here were still alive.* They had lived here, and played here, and cried here, and sung here, *during my lifetime.* Now it was all gone. Finished. Dead. Here, there was no proud achievement. Here man had been defeated, despite a long, hard, bitter struggle. There was the sadness, the sense of ineffable gloom. The presences around me were in the depths of misery.

I looked around the tumbled stones of the three churches, dedicated to Christ, to Brendan the Voyager, and to Columcille, then made my way back to the boat. Nelson was pleased to get back onboard. He had not liked the village one bit.

As I took off into the ocean dusk (I didn't fancy a night there), I wondered to myself how Iron Age people had reached these remote rocks. When the pro-English General Campbell arrived, chasing Bonnie Prince Charlie after the defeat of the 1745 Scottish rebellion, how was it that the islanders had never even heard that a war had been fought? Why were there so many bird beaks on the floors of the cottages? The last conundrum I figured out on the passage to Iceland. The poor souls had used the bird beaks in the place of wooden pegs, to fix the rush thatch to the roofs!

But still, there was something fascinating about the place, named after a saint who is not even on the Christian calendar, something mysterious and yet at the same time hopeful. After all, what else can we do but admire the plain courage of all the folk who had wrenched an existence out of those barren rocks for so many centuries?

St. Kilda is now (1977) a British government wildlife reserve, and there is a rocket-tracking station on the main island of Hirta. I am told there are even more birds there now!

*Now give me a nail and a hammer,*
*And a picture to hang on the wall,*
*Give me a pair of stepladders,*
*In case that I should fall,*
*Give me a couple of waiters,*
*And a dozen bottles of ale,*
*And I'll bet you I'll hang up that picture,*
*If somebody drives in the nail!*

One of Tansy Lee's drinking songs.

# 13

## Background to the Sagas

As is shown in the old legends of the Gaels, and also in the accounts of the Greek Pytheas and the Roman Pliny, the Celts of Ireland and Wales made the long voyages to Iceland and back with surprising regularity, many centuries before Christ. But there was no permanent Celtic settlement there until the 750s, when a hundred or so monks and anchorites, womanless, tiring of incessant Saxon and Norse raids on their coastal eyries, gathered up their parchments, bell, crosses, and tools, and, mustering among them hardy curragh sailors, sailed north to find a safe refuge on the wild, semibarren, volcanic islands of Papey and Papos. The monks knew well the old Gaelic legends. Had not the holy Saint Brendan sailed these waters and had he not told of fiery mountains being spewed out of the sea from the depths of hell and of a blasphemous sailor lost into the red-hot molten rock?

The monks had read of Cormac ua Liathain, who long before had sought his desert in the seas of the wild north. There Cormac had meditated for twenty years to drive the wailing banshees from his Gaelic soul and find his peace in the contemplation of infinite forgiveness.

From the monasteries of Aran, Anglesey, Bangor, Clonfert, and Clonmacnoise, the holy men set sail in their curraghs. Northward they pounded to Iona, off the coast of Strathclyde, there to listen to the clear words of *De Ratione*

*Temporum* and *Librus Regium Questionum*, the works of the Venerable Bede, written far away in Wearmouth and Jarrow, giving them directions garnished from many voyages to the Faroes and Iceland during the past centuries.

With twenty to thirty men in each curragh, the saintly fleet bowled and rolled over the stormy waters, the wind bellying out the Celtic crosses on the flaxen sails. They called at the already established Christian outposts on the lonely Faroe Islands, then pressed on north, to Thule, the last land in the world. They took with them sheep and ponies, corn and beer, oats and flax, and iron tools to carve refuge from the rocks. The men of the fleet sailed on, singing hymns as the stone deadman-anchors were raised, the sails hoisted, and the hide hulls slid away from the Faroes to take the cross of God to the country they thought nearest to hell.

For a hundred and twenty years the Gaelic colony of holy men clung to the steaming rocks of Lon and Sieda. For more than a century the holy fathers, the *papar*, dug into the desolate sands of Skeidara and the earth ledges of the tiny islands of Papey and Papos. They had regular communication with the mother monasteries of Britain and Ireland, with young men arriving to replace the older men dying in hard labor and prayer.

In 860 the first Norseman, Naddod the Viking, blown off course on a voyage from his lonely vikke in Norway to the Orkneys, sighted Thule. But having also sighted an island of fire "risen from the sea," Naddod, wary of meeting the devils of hell, or more of his own breed, turned south and did not land. Upon his return to Norway, tales of his adventure fell upon the ears of a landless Swede, a Norseman, to be sure, but no Viking, loitering around the wooden eating-hall of Harald Fairhair, king of Norway. In short order, Gardar Svarvasson, though penniless, rousted allies from among the idle sea-rovers of Norway and set sail to discover this mysterious land. Rumors of the Christian expeditions of long ago had filtered back to the vikkes, to the lonely Norwegian fiords, over the years. Perhaps there there were rich pickings to be had for the slash of a bloody sword?

The feelings of the Gaelic holy men as they stood on the forlorn shores of the Vatnajoküll, with the black clouds bursting over the Vestmannaeyjar Island out to the southwest, as they stared, horrified, at the blood-red-striped sail of Svarvasson, with his scowling dragon's head bow-stem, charging in from the east, can only be imagined. But Gardar Svarvasson was, first and foremost, an explorer; indeed, he was one of the first of the ancient sea-rovers of whom the record is at all clear.

Following the custom of the Norse, he called a council of war, and, with his twenty-two Vikings, argued the alternatives. They were seeking land for their families; this was not land, this was a desert of hard rock, fit only for Christian lunatics. They would sail on, to the west, and seek good grazing soil for sheep and cattle. They would leave the meager pickings of the Vatnajoküll, this smoking land, to unlucky latecomers.

Up went the striped squaresail, over the shield-bedecked gunwale the long oar sweeps were thrown, and the dragon's head bit into the wind again. Past the long, black, melancholy shores of the Landeyjaer, past the storm-tossed, inhospitable peninsula of Reykjanes and the rocks of the Skagi they pressed with all muscle and flaxen sail, until before them opened up the wide, heart-lifting expanse of the Faxaflói, with the waters shining in the afternoon's pale sun. There they gazed, stupefied, beyond the mountain-rimmed gulf of green, white-spumed waters, at the stupendous cone of Snaefellsjökull rearing up, like the curse of Thor himself, into the cloud-swept skies of Thule.

But they found the pastures cold and windswept between the knurled claws of the Snaefell, and so pressed on north past the snarling mass of Ondverdarness, and finally entered Breidafiord, the broad fiord, where they wondered at the thousand skerries and swift currents, stronger than any they had ever seen. They stared at the seal-covered rocks and skulking reefs, and the seven ax-clefts struck by the gods into the Isharjardajub, a mighty rock heap thrown, defeated, into the sea by the snow-shouldered mount-mass of victorious, arrogant Glama! Gardar and his men plied their iron-banded arms to the sweeps, gliding the knarr into the Kalelen deep-fiord, where the icefalls of the Drangajoküll tumble into the sea like panicked sheep leaping from the mother herd.

Still Gardar was not satisfied, and after a rest of several days, onward to the north they went, with no sign of man, only the birds in their massed thousands as they swooped over the striped sail, only the seals and the walruses as they moaned low in the pale light of the falling sun. On they went, with the North Horn, the Hornbarg, under a stormy lee, to Húnaflói, the great expanse of fish-ridden water with the low land around flatter and richly grassed, green valleys driving inland between the tumbling, stark, rock mountains. Warmer and drier, too, they were, for they were now protected from the southwest fist of the wind. Gardar's men peered beyond the green of the valleys and the soft blues and greys of the mountains. They could see, behind the bluff peaks, the steely, silver-gleaming glint of ice on the high falls.

Gardar now determined to winter on this coast, before returning to Norway with news of his magnificent find. The longship headed east along the coast. He missed the best wintering haven, Eyjafiord, having been blown past it in a night storm, but, just to the east of the mighty upthrust of Skjálfandi, "the Trembler," he entered a long, south-running fiord, where he and his crew built a house. They named the place Húsavík. House-Bay. No Celtic kindness yet in names.

There, at the darkening of winter, for the winds now blew from the north hard into the fiord, Gardar left one of his viking crew, with a thrall and a bondwoman named Nattfari. Gardar sailed on east in the spring, headed for

Norway. A few months later Nattfari gave birth to a son—
the first child known to have been born in Iceland. This is
recorded in the Norse *Landnamabok*, a history of Iceland.

Gardar Svarvasson, never a man to hide his light under a
bushel, named the land *Gardarholm*. The millenium of
peace in Thule was over.

While Gardar was on his way home to Norway, Floki the
Fisherman, a mystic by nature, sailed for Thule from
Stavanger, Norway, with a small crew, a cage of ravens,
and various small animals for sacrifices. Floki was continually making sacrifices to the gods and invoking their assis-
tance in the smallest things (which is probably the reason
for his small crew). He landed in Breidafiord and wintered
there. Floki was no farmer, though he did take some live-
stock. Whether he did this for breeding or for sacrifices is not
clear from the sagas. What is sure is that the fishing that
winter was bad, which is not surprising, considering how
the winter gales storm into Breidafiord. Floki longed for the
spring. When April came, it was still snowing, still cold, so
he left in anger, ranting and raving at the weather, the
gods, and the land, which he called in his spite, Iceland.
Floki returned to Norway and gave his late winter home as
bad a reputation as Columbus gave San Salvador, that
barren stretch of sand, a good one. But one of Floki's crew,
named Thorolf, who had made a very courageous passage
over the wild Flaxaflói in his parted tow-boat, swore to all in
Norway that the new land was so rich that butter dripped
from every blade of grass, and forever after he was known
as Thorolf Butter.

The following year Ingolf Arnarson and his brother Leif,
having killed the two sons of the Earl Atli of Gaular, in
South Norway, had, according to the Norse law, to pay
blood-money. Being penniless, they called together their
thralls and cousins, fitted out a longship, and sailed for
Iceland.

The first year Ingolf and Leif spied out the land, as Gardar had done before. The second year they made another

expedition with settlers, but Leif, in his longship, sailed first for Ireland, where he raided for slaves. Twelve of these, warriors all, he captured and carried to Oraefa, where many fine farms now thrive, nestled between the rocky outcrops of the jökull. The Irish warriors eventually killed Leif and stole away with Leif's women and boat. They sailed to an island off the south coast. There they held out for many months against Leif's berserk avengers, but in the end, defeated, they threw themselves off the high cliffs into the sea, from whence comes the island's name, Vestmannaeyjar—"Irishman's Island."

From 865 on, the Norse immigration into Iceland was regular and steady. With them, the Vikings brought many captives from the Gaelic lands of Ireland, Wales, and Scotland. The anchorites of Papos, Papey, and the Vatnajökull had now retreated into the fastness of Kirkjubaejar, a site so holy that even the Norsemen were afraid to visit it.

Between 890 and 920 events took place which greatly increased the Norse immigration to Iceland. A Viking army, plundering the west of Europe, was battered into defeat by the Gaelic Bretons of Northwest France. The survivors of this army fled, some east, to join their kinsmen in Normandy, some north, to join Hastern and the Great Horde, who were invading Saxon England. Here, with the continuous harrying of King Alfred and his Celtic allies, they were again hammered into defeat, and the Viking array, split into ragged tatters, was thrown back from the Saxon-English shore.

In 902, King Cearbhuil, the monarch of Leinster in Ireland, defeated a Norse army and in 1014 the great Brian Boru finally threw the Viking plunderers out of Baile Atha Cliath (Dublin) and into the sea. The Norse survivors of this debacle sailed for North Wales, the very heartland of the Celts, where they were promptly decimated and flung back in bloody disarray to sulk in their sea-lair of Man. But here the Vikings found no respite, not even in their own flaunting grounds, the North Sea, the Irish Sea, and the English

Channel, for now the Celt had regained his sea legs and the Saxon had found his. With the aid of lessons well learned from the Norsemen, they time and again attacked and defeated the dragon-head ships of the Vikings, forcing them ever northward. These seaborne hammers, struck bloodily year after year from the British Isles, turned the Norsemen's bows towards Iceland, where they arrived in increasing numbers, along with their families and Celtic captives. Gradually, over the next two centuries, the two bloodstrains mixed. The *Landnamabok*, the old book of families and their settlements, drawn up around the year 1000, shows four hundred families living in Iceland, and one-seventh of the names in the book are unmistakably Celtic.

Despite the rockiness of the country, there is almost no stone in Iceland suitable for building or carving. There were hardly any trees, the woodcarving of which would give vent to artistic expression. The only way that the Icelanders could express themselves on a higher level than tilling the soil, fighting, or fishing was through words—spoken and written. The Celtic leavening on this race of hard warriors, farmers, and fishermen gave breath to the greatest flowering of literature the world had seen until the Catholic Renaissance. There is no other viable explanation of how the works, for example, of Geoffrey of Monmouth, and the great Welsh legends came to be translated into Icelandic Norse. So far as is known, there was nothing similar in Norway, which, word-wise, was practically dormant until Ibsen, nine hundred years later.

There were three sources of Celtic influence in Iceland. First, the surviving anchorites of the old Christian settlement, who came into contact with the early Norse settlers. Second, intermarriage between Celts and Norsemen (Helgi the Skinny, prince of Norway, was born in the fourth century of a Norse nobleman and an Irish princess, and one of the foremost chieftains of Iceland, Olav Peacock, was born of Hoskuld Dallakollsson, descendant of Aud the

Deep-minded, and Mael Curcaigh—Melkorka, in Norse—daughter of the great King Murcataigh of Ireland). Third, there were the hundreds of Celtic thralls and bond-women (not exactly slaves, more like indentured servants). These thralls were, as often as not, sturdy warriors captured in battle and held until ransom was paid (which it seldom was, for there was rarely anything to pay it with). Some of the Icelandic thralls had been great and powerful men of influence in the Gaelic countries, men such as those Celts mentioned in the sagas, like Njal, Kormak, and Kjartan. As a result, there are place names of Celtic origin all over Iceland.

But the conversion to Christianity of the wild Vikings proved, in the first centuries of Icelandic settlement, beyond even the vocal charms of the Irish and the Welsh. Soon the whole island was worshiping gods more fitted to its terrible aspect, more amenable to its inhospitable climate, more understanding of its awful wrath. The old gods of the Northmen soon displaced the Son of Man even in the Celtic blood, and Niörd, Tyr, Balder, and Odin were among those worshiped. However, Thor of the mighty hammer and the fertility god Frey, with his great phallus always stiff and erect, were the most feared and respected.

The attempts of the crown of Norway to establish sway over Iceland failed, having been resisted with all the craft, guile, and violence of the Icelandic Norsemen and Celts. Soon a system of self-government was developed. This was the Althing, the parliament, which the Icelanders claim was the first democratic parliament ever established. This is untrue; the Althing was not representative of the people, but only of the more prosperous landowners. It derived its origin from the Law of the Gulathing of southwest Norway, which had as much to do with democracy as the Senate of ancient Rome. The Althing was, in fact, an institute for the maintenance of a wealthy, powerful, and avaricious establishment of land barons.

In any case, it had been preceded as a representative

body by over one thousand years. The Eisteddfodd of Wales was a meeting place where every man could speak and no man could be held in jeopardy for anything said during the sessions.

During the twelfth and thirteenth centuries Iceland prospered as a fount of literature. But the Norse spirit was shortsighted and lazy, always seeking the easy, if violent, way out of a dilemma when it came to day-to-day living. The few trees that grew on the island were cut down, and no attempt was made to keep the cattle alive during the cold winters; instead they were killed wholesale and the carcasses buried in the snow (though this in itself helped the literary effort, calfskin vellum being used for writing the sagas). No attempt was made to develop the right kind of clothing for the climate, nor to resow pasture land.

And so, around the fourteenth century a plague caused the population to stagnate, then slowly decline. Gradually Iceland withdrew again, back behind its curtain of mist and fog, until very recent times, when it became first a staging point of ship convoys during two world wars, and later an important airways crossroads on the great-circle routes from Europe to the Western Hemisphere.

But about seven hundred parchments of sagas and precious translations survived the centuries of isolation. Seven hundred, or about one tenth of the total written. A treasury of lively, human stories, full of Gaelic dreaming, of deep, abstract, oblique meaning in the simplest descriptions. And full also of Norse vigor and humor; the humanness of the characters shines strong and bright across the dark span of the lonely years between us and them.

As I took my departure from the heartbroken islands of St. Kilda, I thought of this long-ago time, and with a slight wind barely moving the vessel over the swells from the west, I settled down to watch the moon set beyond the stupendous cliffs of strange Boreray.

A whole island tipped over on its side. Cliffs fifteen hundred feet high, ghostly white under the moon, with millions of skuas and guillemots clinging to the ledges, so many that the black granite rock looked like some spirit-land rearing straight up into the clouds from the black, night-gleaming, heaving, ocean sea.

Soon the ghost-rocks had dropped astern. We were alone in the night at the edge of the world, with only the rustle of the wind on the stays and the slop-slop of the bows. The boat plunged on into the night, black silver with the moon's west-sinking, until the first flickering spider's touch of pale dawn light, low on the eastern horizon. Before I hove to, to sleep an hour, I searched below the dawn. There, a mere smudge of deeper color in all the other greys, was St. Kilda—the Islands of the Dead. I stared for a minute or so, then, hungry and sleepy, clambered below. It was my last glimpse of Britain for over three years.

# PART III

## Vici
### (I Conquered)

*For my purpose holds*
*To sail beyond the sunset, and the baths*
*Of all the western stars, until I die.*
*It may be that the gulfs will wash us down:*
*It may be we shall touch the Happy Isles,*
*And see the great Achilles, whom we knew.*

Alfred, Lord Tennyson
"Ulysses"

*In the country of the blind, the one-eyed man is king.*

Old Spanish saying.

# 14

## A Rough Passage

With the wind in the southwest, the passage from St. Kilda
to Iceland, for the first two days, was on a broad reach, the
fastest and the easiest sailing. Frequently sighting the
fountain-spouts of whales, the great blue whale and the
sperm whale, in patches of bright sunlight as the dark
shadows of wheeling clouds slid over the rough face of the
ocean waters, *Cresswell* danced and streamed to the northwest. Often, we were accompanied by porpoises, shooting
over to the boat's side at tremendous speed, jumping high
into the air off the tops of the seas. They would convoy us,
sometimes for hours at a stretch, sometimes flashing away
with a squirm of their powerful tails, sometimes drifting
alongside, flickering their bodies every now and again,
seeming to make no effort, yet keeping up with us at a good
five knots.

Down below, I would know when the porpoises were
arriving, for their conversations, their whistling screams of
joy, were plainly transmitted through a mile of water and
through the hull.

Nelson's attitude to the porpoises was exactly the same
as it would have been had they been children. He balanced
himself against the knighthead, on the bow, and jumped
around, watching their every playful move, yapping as
they performed their rolls. He jumped with excitement
when the mothers playfully rammed and nudged the

youngsters against the bow of the boat.

On the third day out there was a radio forecast from the BBC: "Sea areas Rockall, Malin, Iceland, winds increasing to gale force, storm imminent." I was not surprised. Already, the night before, I had picked up a transmission from a trawler to a weathership keeping gallant and sacrificial watch out in the vast deeps of the ocean indicating that the weather was deteriorating seriously. Sure enough, towards dusk, at about latitude sixty north, longitude fourteen west, the sky in the west was coal black torn cumulus, while overhead stretched ragged strips of cirrocumulus, the "mackerel's tails." Away to the east, in a deep purple sky, the moon rose blood red. I hoisted my way up forward onto the heaving foredeck and handed the staysail. Then, after bringing the boat's head up into the wind, I lowered the gaff head and peak and tied two reefs in the main.

Half an hour after all was battened down, the weather slammed down on us, and soon we were in a sea of frenzy. *Cresswell* was still able to steer herself roughly north by northwest, so I lashed the wheel and let her go at that. All that night I was occupied in pumping out the hull, for despite the dodgers, a lot of sea was coming onboard, and I was often knee-deep in icy cold water in the cockpit.

*Cresswell*'s cockpit, unlike those of most modern ocean-going sailing craft, was not self-draining, and no matter how much precaution I took against seas coming onboard, the cockpit, in rough weather, would always take a great amount of water in a surprisingly short time. This was because the boat was a shallow draft hull with almost flat bilges; unlike the modern deep-keel craft, there was almost no room for water taken onboard to stow itself. A ton of water coming in meant about six inches slopping around right through the boat. So it was pump, hard and often. But I had a good old Royal National Lifeboat Institution pump, a great brass monster, which could jerk out half a gallon at a stroke, and the water was soon got rid of. It was heavy work, though, and coldly wet. I was out in the cockpit, almost smothered under two jerseys, two pairs of fear-naught trousers, seaboot stockings, seaboots up to my thighs, apron-type oilskin trousers, an oilskin coat, a sou'wester, and a towel around my neck, lashed to the binnacle with a heavy line tied with a bowline. But still the cold spray continually found its way inside my clothing, and I spent the whole storm, all three days in it, pumping out the hull, tending the sheets, adjusting the wheel, grabbing a bite to eat when the chance arose, which was not often, thoroughly wet and miserable.

With the boat's sails reefed down and the seas growing as the wind drove them from the west, progress was much slower. When she was reefed down, *Cresswell* never made more than 2½ knots, which is about the speed of a man walking at a moderate pace. And most of that was sideways, because she made a lot of leeway, not having a big, deep, outside keel.

These defects in her windward ability I had accepted. I intended to get into the ice, and with a deep keel that would have been almost impossible, as the keel would be crushed between the ice floes; but with a rounded hull and no outside keel the possibility was that she would be lifted upwards by the ice pressure, as you squeeze an apple pip out from between forefinger and thumb.

The action in a small vessel in a storm is a wonder to behold. Every separate part of the hull and rigging works its own way, tremendous forces pulling and pushing every three seconds or so. The strains imparted onto the masts and the running-rigging are stupendous, and unless you are absolutely familiar with every little bit and piece of the craft, unless you know the strength of each block, each wire, each halyard, you spend the time waiting for something to give. And when something gives on a sailing craft in heavy weather, with everything tensioned like a violin string, something else is going to go with it, and something else with *that*, and so on, ad infinitum. This anticipation of something giving way is probably the most worrisome thing of all and is probably the main reason for exhaustion. More so, even, than lack of sleep or hard physical effort. That, and the lack of food due to the inability to cook it. I reckon that many craft have been lost because of exhaustion, both mental, caused by worry, and physical, caused by neglecting to eat properly.

The answer, of course, is always to sail in the best order you possibly can, with all the hull and rigging, sails and gear well maintained, and always to have food available which can be eaten without cooking. Even bars of chocolate or corned beef. Food undeniably tastes better warm and is more comforting; but when it comes to refueling the body, all that really matters is to get the protein inside you.

The storm south of Iceland lasted for three days and nights. Wet, cold, and weary, I watched the skies clearing in the west, grabbed a handful of burgoo, dolloped some out for Nelson, then turned in, with the boat handling herself in a diminishing wind, still under reefed sails.

When I woke it was close to noon, so I hove the boat to and snatched a sextant sight of the sun. We had moved only seventy miles in three days, on a course almost due north! But as the wind dropped to a moderately stiff breeze of about twenty knots, it backed around to the south. I prepared to shake out the reefs and get her once more on a broad reach, this time heading west-north-west, so as to keep plenty of sea room between me and the south coast of Iceland, which, at this time, was about three hundred miles to the north.

I climbed up to the foot of the main mast and let go of the peak halyard; then, holding that under one foot, I prepared to let go of the throat halyard. Suddenly there was a loud crack aloft. I jerked my head up to see what was happening—then everything went black.

The first thing I saw when I tried to open my eyes was blood all over the side-deck and the doghouse side. My head was throbbing and every movement increased the pain. Then I realized, with a shock, that I could only see *through one eye!* The other was blackly blank, and blood was dripping down my oilskins. For the first and only time in my life at sea I was violently sick. Nelson, covered in blood and spew, was still holding onto the bottom of my pants leg, and I could see where his teeth had bitten in so hard that the tough oilskin material was chewed away. He had saved my life by stopping me from sliding over the side.

Slowly, sitting there on the pitching deck with the green seas still breaking in great waves over and against the sides of the boat as she rocked and rolled and pitched and tossed, I came to, grabbing at the handrail, and looked around me.

Through my good eye I saw that the throat-block grommet, the heavy wire cable-strap slung around the mast above and resting on the hounds-bands (heavy blocks of hard timber bolted through the mast), had snapped as I had eased the throat halyard to raise the mainsail. The continual wear and tear, the everlasting rubbing and chafing had worn through the seizing around the throat-block strop and had finally worn away several strands of the wire, making it so weak that it gave way. The peak halyard block, also held on the same strop until then, had exploded loose, and the twelve-foot-long spar, with its heavy iron head-band on the outer extremity, had crashed down and walloped me right over my right eye. I gingerly touched my forehead and eye socket. My eye was out on my cheek! There was a great round thing sitting just below the eyebrow!

Horrified, I took hold of it and, opening my eyelid with the other hand, shoved it back in. The salt of my hands stung my eye socket. For the first time in years I wanted to cry. Nelson was still hanging on to my trouser leg, whining, looking up at me pitifully with *his* one eye.

Slowly I made my way down to the cabin, where there was a small mirror set into the doghouse side. What I saw was a bloody mess. My right eyebrow was split wide open, with an half-inch bloody gap, now beginning to coagulate, while the eyelids were swelling. I forced the lids open and saw that the eye was blood red. I tried to move it and to my immense relief it moved; through the damaged eye I could see a glimmer of daylight. I hadn't lost the sight!

The first-aid gear was kept up forward, with the sail repair kit, and I made my way along the pitching cabin, grabbing the table as I struggled forward, and snatched up both kits, the first aid in its metal box, the sail kit in its blue bag. Back in the companionway, I fumbled around for a match to light the stove and heat up some water. In this I boiled the smallest needle I had onboard and the smallest fishing line, a nylon wisp of baitline, used for catching sprats. Then, with my seaman's knife, always kept razor sharp, I opened the wound up, squeezed the two sides together and put three great big stitches right across it, and tied a round turn and two half-hitches in the end of the nylon line. In the process I was sick three times, until my stomach could cough up no more.

Still covered in blood and regurgitated burgoo, I sat down and, shaking, made cocoa while Nelson stretched out on the opposite berth and looked at me as if to say, "You silly bugger, what did you do that for?"

After turning out the stove, with the boat still wallowing violently, I turned in to steady myself. I rose an hour later, head still throbbing, and spent the rest of the afternoon cleaning up the blood and spewed food.

Next morning, I hauled myself up the mainmast carefully, by the topping lift, seized the strop around the mast (a hard, cold, windy job), secured the blocks, slid down again to the deck, hoisted the mainsail; and we were off again. All in all, this took ten hours in a sloppy, jerking sea, with waves as high as eight feet, suspended atop a wildly waving mast, blind in one eye.

The weather for the remainder of the voyage to Reykjavík was fairly steady, winds of around twenty to twenty-five knots, and on the tenth day out of St. Kilda, I sighted through my one good eye, Reykjanesta, the southwest corner of Iceland, through a misty haze of low clouds sweeping across the Skagi. I left plenty of sea room between *Cresswell* and the long, rocky, dangerous shore of the Reykjanes peninsula, then hove to for the night, ready to sail into port the following day. It was only thirty-five miles away, on the southeast side of the Faxaflói, so there was no hurry. There was no point in entering at night. In this moderate weather the bay would be alive with fishing craft.

I bandaged my head up; fortunately, my eye no longer hurt very much. Apart from bloodstains on deck and a few dents and scratches where the gaff boom had clattered down, the boat was in good order. However, there was sea water in the fuel tank, so the engine was out of commission. I did not feel like siphoning out the tank, a messy job, even in port, and a nauseating job at sea, as I would wind up swallowing about a pint of diesel oil. I left that job until arrival, as the weather forecasts indicated a good breeze on the morrow, which would blow me right into harbor.

The sun rose at around four in the morning; I hoisted sail after breakfast and made my way into the wide Faxaflói, past the port of Keflavík, busy with fishing craft, and so into the harbor of Reykjavík.

With the yellow-jack pratique flag flying from the mainmast, I waited for the customs to come onboard.

"Hello, Englishman!"

"Good afternoon."

"Where you come from?"

"Scotland, Barra."

"Good trip?"

"Fair."

"What happen your head?" The customs man, a jolly-looking fellow around fifty-five, with a red face, pointed at my blood-soaked bandages.

"Oh, I always dress like this."

He laughed. "What happen?"

I told him.

"You go up the hospital; free for seamen. See Dr. Jorgensson; he put you right. Then you come to my house,

we have some schnapps, yes?" He punched my shoulder
playfully.

"Right, mate, you're on!" I would have grinned, but
cracking my face hurt too much.

At the seamen's hospital, Dr. Jorgensson said I had made
as good a job of the eye repair as he could have done. But I
think he was merely trying to cheer me up. It left a wide
scar, which reminds me, to this day, to always keep an eye
on the blocks.

"Now take it easy here, rest for a week," he said. "And
mind you, no strong drink."

"Right you are, sir."

I made my way up to the house of Alpi, the customs
officer, where supper, cooked by his beautiful, merry,
Rubenesque wife, was waiting, with a portion for Nelson.
Then Alpi and I got stinking drunk and finished up flaked
out over the floor of the living room in the warm, wooden
house on the side of the hill overlooking the bay where
Floki had sailed with his sacrificial ravens so long ago.

The schnapps did more for my eye than anything else I
could think of, and in a few days I could see as well out of it
as before, except perhaps when I looked aloft at the rigging
strops. Then I could see a hundred times better.

By now, in mid-June, the days were much longer, and
sunset was not until about ten-thirty at night, so I determined to make sail again from Reykjavík, now that my eye
was good, and head for Greenland, where I would make
the first attempt to reach latitude eighty north. It was already too late to try for Svalbard, unless I was going to
winter there. It would be better to sally up the Greenland
coast this year, and, if conditions there were too hard for
wintering, try to get back to Iceland. Here, I could winter on
the north coast and prepare the boat for the voyage into the
deep Arctic early in the spring of 1960. The idea was to get
to the edge of the pack ice as early in the summer as
possible, so as to be able to shoot the sun right through the
twenty-four-hour day, and then, with a northerly running

current shifting the ice and the boat, to try to drift north over the winter, as far north as possible—I hoped to beat Nansen's record of eighty-four north—then emerge from the ice in the spring of '61.

I would need the boat in good order and a minimum of two years' food and stores. Iceland was the place to get ready to tackle the Arctic!

*I'm a sailor lad in a fishin' boat,*
*Learnin' all about seafarin',*
*An' me education, scraps of navigation,*
*As we hunt the bonny shoals of herrin'.*

> Old fisherman's song about the Icelandic
> grounds. It originates in Yarmouth, England.

# 15

## *Around Iceland Single-Handed*

One evening while we were sitting in Alpi's living room eating liverwurst and jam sandwiches, Mrs. Alpi asked me, "What will you do now, Tristan?"

"Well, love, my eye's a lot better, but it's still a bit early to head up for the Scoresby Sund in Greenland. There'll be far too much pack ice and bergs yet to make the Sund safely. What I would like to do, while I'm waiting around, is have a go at sailing right around the island."

"What island?" she asked.

"Iceland," I replied.

Alpi perked up. "Alone?" he asked, over the sound of Grieg from the record player.

"I'll take Nelson, of course, he's very handy. Keeps a good watch when I heave to, and he's great in a fog."

"My God, but don't you know the distance involved? It's over one thousand miles straight sailing. If you get contrary winds, it will be more like two thousand."

"Yes, but the Maury wind charts indicate a pretty regular shift of wind around the end of June, and I can get to the North East Cape, off Thistilfiord, easily with this southwest breeze. Then I'd wait for a wind shift from southwest to the north, slide around the eastern shore, and be on a nice flat sea south of the island all the way back here."

I was trying my best to make it sound like a weekend cruise around Catalina Island.

153

"But supposing the wind doesn't shift to north; you might be waiting there for a month and miss the short Greenland summer, or at least one precious month of it, and it only lasts until the end of August." He unfolded a chart of the Iceland coast.

"Well," I said, pointing my finger at the island of Grímsey, sitting all alone in the Arctic Ocean about thirty miles off the north coast, "I will wait here. If the wind doesn't shift by the end of June, then I will head direct northwest for Scoresby Sund from Grímsey!"

Alpi frowned. "Hmm, and what about permits to visit Greenland? You know the Danish government is very particular about who visits their colony, and it sometimes takes weeks to get all the permits approved in Copenhagen."

"Bugger the Danish government!" I said, remembering Keanan the Postman. "Anyway, if I clear Reykjavík for Jan Mayen Island and the wind happens to take me into Scoresby Sund, what can they do about it? If they get snotty, I'll plead *force majeure* and then they can't refuse my entry, and in those latitudes they can't very well chuck me out of the port until the weather and I are ready for sailing, can they?"

"You bloddy crazy Valisaman. Don't tell anyone I heard that!"

"Handsome is as handsome does, Alpi."

"Well, have another sandwich, anyway." He passed the tray.

The next two days I spent preparing the boat for a fast sail around Iceland, as well as the estimated year in the Arctic. That's where I would be heading if the winds did not shift to schedule. I took in an extra twenty gallons of diesel oil, ten gallons of kerosene, extra cold weather lubricating oil and antifreeze, and a full set of arctic clothing. Alpi introduced me to one of his friends who had returned the previous year from working with a Swiss geophysical expedition in Greenland. Jokki had a complete set of Eskimo clothing, mostly made of caribou skin.

The suit all together—boots, socks, undervest, under-pants, gloves, trousers, and jacket—weighed only about ten pounds! Only the socks were not caribou skin. These were of blanket material, or duffle. The undergarments were of caribou fawn skin, softer, warmer, more pleasant to the skin than the finest silk or man-made fiber. The boots were of bleached young sealskin. Jokki also threw in a sleeping bag, the real arctic kind, with a short-fiber sheepskin lining. "And mind you sleep naked in this," he warned, "otherwise, if your sweat freezes you might get frostbite."

I got the whole rig for just twenty pounds (fifty dollars then), a real bargain.

With a good forecast of steady southwesterlies, I motored out of Reykjavík. I had cleared the engine fuel lines of sea water, so that my engine was working well, and I had checked and rechecked all the rigging, running and stand-ing.

The first hop, of about 120 miles, was to the deep inlet of Arnarfiord, up in the northwest peninsula, and we had a steady, but rough, passage across the wide mouths of the Faxaflói and the Breidafiord. The coast was very busy, with a continual coming and going of fishing craft large and small, so there was no sleep for me on this passage. By the time I entered the Arnarfiord, I was, as I always am after a few days in harbor, weary. I sailed right into the far end of the fiord, along the blue water, with great high stony mountains reaching up either side of the fiord, to where the icefalls of the mighty massif of Glama reach down to the sea.

I guided *Cresswell* in a little further towards the shore at the end of the fiord and dropped the hook. The first thing that struck me, in the clear air of the sub-Arctic, was the clarity of vision. The snow-clad peak of the Glama was all of ten miles away, yet it seemed to be only a mile. The second thing was the range of hearing, especially on the water. A voice speaking in normal tones two miles away, on a calm day, could be heard quite distinctly.

The next morning, early, there was such a palaver and blowing of sirens as the fishing boats took off out to sea that I could not help but be at my breakfast and have the anchor up and the sails hoisted before even the early rising Icelanders were out milking the cows in the green meadows of grassland rising between the Glama's rough, clenched knuckles.

As *Cresswell* sailed north, past the twin guardians of the Isafiord, the grey glowering heads of the Stigahlid and the Grunahlid, the wind increased, and with it, the clouds. Low, dirty, black, and menacing. But the weather held below gale force that night, until I had rounded the Horncap, the northernmost point of Iceland, and was sailing over comparatively calm waters, with a good stiff wind, southeast, to make the Húnaflói before dark on the morrow.

There are two islands called Grímsey off Iceland, one way out in the Arctic Ocean, and the other sitting just inside the Húnaflói, which is a very extensive inlet biting deep into the north coast of Iceland. With the help of the tide, I beat steadily all day until I could slide *Cresswell* in very cozily 'twixt the island and the mainland. There I rested, for there was not a living soul around, only birds and a few seals lying around on the pinkish rocks of the shore. To the northwest, as I let go the anchor in clear, clean water, shone the ice cone of the Drangajökull, all of thirty miles away; yet with the evening sun shining on the snows almost horizontally, it seemed as if I could reach out and touch it with my hand. My fishing line yielded a great fat halibut that night, but I found it very oily, and the only part I could eat with relish was the fins. It was a pity, because he was a giant, about forty pounds. I boiled up the head for Nelson, and he loved it.

At sunset, around ten-thirty in the evening, the sky turned a mottled green, a soft, pale green, tinged with brilliant orange over the far-off peaks of the Eiríksjökull far to the south. In the rushes and driftwood washed up on the stony beach, eider and harlequin ducks rustled their wings, while from the Arctic Ocean a low, cold sea-ice fog slowly crept in with the night breeze. This sea-ice fog was so low, yet so dense, that, standing in *Cresswell*'s cockpit, with my head in clear, fresh air, looking down I could not see my waist. It was like being afloat in a blanket of cloud. Above, the stars shone much bigger, much brighter than they appear in any shoreside southerly latitude (with the outstanding exception of Lake Titicaca, I was to find out much later). The Great Bear was almost directly overhead, pointing its tail at Polaris, a massive mammal leading a chubby cub over the deep, dark blue velvet of the polar night sky. Polaris was only about twenty degrees north of the vertical. I was about forty miles from the Arctic Circle. The ice floes I saw were far out on the northern horizon, low and gleaming on the grey green sea, but with the wind in the southwest, they were being held back from the shore, or at least their southerly progress was being impeded.

I sighted the seaward Grímsey Island on the evening of the fifth day out of Reykjavík, and I was feeling both pleased and lucky as it hove into view through a low-lying mist. I had had good winds, none over thirty knots and all fair, coming from abaft the beam, pushing *Cresswell*, heavily loaded, at a good rate through the seas.

Coming into the lee of the stark, barren island, I was not happy with the anchoring prospects. The swell all round the island would not make for a comfortable anchor, so, after a short sleep in the forenoon, I weighed anchor and headed for Thistilfiord, on the northeast corner of Iceland.

The sailing was splendid, and, making good time through the night, I decided to press on to the southern side of the Fontur peninsula, where we would be protected not only from the southwest, but also from the north. The following day, after beating hard to windward all afternoon and most of the evening, we at last went to anchor in the lee of high land at the root of the fiord.

I waited there for four days, in a flat calm, until the wind started to ease down from the north. The change of wind was right on time, just like clockwork, and I decided to sail immediately, even though it was night. The four days at anchor were spent resting and tending the gear, repairing a split No. 1 jib and listening to the cries of thousands of skuas and guillemots nesting on the cliffs, watching, again in delight, the magic wonder of the fulmar petrel's flight. The way out of the fiord was, as I had verified on the way in, clear of any obstacles, and I wanted to make a good fast run south, down the east coast of Iceland before the seas worked up from the north. Once past the Vestra Horn, the Western Horn, I would again be in the lee of the land, with the wind coming offshore and relatively calm seas. Temperatures dropped sharply with the coming of the north wind, and I wrapped up well. Now we were off again, bowling along, with the wind dead astern, sailing fast in the offing of the great bay of Vopnafiord; then, as dawn filled out the sky with light, past Seydisfiord.

That evening the great rocky plateau of the Vatnajökull, the ancient refuge of the Celtic Christians from the savage, overbearing Vikings, hove into sight, and I determined to make the next day for anchorage under Oraefajökull, where their original settlement had been fifteen hundred years before.

I had charts for the narrow entrance to the Skeidarafiord, so made my way in without too much bother and anchored behind the island, which almost blocks the river fiord from the sea. I arrived there about four in the afternoon and went ashore, taking Nelson with me, for he had seen rabbits on the shore, and despite his missing leg, the hunter instinct of the Labrador was strong in his blood. I spent the daylight hours of the evening climbing over the rocky ground, looking for traces of the Gaels, but found none except what might have been a flint ax-head. There were a number of piles of stones which, standing alone on grassy slopes, could have been the remains of huts or storage sheds, but there was nothing obvious to my untrained eye. Disappointed, I returned onboard and, after a meal of burgoo and bacon, turned in. It was a warm evening; Iceland in the summer, especially in the southeast, can be as climatically mild as England.

Early the next day, I slid out of the Skeidarafiord and, with the wind still blowing from the north, laid a course for the islands of Vestmannaeyjar, about a hundred miles to the west. The scenery on this sail was magnificent. The seas were quiet compared to what they usually are when the wind blows the long rollers of the Gulf Stream straight up against the wild shores, but now it was ideal sailing, with a good wind and an almost flat sea. To the north, to landward, the tremendous heights of the inland volcanic plateau stood out clearly in the sunlight against the dark clouds interspersed with patches of blue sky. In the northwest the great, volcanic, snow-covered cone of Hekla rose into the sky from a heaving rock plain.

During the night, we passed through a fleet of fishing craft, and I was wide awake the whole time. There must have been a thousand out there, fishing the south coast, taking advantage of the ideal conditions. Their engines thudded, their lights twinkled all around, and often, as I passed about two miles away to avoid their nets, I heard them talking and singing as they tended the nets. On one occasion, I even heard the clashing of cooking pans on the galley stove as supper was served. It is always a worry, navigating under sail through a fishing fleet. The answer, of course, is always to make sure that your navigating lights can be clearly seen, yet are not in a position where they dazzle the helmsman. Also, have an efficient radar reflector.

In the late morning the Vestmann Islands came into view, their high cliffs sparkling in the sun, the green seas heaving around the bases of the cliffs. Green for the Irishmen who, long, long ago, escaped from their cruel lord, Leif Arnarson, and, finally starved into defeat by

Leif's avengers, threw themselves over the high cliffs onto
the rocks below, rather than surrender to the berserk Norse
savages.

Here I anchored again and in the lee, or calm, side of the
islands, with a great swell heaving the boat, spent a fitful
night. I caught a cod and fried his liver. Nelson had the
head, as dogs evidently do not need vitamin C to the same
extent as humans. Anyway, he got enough out of the great
staring eyes, which to him were a tasty morsel.

I left the Vestmann Islands the following day—it was too
uncomfortable an anchorage to consider staying there any
longer, and, besides, the month was passing and the north
was calling. By evening of the next day, I had passed my
earlier track from St. Kilda, and on the night of 30 June,
1959, the first recorded single-handed circumnavigation of
Iceland was completed. It had taken twenty days, with
eight nights at anchor.

As I beat against the northeast wind into Faxaflói and
Reykjavík, I reflected on how fortunate I had been that the
wind-shift had come so propitiously at the northeast cape. I
was tired and determined to rest for two days before making off to Greenland and the north.

Alpi was on the jetty to meet me. His house overlooked
the harbor, and he had recognized the old-fashioned gaff
rig of Cresswell.

"I knew you did it" were his first words, as we shook
hands. "My friend Jokki sighted your boat off the Hor-
nafiord on Thursday, from his ship heading for Copenhagen, and he sent a radio message."

"Christ Almighty, Alpi, the bloody sea's getting like Piccadilly Circus these days. Can't go nowhere without someone breathing down your bloody neck and sending
bloomin' telegrams——"

"Not where you're going," he said, mysteriously.

We headed for his house to scoff smorgasbord and quaff
schnapps.

"I won't enter you in this time," said Alpi. "You've already got clearance for Jan Mayen. We'll let it stand at that."

"Thank God for that, Alpi. All I need now is a heap of forms to fill in."

"You like writing forms, eh, Tristan?" he grinned.

"Yeah, like a hole in the head!"

*She's a tiddly ship, through the ice floes
  she slips,
She's sailing by night and by day,
And when she's in motion, she's the pride of
  the ocean,
You can't see her fanny for spray.
Side, side, Cresswell's ship's side,
Nelson looks on it with pride.
He'd have a blue fit if he saw any shit
On the side of the Cresswell's ship's side!*

The Arctic Ocean song, 1959–61.

# 16

*Mysterious, Misnamed,
and Misunderstood Greenland*

Aeons ago, when all the continents of the world were joined together, before they started to drift apart at the stately rate of two inches per hundred years or so, the miniature continent of Greenland was directly under what was then the equator. Thousands of millions of years before, when the earth was only one-fifth of its present age, the first rocks of Greenland had spewed forth out of the molten core of the world, forming a nucleus around which the five other vast continents, Europe, Asia, Africa-Australia-Antarctica, India, and America huddled, like young cubs feeding off their mother.

This one-time hub of the world's continents, now known as Greenland, eventually was covered by an immense blanket of tropical vegetation inhabited by nightmare monsters like the dinosaur and brontosaurus. That this was so is indicated by the unimaginably vast deposits of coal lying under the two-mile-thick layer of ice. The release of the pent-up power of the ice and coal of Greenland could provide the whole earth with energy for untold generations.

Gradually the miniature continent drifted away, towards what is now the Arctic. By some process which is not yet understood, the nature of the sun changed, and for many centuries the phenomena known as sunspots were very active, shooting great streamers of hydrogen hundreds of thousands of miles into space. This caused a cooling of the earth, especially at the poles. The great Ice Age was upon the earth, and Greenland was covered with a thick, thick blanket of ice. The mother continent of the world was frozen and remained so, entirely, for many thousands of years. It is still thawing out, slowly.

Once the sun, a variable star like all the others, again calmed down, the Arctic regions began to warm up. Eventually the island of Manhattan, which during the depths of the great Ice Age, with a vast amount of the world's sea water frozen into great sheets of ice, had been forty miles inland, had a harbor once more.

Around three thousand years ago one of the periodical warm-ups of the world was in full swing, and the Arctic regions were basking under a climate much milder than is now the case. This happy state of affairs continued until the early sixteenth century, when what we know as the Little Ice Age, which lasted about two centuries, began. Until a few thousand years ago Greenland was a land completely empty of humans. Birds and fishes had arrived thousands of years before, with the first warming. Then the animals— the musk ox, the polar bear, the Arctic fox—had entered the country over the eighteen-mile-wide strait which separates western Greenland from the Canadian islands. After many, many centuries, the Eskimos, a hardy race of people who had learned over untold generations of suffering to come to terms with the cruelest climate on earth, crossed the Smith Sound from Ellesmere Island to Etah, and slowly spread down to the south of Greenland, then up the east coast. When the first wandering Norse sea rover found the shores of Greenland, the Eskimos had just reached the southern tip.

The history of the Norse settlement of Greenland was, after a very promising start, a story of unmitigated disaster.

Contrary to the history I was taught in school, Eric the

Red was *not* the first Norseman to sight Greenland. This dubious honor belongs to a landless, penniless itinerant who first arrived in Iceland about A.D. 919. Too late to grab a piece of real estate for himself, he called together his companions, checked the hull and rigging of his knarr, embarked sheep and pigs for food, and sailed further west. His name was Gunnbjorn, and he returned to Iceland in 920 with tales of the great shore seven hundred miles towards the sunset, which he called *Gunnbjornarker*. This was a very human thing to do, just as it had been for Gardar to call Iceland *Gardarholm*, as it would be later for Columbus to name Colombia, Amerigo Vespucci to name America, Abel Tasman to name Tasmania, and for Cecil Rhodes to call a great chunk of Africa Rhodesia. This is nothing more than graffiti on the grand scale.

Eric the Red, who had the fortune to be "in with the media," which in those days consisted of the saga-singers, was born near Stavanger, Norway. He, too, arrived too late for the great Icelandic land-grab, and, having heard the tales of Gunnbjorn's much earlier voyage, sailed west.

On the shores of Greenland, which he reached in 981, he found willow, birch, and juniper, and short stubby grass in the valleys between the rocky morains. The summer was warm and kind. He returned to Iceland and spent the next four years mustering up twenty-five ships and five hundred settlers. With these, in 985, he established three colonies: one on the west coast of Greenland, which lasted three hundred and sixty years; one on the east coast, which survived a little longer; and one at the southern tip. The last trace of the Norse colonies of Greenland was found, 555 years later, by a German Hanseatic merchant, Jon Greenlander, of Hamburg. He sailed his ship into a fiord near Cape Farewell in 1540. There on the beach he found a man, one lone man, lying face down, dead. The corpse was small and thin, yet dressed in European-style clothes. In his hand he clutched a wooden harpoon with an iron tip.

This was the last descendant of the Viking Norsemen of

Greenland. The last of a race of strong, tall, robust people who had scourged all the known seas of the western world. This stunted dwarf, holding a primitive iron weapon, was the last of the Iron Age men. They had existed only a thousand years.

The Norse colonies died out for two reasons. First, around the early 1500s, the Little Ice Age began, which would last for two centuries; and second, unlike the Eskimo, the Viking refused to come to terms with the change in nature. He insisted on wearing European-style clothes. The skin of a caribou or a musk ox was beneath the notice of the proud Norsemen. Yet it would have saved them. They had encountered the Eskimos, whom they named *Skraelings* (screamers), many times over the centuries, and bloody battles had been fought. They would have done better to have learned how to dress from the Eskimos, who have survived ten thousand years.

During the centuries of Norse occupation of the coasts of Greenland, or at any rate small sections of them, trade into and out of the country by any ships but those of the Danish-Norwegian federation was strictly forbidden by edict from the court of Copenhagen. This, of course, led to the arrival of the Bristol ships, and in short order there was a flourishing trade in walrus tusks, caribou skins, bearskins, sealskins, whale blubber, and bone. Then, in the late 1500s, with the disappearance of the Norse colonists, the trade in slaves began. It is on record that in most years during the late 1500s anything up to one hundred Bristol ships were on the coast, many of them dealing in Eskimo slaves. Where these slaves were taken is a mystery, but I suspect they were used for seal hunting in the Arctic.

Arctic exploration in modern times began with the search by European mariners for the northeast passage to China, in the mid-1400s. Then, with the "discovery" of North America, the focus of exploration was changed to probing for the northwest passage to China. Voyages in pursuit of this elusive goal went on for the next four and a half centuries. Many, such as the Hudson voyage and the Franklin expedition, resulted in tragedy. In the latter, 129 men, in two ships, the *Erebus* and the *Terror*, stuck in the ice and ran out of food. Not knowing how to get to the food which was swimming under them, they starved to death, with the survivors eating the bodies of their comrades, then gradually starving again until there were more deaths, and so on, until finally the last man expired after eighteen months on a sparse diet of human flesh. This was in 1846. A gory story of brave, steady men driven to desperation. The mental state of the last man, huddled in the ragged tatters of a makeshift tent against the bitterly cruel blasts of the Arctic blizzards, knowing he was all alone in the black, everlasting night, contemplating his home and family and the dead comrades he had eaten, is beyond human imagination.

The summer in Greenland is short, only three months' duration. The shore ice and pack ice take all spring and one month of summer to thaw. Then leads, or passages, open up between the shore ice, heaped and immobile, piled up to 180 miles out from the shore line, and the pack ice. The moving pack ice floes are anything up to three miles long and six feet thick. By the end of July these leads may be a few miles wide. Between the ice floes the sea is calm, and in a favorable wind the sailing is magnificent.

The difficulty is finding the right leads, because many of them are dead ends, which get progressively narrower and finally, after many miles, wind up in a field of solid ice. The main risk is being caught in the passage between the shore ice, which is fixed and solid, and the pack ice, which might be moving at a great rate, carried south on the southerly running Greenland current. If the pack ice forces a small craft against the shore ice, she will be ground to bits in a matter of minutes.

But in nature every situation has not only disadvantages, but advantages, too. In the arctic summer it is broad daylight for most of the clock around; and in the twilight, which lasts for only an hour before the sun again rises, the sky is

usually so clear that with the starlight alone it is possible to
see many miles and even read a newspaper.

The shore ice, frozen across the mouths of the fiords in
the cold winter, begins to break up in early June, and by
mid-July there are clear entrances and long leads between
the pack ice. It was for this reason that I delayed sailing for
Greenland until July 2.

As I took my farewell of Alpi and his wife, together with
some of their friends, they said to me, "Now don't forget, *if*
you get to Ella, look up Mr. De Limos. He is a very good
man and will help you."

"I'll be sure to do that *when* I reach Ella. So long, Alpi,
don't take any wooden kronor!"

I sailed out of Reykjavík in the early morning, the last
town of any size bigger than half-a-dozen huts that I would
see for another twenty-two months.

*Cresswell* was soon out of the fishing fleet, heading across
the Denmark Strait, which is probably, after the Mozambique Channel of Africa, the widest strait in the world,
about eight hundred miles. The first five days were lively,
with a northeaster blowing over my starboard quarter, but
then the wind died and for two days I was becalmed. By this
time maverick ice floes had become a common sight, and,
sitting there fishing, waiting for a wind, I would sometimes
have to start the engine to move out of the way of a floe.
They were moving very slowly, about half a knot, to the
south. On the second day, becalmed, I motored over close
to one of them. The sides of the floe were not protruding
underwater, so I tied the boat up to two spikes which I
drove into the ice. With the boat safely secured, I took
Nelson for a walk in the sunshine. It was warm enough to
wear only a shirt, with the sleeves rolled up, shorts, and my
British army boots. I felt rather like a Lancashire collier on
the beach at Blackpool.

The seas were calm, almost Mediterranean blue, and
looking over the sides of the floe, down into the green
depths of the Arctic Ocean water, I saw thousands of

shrimp floating around. There was no other sign of life. After an hour's stretch, I untied the boat, withdrew the spikes, and set off again, clear of the floe. Once well away from it, I set to making a shrimp net from a plastic mosquito net and some box-wire lashed onto the end of the harpoon handle.

"Well, old mate," I said to Nelson, "one thing's for sure—if it's like this all the way, first of all we won't starve for fresh food, and secondly we won't get very far to the north!"

By this time I was at latitude sixty-nine. I remember it quite well, because that evening I caught a halibut, a big one. He weighed on my hand scales exactly sixty-nine pounds. Again, he was much too oily to eat, so I boiled up his fins, which I ate for supper, while Nelson had his head. I tried giving him the head raw, because I wanted to see if I could persuade him to eat uncooked fish and thus save on cooking oil, but he turned his nose up at it. Then I cut off the best bits of the halibut flesh and pickled it in lemon juice made from pure lemon crystals. After a week of marinating, the halibut had given off a lot of oil, and the tang of the lemon detracted from the greasy feel of the meat.

After three days of calm, dodging the ice floes, which were passing more frequently, the wind piped up again, this time from the southwest, and soon we were off, under all working sail, in a calm sea, with a good breeze.

On July 9 I was sailing due west along a wide gap between two great fleets of pack ice. They were moving south, which meant that my actual course was to the southeast. I was concerned about this, because to the south of Scoresby Sund, my destination, there is no possible haven for a couple of hundred miles. Nothing except the high-cliffed, barren, inhospitable coast of King Christian IX Land, with the well-named Cape Cruel jutting out into the shore ice.

But on the eleventh a lead to the north opened up and I changed course, with the gentle breeze astern of *Cresswell*. There was a mist on the western horizon, hiding the land, which otherwise I would have seen, even from fifty miles off. Although I knew my position from the sun sights, which, despite the lack of a clear horizon because of the pack ice floes, were reasonably accurate, I did not realize that I was actually sailing up the so-called shore lead—that is, the gap between the fixed shore ice and the moving pack ice. But, luckily, there was a very wide shore lead, and so I had no problem, apart from fatigue and eyestrain, in reaching Cape Brewster on the fourteenth of July. There, the wind dropped, and I spent almost a whole day motoring between gleaming, gigantic icebergs passing through the mouth of Scoresby Sund on their way out to sea from the ever moving glaciers.

The colors were fabulous. All around us the mountains and glaciers reared up to the blue sky—greys, greens, and silvers of every shade. The Sund itself was sparkling blue, as we always imagine the Mediterranean to be and as it so rarely is. Proceeding majestically through all this were great white, gold, pink and green, yellow and pale blue mountains of floating ice, some of them a mile or more in length and up to a thousand feet high!

Soon, under the gossamer, spider-web, cirrus sky that presages the aurora borealis and a high wind, I sighted, away to the north, the wireless aerials of the radio station at Scoresby Sund hamlet, a little collection of wooden buildings, neat and tidy in the Danish fashion. By supper time I was at anchor, awaiting the arrival of the powers-that-be.

"Good evening, where have you come from?" He was a slender, yet big-boned man dressed in a lumber jacket and khaki trousers with sealskin water-boots. His florid face had the broken blue veins of a European who has spent many years in a cold climate, an appearance very similar to the symptoms, in more southerly latitudes, of alcoholism.

"Hello, pleased to meet you. I've come from Reykjavík."

"Have you permits to navigate in Greenland?"

"Well, no. I cleared for Jan Mayen, but as I was becalmed

and lost my way, I decided it would be best to head in here!"

"O.K., it's a good story. I'll believe it. But don't stay here too long, in case one of the inspectors arrives from Denmark, or there'll be hell to pay. As soon as you're ready, make out again for Jan Mayen, yes?"

"Yes."

"Meanwhile, welcome to Greenland!"

"*Mange tak!*" I mustered up one of my few Danish phrases.

"Hey, that's good, come for supper later on! But don't bring your dog ashore."

"Don't tell me you have quarantine regulations here?" I said.

"It's not that. All the dogs here have tapeworm, and he'll soon catch it from them."

"Thanks for the tip. I'll be over in an hour, as soon as I've squared everything away. No shore leave for you, old son," I said to Nelson.

That night I ate with the wireless crew, who had been on this tour of duty for almost two years and still had another year to go before returning to Denmark. One of them, who was to be married upon his return home, said that he loved the land so much he intended to return with his wife and settle down.

I spent two days in Scoresby Sund cleaning out the bilges, decarbonizing the engine cylinder heads, checking the rigging and sails, and storing onboard fifty pounds of charcoal fuel for the small solid-fuel heating stove. In the late afternoons I went climbing over the rocky hillsides among the brilliantly colored, lichen-mossed rocks, along the shores littered with great boulders brought down by the ancient icefalls, watching the musk ox, with its straggly black hair, like a horse's mane, the large bearded seals and the smaller hair seals basking on the flat rocks at the water's edge of the deepest fiord in the world—Scoresby Sund,

4,600 feet deep, with vertical walls of rock around it rising straight up to heights of 6,500 feet. Beyond the sheer cliffs on the high plateau, the great snowy mass of Petermanns Peak reared its head 10,000 feet above the fiord! A giant's playground. Over to the west, the Stauning Alps rose 9,000 feet, and this seemed low, for the icecap around the base of the mountains is 6,000 feet deep!

This part of the Arctic, on the east coast of Greenland, is unique in that it has short, intensive summers, when the temperatures rise up to nine degrees centigrade. For this reason, among others, the tremendous, seemingly limitless glaciers of the country are among the most productive in the world, calving off many thousands of huge bergs all year round, but especially in the warm summer. And for this reason, also, the waters off east Greenland are among the most dangerous to shipping of all the Arctic seas.

At the head of the northwest fiord of the Sund is one of the fastest moving ice-masses on earth—which calves off anything up to fifty bergs a day in the warmest days of summer. And these can be over a mile in length! What a source of energy if only it could be harnessed!

As I climbed over driftwood washed up on the shore after floating on the currents all the way from Siberia, I reflected that the first strikes, the first probes north, into the East Greenland ice by sailing craft had been made by a British expedition from Liverpool, in the year 1824. They had reached Shannon Island, named after one of their leaders. I intended to penetrate the ice fields further north, if possible to latitude eighty-four north, which is the furthest that the great Norwegian Nansen reached in the *Fram* sixty-six years earlier. The odds were against this, but if I didn't outdo Nansen, at least I'd beat the Liverpool expedition! Scoresby Sund is on latitude seventy-two north. There were only thirteen degrees between me and the furthest north under sail! Only 780 miles! By ocean sailing standards, a mere eight days' sailing!

*Out of the night that covers me,*
*Black as the pit from pole to pole,*
*I thank whatever gods may be*
*For my unconquerable soul.*

*In the fell clutch of circumstance*
*I have not winced nor cried aloud.*
*Under the bludgeonings of chance*
*My head is bloody, but unbow'd.*

*Beyond this place of wrath and tears*
*Looms but the Horror of the shade,*
*And yet the menace of the years*
*Finds and shall find me unafraid.*

*It matters not how strait the gate,*
*How charged with punishments the scroll,*
*I am the master of my fate;*
*I am the captain of my soul.*

William Ernest Henley, "Invictus."

# 17

## Tooth and Nail, Head-On!

My aim, upon departing from Scoresby Sund, was to sail north as hard and fast as possible through the ice fields, along the shore lead, between the shore ice and the pack ice. My destination was Kap Bismarck, on the coast of Queen Louise Land, approximately 380 miles north, on latitude seventy-six degrees, forty-five minutes north. If I made a swift, easy passage, I should arrive within two weeks. If, on the other hand, the passage was slow because of ice obstacles and hazards, and I arrived late in the northern summer, I would winter near the Danmarks Havn wireless station, in a small bay which might or might not be ice free. Then, when the ice broke up the following summer, I would press on north up the coast of Germania Land and attempt to buck the current and the ice to a point north of latitude eighty-four, the furthest north ever reached to date by a sailing ship.

If the passage was fast, I would call briefly at Kap Bismarck, then press on further north while the ice was still fairly loose, hoping to reach the magic eighty-four-degree point that same autumn. Then, the ice would seize the boat and, on the current, carry *Cresswell* south again over the winter, back to civilization. If the drift back south was slow, I still had a good chance of weathering it out, for there was two years' supply of food onboard, and plenty of seals around.

The yearly inspector's ship was expected to arrive any day, and as I was eager to beat the coming winter in late September, I sailed out of Scoresby Sund anchorage with few regrets, apart from losing the fine company of the Danish radiomen and meteorologists, who had been hospitable and informative.

I motored out of the Sund through the loosening pack ice, dodging mountainous icebergs floating out into the Arctic Ocean. Once clear of the shore ice, which extended about forty miles, I found a wide-open lead to the north, though well dotted with isolated ice floes of all sizes. I was headed for the radio station at Myggbukta, on the coast of Hold with Hope peninsula, about 160 miles north. After three days and nights of hard sailing, in a flat sea, with the south wind dead astern, I was off the island (∅) of Bontekoe, where I moored onto an ice floe which had found its way around to the southern side of the island and gone aground. Here I slept fitfully for one "night." I was concerned in case another floe should come around the island and trap *Cresswell* against the one she was already moored to. After a few hours' sleep I decided to stay at Bontekoe ∅ for one more day, carrying out the necessary chores which had been neglected during the three-day passage north, when I had been on the wheel practically the whole time.

After the work was done, I took a good look around, though I did not leave the boat. I could have climbed over the piled up ice on the southern shore, but I was wary of possible accidents and also of the boat's breaking loose from the floe, if the wind shifted. During the day, it was warm enough to wear my normal sailing clothes—jersey, sheepskin jacket, long cotton underpants, and blue jeans, with long stockings and sea boots. But at night it turned cold, and I was glad to be in the sleeping bag for the short "dark" hours.

I watched the broken-up bits of the great pack ice field as they floated by the island—long ice fields, several miles across, which took hours to pass; "ice cakes" only as big as a motor car; chunks and the slushy "brash," melting on the sides of the larger floes and sinking into the ocean. On many of the floes and fields, there were seals, sometimes in small groups, sometimes alone, and I watched them through the binoculars as they woke from their brief naps and popped their heads up for a startled look about for marauding bears.

Over to the west, as soon as the sky clouded over, a strange phenomenon appeared. A perfectly recognizable map of the terrain below was reflected on the white bases of the clouds. It tallied up quite well with the information I had on the charts. Water of the fiords and leads showed up black on the surface of the clouds, while the ice and snow was a mottled grey color, and the vegetation, lichen on the rocks ashore, reflected a yellow or brown. It was as if someone was holding a huge mirror in the sky. This is what the Danes called the "ice-blink." "Very useful," I said to Nelson. Now I knew how to find a good water lead in cloudy weather.

By this time I had taken to wearing snow goggles, because the summer sunlight, which strikes a glare through the dry, clean air, made the ice of the floes shimmer with blinding light. After suffering a headache, I soon realized that snow blindness is in fact the result of eyestrain caused by the constant, instinctive seeking of shadows which, because of the angle of the sun's rays, are almost nonexistent. Man's greatest aid to judging distance, in normal conditions, is the effect of light and shadow. If the shadow effect is changed, as it is, for example, in moonlight, or under fluorescent lighting, then our eyes search continually for the normal references, straining themselves to gauge distance. The effect of the reflection of light from the ice is also a cause of blindness, but a minor one compared to trying to find normal seeing distance in abnormal conditions.

The thought of the continual procession of bergs and ice fields across the top of the world, for thousands of square

miles, was, at first, somewhat terrifying. I was relieved that
there was no one else with me. Eventually I realized that the
so-called Arctic hysteria, the feeling of panic which explor-
ing parties have reported, is, in fact, only a form of mass
hysteria transmitted from one nervous member of a group
to the others. Being alone, I stood a much better chance of
avoiding this affliction. I decided to consider only the immediate environment, and to hell with the rest of the Arctic.
That could look after itself.

When I left the ice-floe off Bontekoe Ø and headed north
for the radio station at Myggbukta, it was obvious that I
stood no chance at all of getting to the shore. The ice was
one solid frozen mass of heaped-up, stranded floes and
bergs, with ledges and needlepoints jumbled up
higgledy-piggledy into the sky as far as the eye could see.
The nearest I could approach the shore of Gausshalv Island, where the radio station was located, was about thirty
miles, and I dared not chance walking over the shore ice for
that distance. I decided to carry on north.

Here I had to turn my course east, out into the ocean,
towards the moving continent of pack ice floating down
from the North Pole, looking like an army on the move—
horsemen and gun carriages, coaches and long lines of foot
soldiers marching across the rim of the world.

After heading east for forty miles offshore, I eventually
found the edge of the fixed mass of shore ice and, picking
my course carefully, headed again north. There was little
wind on this passage, and progress was painfully slow. I
did not use the engine, as I wished to conserve fuel for
emergencies, in case I was trapped in thin ice. The wind
was so weak that it took me almost ten days to cover the
eighty miles to latitude seventy-four, away out over the ice
piled up on the Home Foreland. I was still in an area where
the British Liverpool expedition of 1824 had left marks,
right up the coast, in the names of headlands and islands.

At latitude seventy-four progress was almost halted altogether, for the pack ice was much closer to the shore ice,

and the shore lead, so-called (though it was anything up to two hundred miles out to sea), was very indistinct. Many times I headed up one lead only to find myself in the middle of a solid field of ice many times bigger than a New York City block. Then I would have to turn the boat around and motor out against the southerly breeze, running with the current to escape the mass of ice closing around the boat.

It was now the first week in August, and there was already a noticeable change in daytime temperatures. After two more weeks of struggling to find my way through this maze of icy jigsaw puzzles, the wind changed to the north and the temperature fell below freezing. I donned my fawnskin underwear, a shirt and an extra jersey, the Eskimo-made caribou-skin jerkin and trousers, and the sealskin boots.

Until the eighth of August there had been light twenty-four hours a day. After that the sun was down below the horizon for rapidly increasing periods of time, so that by the end of August, daylight and darkness each took half of every twenty-four hours, as they do below the equator. As the skies were mostly clear of cloud, I was still getting quite accurate sun sights. However, I had difficulty in finding my course through the ice, for there was rarely any ice-blink, which would have indicated water passages.

I reached Pendulum Island, at latitude seventy-four, forty-five north, on August 18, and, to my delight, found clear water running north, ahead. There were still many, many ice floes around, and after a brief rest (tied up against a floe in fairly open water), I pushed on, ever north, using the engine, as there was rarely room to beat against the wind. Progress was slow, as the engine was only ten horse-power and *Cresswell* was heavy with stores. Hammering against the strong north wind and current, I could not make more than two knots over the ground, and most of that to east or west, dodging the floes and bergs, which were becoming disturbingly frequent, especially at the end of the easterly legs.

When I reached the edge of the shore ice, off Kap Philip Broke, the southeastern cape of Shannon Island, at latitude seventy-five north, I saw my first polar bear. They are difficult to spot except when they are fairly close, say about three hundred yards. The dirty yellow color of their fur blends in perfectly with ice which is more than one season old, but I happened to be scanning the inshore side of the ice, as best I could, with the binoculars, when suddenly a slight movement in one hummock of piled-up floe caught my eye.

It is difficult to gauge distance in clear air over ice, but I reckoned he was about two hundred yards from the boat, walking on all fours. From fore to aft he was all of ten feet long, and he looked as if he weighed a ton. By this time, with the wind coming south off the ice, Nelson had picked up his scent and went rigid, sniffing the air, the classic pose of the hunting Labrador. When he sighted the bear with his one eye, he jumped and disappeared down below.

I had been warned about bears out on the ice by the Danes in Scoresby Sund. They had told me that a polar bear ashore was, like the grizzly bear out of the woods, a timid beast, who would avoid any encounter with an enemy. But once out on the floes, he was king of all he surveyed. He had only seals and wolves (possibly) to deal with, and he became a hungry, arrogant, violent, very dangerous wild beast, whose weight alone was enough to knock the life out of the strongest man. I put *Cresswell* on a broad reach, out to the east, adjusted the sails, for there was a perfectly clear stretch of water ahead on that course, then went below to make hot chocolate and warm myself.

"Thank God there's water between us and him," I said to Nelson, who was cowering under the cabin table. He bumped his tail in the floorboards. But I was disturbed by the thought that if I did not fetch Kap Bismarck and got stuck in the southward drifting ice pack, one of these brutes, or maybe even more than one, might get wind of us and attack.

By August 30 I was on latitude seventy-five degrees fifty minutes north—only sixty miles south of Kap Bismarck and safety. But try as I would to find a clear passage, it was almost impossible. Stretched right across the northern horizon was a solid barrier of piled up shore ice, rising in hummocks up to three hundred feet above the ocean level, along with a moving mass of pack ice and bergs, some of the latter up to nine hundred feet high and three miles from bow to stern.

Choosing one seemingly promising narrow lead running slightly west of north, hardly wider than three times the beam of *Cresswell*, I pressed on. By now the tops of the ice floes were well above deck level of my boat. I was, therefore, most of the time protected from the wind to about a third of the way up the mast. The engine was pushing the boat at four knots over the ground, going flat out, while the ice floes, moving on the current, were traveling at around a knot and a half. Our combined speed, therefore, was around six and a half knots—eight land miles per hour. All day, all night, for two days, I stayed at the wheel continuously, without a break, wending my way through these never-ending walls of gleaming ice as high as a garden wall, sometimes in a narrow passage hardly wide enough for the boat, sometimes in wide stretches.

I was still cold, even though I had thrown two blankets over my Arctic clothing and rigged up a windshield of canvas, forward of the wheel, to keep off the boat's own wind, created by her speed. The rigging was frosting up. This was a great worry. Every time I reached a stretch of wide lead or clear water, I had to lash the wheel, leave the boat at the mercy of the current, climb the masts, and knock off the ice with a small ax.

Doing this became a nightmare of cold and superhuman effort, short of sleep as I was. High up the mast the north wind blew intensely cold, frosting up all my clothes, with my breath forming an inch-thick layer of solid ice over the thick scarf tied up around my head between the goggles and the collar of my jerkin.

Not to have knocked the ice off the rigging would have been to commit suicide. It formed so quickly in the wind that within three hours it could create such a weight high up on the craft that it would overcome the weight of the ballast in the keel and capsize her. *Cresswell* would sink immediately. If I did not drown right away, I would freeze to death. If I managed to clamber onto the floe, I would both freeze and starve to death anyway in a long, protracted agony over a couple of days. Getting rid of the ice was a matter of staying alive.

By the morning of September 1, I was almost falling asleep on my feet. I had reached latitude seventy-six degrees ten minutes north. Bismarck station was a mere thirty miles away. Perhaps there was just enough clear water ahead to make it to Bismarck and sleep in safety. Perhaps around this next cape of ice, perhaps around the corner of that berg, the ice would clear just enough to get me thirty miles. Thirty miles in an ocean-crossing sailing yacht was a mere six hours' normal sailing; in a motor car, half an hour on a good road. Thirty miles—the difference between safety for the duration of the bitterly cold winter, and extreme discomfort, danger, and possibly even death, a cold, lonely death, in the ice. I pressed on, more by willpower now, for my physical strength was ebbing with lack of sleep. I was about three hundred miles nearer the Pole than the northernmost tip of Alaska.

Suddenly, my fate was decided for me, though I did not realize it at the time. The lead I had followed for the past day of cold torture ended up in a perfect wall of ice. I turned a corner, and there I was, like being in a harbor. By this time my fuel stock was so low, and the engine so cold, that getting out of this impasse under power was out of the question. I decided to take a chance. I tied the boat by a bowline only from the end of the cul-de-sac and went to sleep. I slept four hours, dead to the world.

When I awoke, feeling much stronger and more confident, I climbed onto the floe. Earlier it had been difficult to mount the floe to drive the stake in, as I had to cut steps out of the side with an ax in order to get on top. I had been too weak to jump up. Now it was much easier, and the sky had lightened into a grey twilight. The wind, however, was still screaming over the floes from the north, and once on top of the floe, it was a job to remain upright.

I looked first to the north; what I saw was one of the bitterest, most disappointing sights I have ever seen in my life.

There, only forty yards from where I stood, on the other side of an isthmus joining two huge fields of jammed-up pack ice that stretched away as far as I could see east and west, northeast and southwest, was another lead heading north, and away, at the end of it, at its mouth, was a great stretch of clear water right across the north horizon!

"Goddamn it, bugger it, and blast it!" I cursed myself, the floes, the forty yards, everything. Then, more in anger than in desperation, I clambered back onboard, grabbed the big tree-felling ax, and started to hack away at the ice. But after a few minutes the foolishness of trying to carve through a forty-yard-thick wall of ice twelve feet deep became obvious. I sat down on the ice. Tears were futile in this temperature, for they would freeze as soon as they left my eyes. Then I thought of what would happen if these two fields of ice, each higher than the boat, came together.

There was only one solution, for sailing back south was out of the question. It would take days to overtake the miles and miles of ice fields, and during those days they could crush together anyway, especially if the westerly field hit the fixed shore ice. I would not stand a chance. If I stayed where I was, I was a dead man; if I tried to sail south, I was probably a dead man. The third alternative, difficult though it might be, was the only solution. I must try to get the boat up onto the ice floe, about seven feet above sea level. But how?

There was only one possible way. I must hack a slipway out of the ice, wide enough for *Cresswell*'s hull to slide up, then I must lighten her bows, get her bows onto the ice whilst the stern was still loaded and low in the water, then unload all her other gear, and drag the empty hull up the incline.

And this is what I set to doing. I hacked away with the ax and shifted tons of ice, solid hard ice, until, after nine days' steady hard labor, I had a "ramp" leading from just below water level, back through the ice floe at a steady incline of about twenty-five degrees, back almost to the other side of the ice-floe isthmus. I worked all the daylight hours, axing, throwing, shoveling, slashing, until a fairly smooth ramp was created.

On the ninth of September I unloaded all the stores, all the sails, all the tools off the boat, having made a ladder out of some spare lumber, so I could climb off the deck straight onto the "deck" of the floe.

With the forefoot now above the waterline, I turned the boat bows onto the ramp and dragged her until the keel, just an inch of it, was resting on the ice. Then, I started to unload the midship parts of the boat, lifting the forefoot even higher above the bottom edge of the ice ramp.

Then, with much labor, I dug a five-foot hole in the ice at the inner end of the ramp, and into this I dropped the eighty-pound hurricane anchor. The chain from the anchor was secured to a three-inch-diameter nylon storm running line, a hundred fathoms of it—six hundred feet. I filled the anchor hole up with salt water and had a short sleep after a hearty meal of corned beef, rice, and porridge.

When I awoke the salt water in the anchor hole had frozen solid, and I had a good "deadman" to pull the boat up against. I had no winches in *Cresswell*, so the whole thing had to be done with blocks and tackles, five of them,

six-inchers, with three sheaves apiece. I dug footholds into
the top of the floe, reeved the storm line through the blocks,
and set to pulling four and a half tons up the twenty-five-
degree incline. It took me five days to get the forefront up to
the chain, a matter of twenty-eight yards or so. The bottom
of the keel was then only about a foot below the top of the
floe. She was out of danger. She was sitting almost on top
of the ice, exposed to a bitter cold wind, covered in frost and
driven ice, but she was safe. That was the main thing.
Wearily I reloaded my stores onboard, except for some of
the cartons of corned beef, which would take up valuable
space in the cabin. These I covered with an old sail, pegged
down into the ice. Then I noticed that the northern exit from
the floe had jammed up solidly with ice floes.

"One good thing about this situation, old son," I said to
Nelson, as I clambered below to get a long rest, "at least we
don't have to worry about the rigging freezing up now."
But the ice would still have to be knocked off regularly, at
least twice a day, to prevent its weight snapping the masts.

I made a big pot of burgoo, so I could rest thoroughly
during the next day or two, and tacked up all my mutton
cloths on the inner lining of the hull around the cabin, then
fixed felt pads over the portholes and the skylights, while
the tiny cabin warmed up with the heat of the cooking.
Then I went topsides to have a last look around.

The wind had died at last, and there was little noise
except for the distant cracking and crunching of the ice. The
sun had dropped over the southwest horizon, changing the
sky to pale blue, deepening into turquoise, Prussian blue,
then Stygian black. In the north and east the stars shone so
bright, so close, that it seemed as if they hung around my
shoulders. The dryness of the atmosphere made the rays of
the stars diffuse into each other. The effect was like standing under a great chandelier of a billion-trillion shining
candles.

I decided it was too cold to piss in the open air. I would do
it in the big wine demijohn, hermetically sealed, which I

used in inclement weather. I touched the mizzen shrouds with my mittened hands. Small bits of glistening ice fell off the rigging wire. I made a mental note to clean my ice goggles later. I had removed them, for the twilight was deepening. The smell of a good stew simmered up the companionway hatch.

Although I had failed to reach Nansen's latitude of eighty-four degrees north, I had got very close—within eight degrees. I had reached a point only 850 miles from the North Pole itself, and despite the potentially terrifying situation *Cresswell* had been in only two weeks previously, she was now reasonably safe, unless the ice under her broke up.

As I turned to go below, I saw the bear. Twelve feet long, padding silently, swiftly over the snow-laden ice. He was only fifty yards away, coming straight at the boat!

*Weary with toil, I haste me to my bed,*
*The dear repose for limbs with travel tired;*
*But then begins a journey in my head*
*To work my mind, when body's work's expired.*
*For then my thoughts, from far where I abide,*
*Intend a zealous pilgrimage to thee,*
*And keep my drooping eyelids open wide,*
*Looking on darkness which the blind do see.*
*Save that my soul's imaginary sight*
*Presents thy shadow to my sightless view,*
*Which like a jewel hung in ghastly night,*
*Makes black night beauteous, and her old face new.*
   *Lo, thus by day my limbs, by night my mind,*
   *For thee, and for myself, no quiet find.*

Shakespeare, Sonnet 27.

# 18

## *Alone on the Ice*

"Jesus Christ Almighty!" I said under my breath to Nelson, who was also on deck to perform his ablutions over the side. But he had gone stock rigid, his ears quivering, his eye glaring at the monster advancing towards us. Then, without thinking, I was down the companionway ladder, grabbing Nelson as I went.

For a second or two, slithering down the ladder, my mind was in a dither. Instinctively grabbing my harpoon, an eight-foot-long ash shaft with a fine, greased steel tip sharpened to a needlepoint, from its stowage on the deck head of the cabin, I turned to mount the ladder. Then my mind started to work. Fast.

"Move!" I shouted to Nelson. "Move, you silly sod. Make the bastard think you're a fox! Move!" Nelson jerked out of his stupor and jumped, then ran as fast as his three legs would carry him up the side-deck, to the fore deck, where he stood his ground, snarling.

By now the bear was hauling himself upright, with his great paws clawing at the guardrails. As his head, with its fierce fangs and glittering, menacing eyes, appeared over the gunwale, I jabbed at him with the harpoon from where I was standing in the companionway. My idea was to fight him off from there, where the lower part of my body was protected and I could duck if he made a swipe at me.

The bear jerked his head and body back in surprise, his

187

great massive claws tearing away the upper wire of the
guardrail, bending the one-inch-thick galvanized iron
stanchions as if they were putty. Then I realized that this
huge creature could, if he wished, literally tear the boat
apart with his strength. At the same time Nelson made a
gallant charge towards him aft along the side-deck, yapping, snarling, and barking. All hell broke loose. The bear
recovered from his shock and rebounded back, his whole
body thumping against the hull, which slid sideways, the
keel jarring against the side of the ramp. I reacted fast and
jabbed at his right paw, which was tearing at the canvas
deck cover, the huge nails ripping into the covering clear
through to the wood underneath. The harpoon struck
home. It went through the bear's forefoot and stuck in the
wood underneath. The bear let out a roar loud enough to
shake the boat to pieces. Then he ripped his paw, harpoon
and all, out of the deck and dropped down onto the ice. The
harpoon went flying, clattering over the floe. I could feel his
breath, hot and oily, like a cloud of steam from a locomo-
tive. For a second or two Nelson and I stook stock-still,
petrified with shock and alarm. The bear crawled on all
fours around the side of the boat, bumping the hull with his
shoulder. Then I remembered the Very rocket gun.

This is a device, shaped like a pistol, with a barrel eight
inches long and an inch and a half bore, into which flare
rockets are loaded. Fired by mariners in distress, the rocket
will rise into the sky up to four hundred feet and slowly
descend, its phosphorous flakes burning all the way back
down to the sea's surface. When I had sighted the first bear,
off Shannon Island, I had loaded the Very pistol in readi-
ness for just such an attack as this. Now I slithered below,
fumbled at the fireworks box, and grabbed the pistol, my
hands shaking badly.

The bear had climbed up above the ramp on the other
side of the boat and was pawing at the gunwale with one
forefoot, while swiping at Nelson, who was trying to lure
him forward away from me. I climbed the ladder and

turned to face the bear. Holding the Very pistol in one frozen hand, I slammed down as hard as I could on the doghouse roof with the other, fist clenched.

The bear turned his jaws towards me, showing his great fangs, his hungry, wicked eyes crackling with anger. I fired, sending the rocket straight into his throat, a great stream of red light particles. With a grunt, the bear threw himself backwards onto the ice floe, rolling in agony, for the phosphorus of the flare was burning fiercely in his gorge. Then, jumping up and down with tremendous force, he beat the ice with his paws, all the while weaving his upper body from side to side, while Nelson slithered onto the ice and snapped at his hindquarters. After a few more mighty thuds on the top of the ice floe, which actually shook the boat, the bear took off fast across the ice and dove into the water on the other side of the floe. This did not save him, however, because phosphorus burns underwater. There was a mighty splash in the distance and he disappeared.

Shivering with fright and excitement, I went below, still holding the pistol. Once below I found that my fingers were stuck to the rocket gun. Frostbite! I grabbed a flannel cloth in the galley, threw it into the still simmering stew, then fished it out again with a fork and slapped it, steaming, over my hand. I didn't feel a thing for about thirty seconds, until the circulation was restored, and then the hot stew started to scald the hand, and I knew it was safe. I checked my face, which had been exposed just below the eyes, above the icy scarf. There were two fish-belly white spots, one on each cheek. I repeated the burgoo-stew treatment, in my hurry splashing the hot, gooey liquid onto my eyelids, and in a few seconds the cure was made. The pain almost sent me through the roof.

By this time Nelson was back in the cabin, still shaking with fight-lust.

I threw him a bone and some hardtack, then, after closing the companionway door and hatch cover to try to warm the boat up again, I collapsed on the berth. "Jesus!" I thought,

"I hope there's no more of *those* around!"

Wearily I stood at the galley and doled out some stew, but I couldn't eat much. I felt sick with concern and relieved at the same time.

Sleep, when it came, was fitful and full of fantasy. But before I dropped off, I made two resolutions. One was that I would not, while on the ice, sleep more than two hours at a stretch, and then would always leave Nelson on guard in a box in the cockpit to protect him from the wind. The other was that before sleeping I would always, whenever possible, search the floe, out to a perimeter of a thousand yards, for signs of bear.

The Danes had told me that bears generally haunt broken floes and areas where there are many seals, and that, usually, where there is a bear, the white fox is never far behind, eating the scraps of seal left by the bear. Not only the tracks of bear in the ice would warn me of their presence, but also the much smaller spoor of the fox.

Seals are the bears' only food. They are supposed to catch fish, but none of the Danes I met in Iceland and Scoresby Sund had ever seen a bear fishing, neither had any of the Eskimos I met later. There is a conundrum here. If, as the dieticians tell us, fat is only fuel, and protein is the body-builder, how is it that the bear, whose only food (evidently) is seal meat, which is practically all fat, manages to build up such a huge, strong body?

During the short days which followed, I remembered everything that the Danes told me about bears. How they stalk a seal, with their great bulky bodies splayed down on the ice, surprisingly flat and inconspicuous from nose to tail. If it's a bearded seal, a great heavy animal, weighing up to six hundred pounds, the bear will satisfy his appetite, then he will leave the rest of the carcass and amble off to sleep. After two or three days' rest, he will return to the frozen seal remains, a great mass of solid hard blubber and bones, and gnaw it, grinding the rock-hard mass between his teeth till there is nothing left. That is if the foxes have not gotten to it while the bear is sleeping.

The bears are usually followed by the fox, as the lion is followed by the hyena and the jackal. But the two ignore each other. The bear knows he cannot catch the swift fox, and the fox knows the bear is too slow for him; so as he follows the bear, the fox runs around and around, playfully teasing the great, lumbering king of the Arctic. Ashore, the white fox tends to treat man in the same way as he does the bear, running round him with not a care in the world. The fox confuses man with the bear. The bear confuses dogs sleeping or lying down on the ice with the seal. The bear also confuses a still man, sitting or lying down, with the seal. The bear confuses a standing or running dog with the white fox. How he sees an active man is not quite clear. It is either as another bear or as another type of hunting animal. Whichever, out on the ice floes the polar bear will attack, because he cannot stand competition in the fight for survival.

During the short daylight hours, I obtained fair sun sights, and it was soon evident that the drift of the floe was more or less due south, at the rate of around half a knot. That is about twelve miles a day, but as the days progressed, this seemed to be slowing down, until by the end of September, it was down to six miles a day. The great ice field was moving steadily and surely, and I was by then at around latitude seventy-three, which put me somewhere near the wireless station at Myggbukta and Ella Island. I kept the boat clear of ice and driven snow as best I could to make her show up against the whiteness of the floe, in case a plane passed overhead. One day, during the twilight, I actually saw a flying boat heading northwest, but it was far away on the southern horizon, and with the bear threat I did not dare waste my signal flares trying to attract his attention. I had only eight flares with me and no idea how many bears might show up. But fortunately none did, although on two occasions I saw them through the binoculars, walking over distant ice floes.

By the first of October my floe, which I had christened *Ark Royal*, had started to break off here and there, with loud cracks, groans, and wheezes. The lead to the north of *Cresswell* was once again widening up. *Ark Royal* was shaped something like an hourglass, with the two sand vessels pointing east and west and *Cresswell* sitting on top of the narrow stem. If the western edge hit against the solid shore ice, the two "sand vessels" would part company, which would split the floe just about where *Cresswell* was.

I made plans to get *Cresswell* back afloat. It was pointless to slide her back down the ice ramp into the southern lead, for it no longer existed. Where the lead had been was a long line of tossed-up ice cakes and chunks piled up into the air for a distance of about two miles!

The only reasonable course was to dig another ramp through the ice over into the northern lead, then slide *Cresswell* down it and try to emerge from the ice field by way of that route, which seemed to be fairly loose, being low, flat, "young" ice, newly formed. If I could get her afloat again, there was a chance I could get out.

I was out on the ice, huddled up in my Eskimo gear, with a screaming storm coming up from the south, blowing ice particles so strong that I could feel them drumming on my caribou-skin jerkin, even through the inner layer of thick hair. Nelson circled me slowly, keeping watch just within visibility range, about fifty yards. I was probing the ice with the harpoon, plotting the course of the new ramp. Ahead, through a momentary gap in the flying ice, I saw a black lump stretched out on the floe, not more than fifty yards away. A seal! I dropped down flat onto the ice.

Nelson was behind me, out of eyeshot of the seal. I lifted my head up and looked around, trying to appear like a seal, jerking my hooded head in quick, sniffing motions. Nelson sat down in the driving ice. He had sensed something was afoot, even though the wind was blowing at an oblique angle from our side to the seal's. I waved my hand down and Nelson dropped prone, his nose twitching.

There, in front of me, was a highly sensitive animal, with built-in natural alarm systems; an animal which never slept for more than three minutes at a time, which continually was on the lookout for foes, and which could move with surprising speed over the ice and into the safe water. Behind me was another animal, highly intelligent at stalking, hunting, and recovering, courageous and bold, but crippled. His missing eye did not seem to affect his sight much. The trouble was the missing forefoot, which deprived him of the hunting dog's speed, though only by a small margin. In between was me, man, intelligent enough to develop weapons capable of killing a seal from a mile away, yet reduced now to becoming a seal himself until he could get near enough to strike.

Soon I was within forty yards of the seal. He raised his smooth head up, with his shoulders supported by his flippers, and slowly looked around. Then he dropped down on the ice. I watched him for a few seconds, then inched forward again. Every five minutes or so I raised my head, just as the seal was doing, and gazed around. Nelson stayed prone, but he too was slowly slithering forward right behind me, keeping my body between him and the seal. After another hour of inching forward little by little, I was within twenty yards of the seal. After several hard stares, each lasting about a minute, he no longer looked my way. He still rose up on his fins and looked around, but only at the quarters of his vision away from my direction. Then I realized that he had made up his mind that I was another seal.

I scrabbled quietly forward, keeping as close to the ice as I could. By this time my dark goggles had started to steam, and I longed to take them off and clean them, but of course this would have warned the seal. I moved ahead again, perched up, looked around. Nelson had stopped moving with me. He was too crafty to come near enough for the seal to see him and think he was a fox following a bear. Another hour, another ten yards, then a slow nudging forward over the smooth, twilit ice. The next five yards took about twenty minutes to cover, as I moved a little faster because the seal seemed to be getting restless and I was concerned in case he should suddenly take off.

By this time I could study him at close quarters. He was about nine feet long and must have weighed a good four hundred pounds. He was a bearded seal, what the Eskimos call an *ugrug*. Every now and then he would rise up, like a huge slug, and search the area away from me. At intervals his tail flapped lazily against the ice. He looked fat and satisfied; there was enough food on him to give me energy to build ten ramps. I edged closer, trying to make the same breathing noise as he, a sort of heavy wheeze, like a person snoring in his throat.

Fifteen feet away I raised my feet and slapped the ice, just as he was doing with his tail. As he rose to look around away from me, I slowly lifted the harpoon and flung it, hard as I could, straight at his neck. It went right through and he dropped like a stone, with no twitching, no jerking, nothing. His huge carcass just collapsed on the ice.

"Come on, boy!" I jumped up and fell on the harpoon handle, twisting it out. Nelson was up in a flash, snapping and snarling, standing just clear of the seal's head and throat, his back teeth bared, ready to bite. I plunged the harpoon again into the shoulder, as deep as I could. There was a slight resistance as the steel barb entered the tough skin, then it slid right in like a dart into a slab of lard.

Satisfied the seal was truly dead, I looked around for bear and then trudged back to the boat for a bucket and a box. In another two hours I had enough blubber laying alongside the boat to feed a small ship's crew for a fortnight and more.

After a meal and a reconnoiter around our perimeter, I had a sleep, with Nelson on guard, gnawing at a huge chunk of raw seal blubber.

Once awake, I started to dig the new ramp. A weary,

backbreaking job. On the first one I had great difficulty shifting the huge slabs of ice with mittened hands. I made a "longshoreman's hook" out of a great shark-fishing barb by fixing a wooden handle on it, and so I could now grab onto the ice and drag it clear. It took until October 15 to complete the ramp. For two days I was immobile, taking refuge from a raging blizzard. The next task was to start moving the boat.

The first thing was to dig out the hurricane anchor, then plant it again into another hole astern of the boat. Then the fifty-pound fisherman anchor had to be dug into yet another five-foot-deep hole just over the top of the ramp, about ten yards down. The idea was to use the fisherman to slide the boat forward, until she was sitting, bows forward, on top of the ramp, then brake the slide down into the water with the storm line secured to the hurricane hook.

Much easier said than done, but on October 16 all was ready and I started pulling the boat, using the great blocks, or pulleys, as landsmen call them, to inch the boat along the ice, after unloading two and a half tons of removable gear and food onboard. On the seventeenth, after many hours of hard labor in the freezing cold, interspersed with heavy meals of boiled curried seal blubber, biscuits, and porridge, with great dollops of strawberry jam smeared over the lot, the boat was teetering on the top of the ramp. I married up the brake line to the hurricane hook, gave the stern a mighty heave, grabbed the brake line to control it, and she was away, just like a ship being launched, only *Cresswell* went bows first. I had left a good amount of weight in the stern, and as she hit the water, the empty bows danced up into the air, the stern swung around sideways, and she was afloat, checked by the heavy line from colliding with the small ice floes in the water.

Then, using the ladder with a plank lashed along its length, I reloaded the boat, dragging the stores over the ice on a species of sled which I had knocked together during the comparatively idle day-nights on the floe. With me pulling on one rope and Nelson grasping the other in his teeth, we soon made a quick job of shifting and restowing all the gear. It was not easy, as it was very dark in the boat, with just two small kerosene lamps flickering.

After a short sleep and another meal, I went out to try the engine. It was frozen solid, despite all the attempts I had made to keep it warm. I had even constructed a chimney from the galley to the engine compartment to conduct warm air, but to no avail. The blowtorch onboard refused to operate despite an hour's fumbling with frozen fingers. There was only one solution. I laboriously dismantled the cabin stove and chimney and, in a matter of hours, had it fitted up in the engine compartment, with the fumes going through the engine exhaust outlet. This did the trick, and early on the eighteenth I had the engine running and was moving slowly out, through thin new ice, to the northwest. As I was on the lee side of the *Ark Royal* ice floe, the sea was flat calm, and by running the engine flat out, I shoved my way between the thin cakes floating like shining waterlilies on the surface of the freezing sea.

Sunrise on the eighteenth of October was around eleven in the morning, and there was daylight until around one in the afternoon, then twilight until about four. I made good time, for *Cresswell*'s hull was tough as an ox and I rammed my way through thin ice. Gradually the lead widened. Once I broke out of the pack ice field into comparatively open water, I intended to head south, and so out to a point where I could turn east for Iceland, or perhaps even make my way into one of the Greenland fiords, to winter there.

Suddenly, again, my fate was decided for me. There, on the western horizon, was a smudge of smoke, coming closer. I fired off one of my emergency signal flares. As I gazed at the ship's hull, which by now was plainly visible, with the lights shining from her cabins, I saw a brighter light flashing away from where I imagined the bridge was. They had seen my flares!

I patted Nelson on the back of his head. "Now behave yourself, mate, we've got company coming!"

The ship was soon very close, having broken a wide swath right through the thin ice. She was wearing the Danish flag and her name was *Gustav Holm*, her port of registry Copenhagen. Seeing my tattered, barely recognizable red ensign, one of her officers sang out in English over his megaphone.

"Where are you coming from?"

"Reykjavík—I was trying to make for Jan Mayen Island, only I got stuck."

"We can see—how was your trip?"

"Up and down, up and down."

He laughed. As the ship edged closer, I distinctly heard him say to the others crowded on the bridge deck, "Bloody Englishmen. Bloody crazy fools!"

"Hey, up there!" I hollered, between cupped mittens. "Hello, up there!"

"*Ja?*" he replied, bending down low over the bulwark, his gloved hand around his ear. I could plainly see his cleanshaven face under the clean parka hood.

"*Ja?*" he shouted again.

"*Welshman, if* you don't mind!"

*For I'm going back to the frozen North,*
*To the land where spunk is spunk——*
*Not a trickling stream of lukewarm cream,*
*But a* solid frozen chunk!

> Last verse of "The Ballad of Deadeye Dick
> and Eskimo Nell." There are ninety-two
> verses of this, written by an anonymous
> bard in the early 1900s and traditionally ren-
> dered at Royal Navy "Sods' Operas."

# 19

## *Trapped!*

Clumsily, in my sealskin boots and Arctic gear, I clambered up the rope ladder which had been cast over the weather-streaked side of the *Gustav Holm*, clinging to the lines which were already stiffening in the cold. It was no strain, for my arms, after six weeks of hauling and digging in solid ice, were like steel-wire rope, and I soon clattered on deck, watched by the astonished crew and passengers.

I was met by Captain Svensson, who, shaking my mitten heartily, led me up to his cabin under the bridge. Soon I was doffing my caribou-skin jerkin in his warm cabin. My shirt underneath was filthy and stiff with frozen sweat. My beard was eight inches long.

"You have a bath, and I will get your clothes cleaned up," said the captain, who was surprisingly young, about thirty. And then I realized that when ships' captains appear young, it is a sign of one's own advancing age.

The steward showed me into the bathroom, and I looked around in wonder. This was the first bathroom I had seen for months, ever since leaving Iceland. The marvel of hot water pouring from a faucet at the turn of a tap delighted me. For half an hour I soaked in sudsy hot water; it was the first time in weeks that I had been really warm. Afterwards I inspected myself in the mirror. My eye had completely recovered from the blow on the voyage up from St. Kilda, and although tired, I felt fitter than I had for years.

"How was the bath?" asked the captain when I had done.

"For a small-boat voyager," I told him, "there is no finer welcome, no greater luxury."

The dinner, with the passengers and crew, was in the Danish fashion, and that night there was boiled ham. As usual among Northern Europeans, there was far too much on my plate for me to eat, and, as usual, I had to make apologies for my small needs. But the aquavit went down well, though I was careful not to overindulge.

During the meal the captain said, "You know, I can easily lift your boat out of the water and carry her onboard to Reykjavík."

That was the last thing I wanted. The authorities there had charged me mooring fees at fishing boat rates, a fantastic sum, about ten dollars per day. As I had not been in Icelandic waters for commercial reasons, as I had not been exploiting their fishing grounds, and as I had been out at anchor the whole while, using the port facilities only to the extent of drawing off forty gallons of water, this was daylight robbery. Besides, I was 360 miles north of Reykjavík, and if I could winter on the coast of Greenland, I would be in a favorable position to try another probe north early next summer, 1960. Generous as the captain's offer was, if there was rough weather it would not be possible to lower *Cresswell* back down into the sea before the *Gustav Holm* reached Reykjavík, and then, with the shipping company watching all, I would have a fat freight bill to pay, and my coffers were exceedingly low.

"Thank you very much for your offer, Captain Svensson, it is most kind, but I think I will try to get into one of the Greenland fiords. Our position now, you said, is about sixty miles southeast of the King Oscar fiord. What about if I try for there, go up the fiord and reach Ella Island? I can winter there, at the radio station."

He shook his head. "Impossible. We've just come out from there and it was all we could do to force our way through the piled-up shore ice in the fiord. We were very lucky not to be frozen in ourselves. You would stand no chance." After dinner, he led me up to the bridgehouse and showed me a chart of Eastern Greenland.

"Look," he said, "if you are determined on this, your best chance, probably your only chance, is to try to get into Scoresby Sund. There are a lot of bergs coming down from the glaciers inland, but the latest information is that the shore ice is still fairly loose. The pack ice is still moving, so there's a good chance you can find your way in to the wireless station. Anyway, I will signal them and tell them you are heading there, and if you don't reach there in a couple of days, they can set up a search with the Catalina flying boat from Angmagssalik."

"Sounds fair enough to me, captain. Look, I don't want to hold you up any longer. You have been most helpful and kind, and I surely do appreciate it. *Mange tak!*"

I climbed back down to the deck of my boat, gave Nelson a pat, cast off the lines, and was away. The *Gustav Holm* slid away to the southeast while her passengers and crew lined up, waving to me as she eased through the thin ice pack. Then I set off to follow the passage she had already broken up between the point where she had encountered me and the coast of Greenland.

The weather was cold, with a bitter wind of about fifteen knots blowing from the northeast. I soon had all working sail up and in two hours was out in fairly open water. After another twelve hours standing at the wheel in the freezing cold, trying to dodge behind rigged-up canvas shelters, I sighted, away to the southwest, the red light atop the Scoresby Sund wireless mast and, feeling my way around the edge of a great mass of broken-up shore ice, entered the great sound. Now I was within a few miles of a good wintering haven, and there would be company and warmth over the coming months of night.

But try as I would there was no passage through the ice to the shore. In the pale light of the twilit day, I estimated that the nearest I could approach the station was eight miles.

There, on the edge of the shore ice, I would be completely exposed to all the winter storms and to the huge, monstrous icebergs as they swept out to sea. There was only one thing to do; I must try to penetrate into the great long fiord and find a suitable spot, no matter how isolated, where I could perhaps beach the boat, thus keeping her from being crushed as the shore ice piled up. And so I made up by the Scoresby Sund, watching the tiny red light of warmth and cheer fading away beyond the shore fog. Even though I was shining a light, I knew the people in the wireless station would probably not see me through the fog. Then I remembered the great brass foghorn. I gave six toots on it—"*Dah dit dah; dah dit dah*: I wish to communicate with you"—then listened. No reply. Another six hoots, then I heard them— eight miles away. That's how noise carries in the dry Arctic air. They were signaling back slowly, in straight Morse. Their hoots were deep and melancholy. I listened carefully.

"*Dit dah dah; dit dit dit dit; dit; dit dah dit; dit. Dit dah dit; dit, dit, dah. Dit dah dit; dah dah dit dah*: Where R.U. Interrogative?"

I gave the hooter handle heavy jerks. "Due south; going up fiord; try Syd Kap."

The answer came after a brief pause. "C., *dah dit dah dit*, yes; R.AR. Message received. Ends."

That was the last communication I had with anyone but the Eskimos for well over a year. Slowly, I wended my way upstream under sail and engine, dodging the ice floes and bergs, this way and that, under the moon and stars, with the ice mountains gleaming and sparkling nine thousand feet up above the wide fiord. Progress was slow, and it was another two days before I sighted the umiak, forty feet long, made of skins, with five Eskimos onboard. They paddled over to meet me, for they were against the wind, and I was under very short sail, for fear of colliding with a floe. They waved and pointed towards the shore. At first it seemed there was nothing there but bare rock, but then I saw the huts, three of them, sitting on a small headland.

There were some children running over the ice on the shore. To the east of the huts, a smaller fiord dropped back from the main fiord. I sailed along it for about three hours. It was free of ice, right up to the beach!

After starting the engine I made my way in. I dropped the sails and slowly, holding the string to the very primitive throttle arrangement I had rigged up, steered the boat head on, at right angles to the pebble beach. She touched; then, with a rumble, her speed carried her gently about five yards onto the beach as she slid on her three keels. There is very little tide in Scoresby Sund, so there was no fear of the boat refloating and being carried away by the tide; in any case, I secured her with a stout mooring line to a nearby boulder. Then I went to sleep.

When I awoke there was a full storm heading in from the northeast, but going on deck it was obvious that I was in a very good spot, protected by high mountains all around, except due south, where there was a fetch of about thirty miles from the range of mountains which stretch out west to east across Knud Rasmussen Land. If there was to be any danger here, it would come from the south. While I made breakfast of eggs and bacon, courtesy of the captain of *Gustav Holm*, I thought about this problem.

The answer was soon obvious. The beach I was sitting on sloped up to the land at about the same angle as the ramp on the *Ark Royal* ice floe. About sixty feet ahead of the bows was a line of boulders, quite high, about thirty feet on average, and over at an angle of forty-five degrees north-west of the boat, about eighty feet away, was a gap. Behind that, when I went to look, I found sand. Further up, there was a slope of smooth rock, also strewn with lichen-covered boulders. There was no sign of a glacier above the rock hillside. Climbing up it, in the cold starlight, I was reminded of the great water catchments which cover the southern side of the Rock of Gibraltar.

I would haul the boat up through the gap and settle her in behind the rocks which followed the line of the shore.

There she would be protected from all winds, from any high seas brought in by a south wind, and from any ice which might drive ashore with the wind.

There was a problem here though, because unlike the glassy smooth ice of the floe, which had made it comparatively easy to slide the boat, the pebbles and sand would be much more difficult to haul the weight of the boat over. The first thing I would need was long balks of timber, two of them, to lay up the beach, then three heavy rollers. Securing the blocks to the rocks was simple, with a rope lashed right around the base of one of the boulders.

Even after the storm died, there was no sight of the Eskimos, though far in the distance, from the west, the sound of chopping and hammering carried over in the wind. I estimated that the Eskimo hamlet was about twelve miles away. I dared not leave the boat in the position she was in, half-ashore and half-afloat, so I started to make ready to haul her up the beach, first landing all the removable stores over the bow onto the beach, all two and a half tons. While I was doing this, the thought came to me that perhaps I could use the spars, the masts, the gaffs, and the booms to roll her up the beach. The mainmast was hollow for half its length only, but very strong; the mizzenmast completely solid.

It took me three hours to lower the mainmast and the mizzenmast; with a long line reeved through a block way up the beach and back to the mastheads, I had then to take the pins out of the tabernacles and slowly ease the mainmast down. The difficulty was to prevent the mast from crashing down once it was past an angle forty-five degrees from the vertical, so I rigged another line, from the mizzen head to the mainmast top, and, while easing away on the shore line, hauled in on the triatic line. Then, once the mast reached the critical forty-five-degree angle, the mizzen took the weight. Lowering away slowly, or "handsomely," as sailors say, with the triatic line, the whole of the mast was soon down on deck. Then, securing the shore line to the base of the mast, which was lying foot forward by now, I heaved away and dragged the mainmast over the bow onto the beach.

The mizzenmast was comparatively simple to lower, being only two-thirds the height of the main and only half the diameter. That, too, was soon lying up the beach. I packed the underside of the two masts with sails and blankets. Now I had my "railway"! The booms and gaffs were soon lying at right angles across the masts and I had my "wheels." Then I started hauling, with the three keels of the boat, only six inches deep below the hull, resting on the booms. She moved slowly but steadily as I hauled away, using the same five-block purchase I had used on the ice floe, and after six hours or so she was high and dry on the beach, close to the rock gap. Then I made ready to slew her around the corner of the far rock and tuck her in on the sand. But first I had a good meal of corned beef and rice, then a sleep of four hours or so. By the time the four next meals had been eaten, she was lying cozily tucked in, low behind the rock barricade, bows facing northeast and the masts and booms stowed on deck to make a frame for a tent rigged up from the older, spare sails and the canvas awnings. Between the booms I packed boxes of food stores to provide plenty of holding and supporting surface for the tent, which would soon be supporting snow and ice. This took another day.

After another meal and another sleep, with the wind again howling outside, I unshipped the heating stove from its engine-room berth and repositioned it in the cabin. It was the twenty-sixth of October. The sun had disappeared altogether, and there was only about two hours of pale, ghostly twilight. Other than that, all was night. When it was clear, bright with the reflected light of the moon and the stars from the ice and snow of the great massifs overhead, it was a sight of beauty; but when the sky was overcast or foggy, pitch-black and cold, with the bitter Arctic winds blowing blinding blizzards of snow and frozen rain, it was misery in the extreme. But I was ready; my winter haven was prepared. I set out southwest along the frozen, rocky beach to find the Eskimos.

Traveling on foot along the shore was much more difficult than I had imagined. Often there were rock tumbles, or crushed ice right up on the shore, which meant a long detour inland, up slippery, almost vertical, cliff faces. I had left Nelson onboard, on a loose line. The wind was slight, and I made good going. Considering the icy and rocky terrain, I thought I could reach Syd Kap in fourteen hours. I had taken along my sleeping bag and a small sea bag with some baked beans, corned beef, and sugar, just in case I got stuck in a blizzard—or, if the Eskimos were friendly and hospitable, I could exchange it for some food.

It is awkward to account for the passage of time when the "days" are so short, and the only way it can be done is by the twenty-four-hour clock system, used by seafarers and airmen. The normal days and nights fuse into one during the Arctic winter, and much of the time the visibility is better in the "night" hours than in the "day." I left the boat at 1600 hours and plodded first along the pebble beach, now mostly iced over, for two hours. Coming to a rockfall of huge boulders fallen down from the mountainside onto the shore, much too smooth and slippery to climb over, I wended my way up the steep rise of the moraine to circumvent the rocks. On my way down again, the wind piped up from the north and the sky darkened, with great masses of black clouds overhead. In a matter of minutes, there was a raging blizzard, snow sweeping down the mountainside out into the fiord below. A little later, as I took my bearings, worried lest I be marooned in a drift, visibility dropped to a matter of feet. All was black, with white snow swirling around. I could tell my direction because of the fall of the land and the direction of the wind, so I made my way slowly down to the upper edge of the rockfall. By 2350 I had found a gap between two boulders, one resting on top of the other, and crawled inside, freezing cold and shivering, despite the extra jersey under my parka. There was a space about eight feet long and as big as a coffin between the rocks, and in this I laid my sleeping bag, then crawled inside and scoffed another can of beans mixed with some sugar. Then I went to sleep with the driven snow and ice whistling past the end of the opening between the giant boulders.

I wasn't too worried about animals, as I had heard that bears were timid ashore and avoided man, even a sleeping man, while foxes or wolves mainly traveled alone. I packed some driven snow around the bag and dropped off, exhausted.

When I awoke the scene outside was beautiful. The wind had dropped entirely and all around were huge hummocks of snow under the moonlight. It was 0400 hours on November 1. I ate a can of corned beef and swung myself up onto the top of the boulder I had slept under. Peering all around in the freezing night, I found to my horror that I was trapped! The pile of boulders, about half a mile above the shore line, was completely isolated, surrounded by snow drifts of twenty feet or more. I scampered below again, into my rock cleft, lit a cigarette, and had a think. My hands shook as I doffed my outer mittens.

There were five cans of corned beef and three of beans in my pack, four packets of cigarettes and two pounds of sugar, which I had hoped to exchange with the Eskimos for useful items like seal oil. There was the harpoon, a can opener, a flashlight and a seaman's clasp knife, and six boxes of matches. And that was it. The chances of Eskimos coming within sight of me during the next few months were nil. There was only one thing for it, I must dig my way out through the snowdrifts!

I clambered again onto the top of the boulders and looked around. The nearest other rocks clear of snow were down towards the shore, about half a mile downhill, as far as I could tell in the darkness.

Back down in the rock crevice, I opened up two cans of

corned beef, laid the food down on the icy stone, and
opened up the cans with the can opener, flattening them
until they were sheets of thin metal. Then I punched holes
in the metal with the seaman's knife. The next bit was
tricky, because it meant completely undressing, cutting
thin strips of my fawnskin underpants, made like long
johns, and getting dressed again fast. The cold, as I took the
clothes off, burned me all over.

With the thin strips of leather I lashed the plate metal to
my harpoon handle. Now I had a primitive shovel. Then I
set the sleeping bag, with its orange cover, out on the snow,
pegged with slivers of wood hacked from the harpoon
handle, as a signal for any casual observers from the air or
the sea, and started shoveling. I made up my mind to follow
a strict schedule: six hours' shoveling, back to the "cave,"
an ounce of brown sugar, a quarter of a can of beans, a
spoonful of corned beef, two hours' sleep, then back to
shoveling. I reckoned that if I followed this schedule, there
was a good chance of reaching the lower boulder crop
inside a week. That is, if the drifts were not deeper down on
the lower stretches.

I started shoveling at 0600 hours on the first of
November. It was heavy work, for I had to dig a path about
four feet wide at the top, narrowing to about a foot where I
could walk on the packed snow. At first I made my way
forward at around fifty yards a session, then the snowdrift
depth shallowed off to about ten feet, and I drove forward
at one hundred yards a shift by 1200 hours on the third of
November. But I was not very happy, because the heavy
work and expenditure of energy without adequate re-
placement were beginning to tell. Sleeping inside the rock
cleft, I was reasonably warm as long a I stayed still, but if I
moved in my sleep the heat from my body melted the thin
layer of ice inside the bag, making everything damp. This
dampness in turn evaporated with the heat driven off and
formed more ice on the part of the bag I was not resting
against.

By the fifth of November I began to slow down. My determination to get out of my snow prison had not diminished, but it was obvious, from the ground I was covering, that I was sleeping longer and digging less. Once I conked out for five hours. Very unusual for me, and an obvious sign that something was wrong. Then sitting on the rock bed in utter silence, I heard it. A plane!

I grabbed the paper bag which the sugar had been in and went outside, onto the inner end of my dug channel. The bag was fairly large, of brown paper, and I had smeared it with grease from the corned beef and left sugar grains stuck to it. As the plane passed over the Schuchert Elv, from east to west, low over the water, I lit the paper bag and tied it to the end of the shovel. In the windless night it burned brightly for about a minute. After my eyes recovered from the glare of my signal, I peered after the plane. It carried on its course for a full minute. Exhausted and bitterly disappointed, I sat down on the snow, determined to dig on. By this time I had about two thousand feet, maybe seven hundred yards, still to go to the rock outcrop on the shore. I stretched up above the level of the snow, balancing on a rocky ledge protruding from the base of the home boulder, gazing after the plane. He had changed course!

He was coming straight for me. I kept shining the flashlight directly at him, and when he passed over the shore, his big landing lamp replied, shining a beam down on me, then on the trail I had so laboriously dug through the snow. Then he sent a white flare into the black sky, a parachute flare, which for a full five minutes lit up the whole scene, like daylight. He waggled his wings, then turned to the southwest, still shining his spotlight on my boulders.

I had been seen! To celebrate I ate a whole can of corned beef, then smoked a cigarette. "Shall I just sit here and wait?" I wondered. Then the answer came loud and clear—"No! Keep moving, keep digging. It's probably the one thing that's kept you alive and sane, so keep at it!"

The Eskimos arrived three hours later. I saw their long umiak wend into the shore ice. They clambered over the ice and the rocks, then four of them, mere black dots on the white snow surface, made their way, waddling on snowshoes, to the lower end of my trench. They came trudging up the trench, grinning. Two of them spoke Danish. *"Goddag, Goddag!"* they cried, grinning all over their faces.

I grabbed the mitten of the first one to arrive and shook it. I was too excited to speak anything else but English.

"Jesus Christ, mates, am I pleased to see you!"

All four grinned as they recovered my gear and fitted a pair of snowshoes on my feet. Then we set off down the trench. I tapped the rock-solid sides of the trench as we came to the far end. "It's a long way to Tipperary," I said, quietly. The Eskimo leader, Untuk, looked at me quizzically. I offered him an ounce of frozen brown sugar from my jerkin pocket. He accepted it, smiling, sniffed it, tasted it, then swallowed the lot, patting me on the shoulder.

I wasn't too concerned about Nelson. He wouldn't starve; he knew where the burgoo pot was, and there were plenty of peanuts in the engine compartment, where I'd left the hatch loose so he could get at them if I was away too long. But I reflected what a bloody fool I'd been, not to have brought the alarm flares, pistol, and snowshoes with me, and how lucky I was.

*Wise men make life happier and more endurable by lightening their troubles with remembrances of their blessings, whereas most people, like sieves, let the worst things remain and stick to them while the best slip through. . . . And as for the things which are not by their nature evil but are made painful wholly and entirely by sheer imagination, we should treat them as we do the masks that frighten children—bring them near, put them in the children's hands and turn them over until we accustom them not to mind them. So by bringing our trouble close to us and using our reason we may discover how ephemeral and flimsy and exaggerated it is.*

Plutarch, "Exile."

# 20

## Safe and Sound

When the four Eskimo rescuers and I reached the edge of the shore, clambering over the rocky boulders and over the jumbled-up shore ice, then trudging another half-mile over the flat cake ice out on the water's edge, we met up with a waiting party of six more—three men and three women—though to be truthful I couldn't for the life of me tell the difference until they started to talk. They were all dressed more or less the same, all of fairly short stature, all with the same chubby faces. Carefully they handed me into the boat, where there were three more women. Then, with a female hugging each side of me and blankets thrown over my shoulders, we set off, with the women paddling the umiak out to sea, until they had enough sea room to hoist the sail.

The chief of the crew, who seemed also to be the oldest (though it is difficult to tell with Eskimos, as they do not show signs of age until well into their fifties), asked me in Danish how many passings of the moon I had been stranded. I counted up and it came to eight. Eight days! Then I came to the conclusion that if I had not attempted to dig my way out, if I had just sat there, moping, hoping for rescue, I probably would not have survived. The cold alone, after two hours' sleep, was enough to make one wish to die. The action made effort, effort made heat. The action also stopped me from feeling too sorry for myself, and self-pity is very dangerous.

He patted my head, then felt under my mouth-scarf of thin silk, which was covered with a layer of ice. He felt all around my face, then, coming to my beard, let out a yell and laughed. I dropped the scarf and the beard fell out, all ten inches of it. The Eskimos burst out chattering and laughing, until I covered my face again from the cold.

As we made our way down the Schuchert Elv fiord, dodging bergs and floes, I observed the umiak and how it was handled. The ladies sat on each side of me, paddling and warming my uncovered hands on their stomachs. Perhaps inspecting the boat would keep my mind off where my hands were.

The Eskimo boats, the umiak and the kayak, are not just vessels made to float and move through the water. They are highly efficient machines. They belong to the same family of membrane and frame vessels as did the ancient Irish curragh and the British coracle, which themselves were highly efficient, ocean-worthy vessels.

The curragh had more or less the same lines and appearance as the Iroquois bark canoe, but the umiak has the characteristics of the dory, one of the most seaworthy of all vessels. Therefore it follows that as the dory is more efficient than the bark canoe, especially in any kind of rough sea, then the Eskimo umiak must be more seaworthy than the ancient curragh.

Like the dory, the umiak is double-ended. The keel is carved out flat from a piece of driftwood and so are the pieces of wood lashed from fore to aft along the gunwale which keep the frames in position. The Eskimos told me that some of the umiak lashings are of long strips of whalebone, but the one I was in had rawhide lashings, very well served and tied.

I noticed that the men did not paddle the boat, but only steered or handled the sails. I later found that the Eskimos consider paddling to be women's work, and they even call the umiaks "the women's boats." The kayaks, smaller, more fragile, and much harder to handle, were known as "the men's boats," though I did occasionally see women handling kayaks at Syd Kap.

At Syd Kap I watched how the skin boats are made. When a seal is caught and killed, the skin and blubber is removed. The Eskimos put the skins into tubs until the hair rots away on one side and most of the blubber on the other. When the boatbuilder guesses that the rotting is enough, he scrapes the hair from one side and the blubber from the other. The skins are sewn together while still wet, the seams overlapping, and the stitching very fine indeed. The thread used is seal sinew, which swells when wet.

Then the pliable, wet skins are stretched over the frame of the boat. When a kayak is sewn together, the two sides must be held while the last seam is sewn. This is because the kayak is an enclosed vessel, about as wide as a coffin and twice as long. The wet sealskin cover is sewn up reasonably tight, and when it dries becomes as taut and resonant as a drumhead. Umiaks may be built of large sealskins, walrus or white whale hides, and it is a tough job to stretch these hard skins tight enough. This is done by pulling the skins over the gunwale of the frame and over-lapping it back onto its own part, then sewing one part to the other.

Before the Eskimo launches his skin boat, he leaves it out in the rain or snow for a while, to dampen it. After that it is as tight as a drum and no water will leak in. Because the sinews, with which the skins are sewn, rot after three or four days in fresh water, the skin boat is dragged onshore to dry out, turned upside down and placed on stones to allow ventilation. Overnight the sinews are restored, and the boat is good for another three or four days. When the boats are not in use, they are taken ashore and stood on their sides as extra protection from the wind. In salt sea water the umiak or the kayak stitching will last for ten days before having to be completely redried.

The Eskimos told me that the umiaks made of walrus skin are not as good as those made of white whale hide. The walrus skin rots faster and is much harder to stitch. The average life of an umiak is about three years in fresh water, but longer in sea water. The kayaks last a shorter time, but this is probably because they are used more often.

The umiaks I saw at Syd Kap carried an amazing cargo load, sometimes as much as four tons. The thirty-five-footers carried up to twenty passengers. This is because of their high sides. They could come right inshore because of their flat bottom and could be dragged up on the ice because of their light weight when unloaded; no more than half a ton. I realized that in choosing *Cresswell* for the Arctic cruise I had unwittingly followed the path of the umiak, for *Cresswell*, too, had all these attributes, with the exception of the light weight—being constructed of wood, she was heavier.

On the way to Syd Kap the umiak was forced by piled-up pack ice to take a detour down a lead quite close to the shore. She grazed a sharp rock which put a gash into her starboard bow. I was amazed to see one of the women get out a sewing needle made of whalebone, some sinew from a seal, a small sealskin patch, lean over the bow, and sew a patch on!

The sail used was a square sail, and I wondered if the Eskimos had learned of that from the Norsemen, or whether they had figured it out before the arrival of the Scandinavians. The Eskimos told me that they had tried out fore-and-aft sails, but that with an umiak they were dangerous in the swift gusts of the fiords, and that some fore-and-aft-rigged boats had been lost, but hardly any square-riggers.

I learned later that when the Eskimos take the umiaks up the rivers, if they come to a shallow part, they half unload the umiak, with its four-inch draft, then they get out into the water and lift the boat over the shallows! When they haul against the current, they secure the towing line half-way up the mast at one end, then to a dog team or some men at the other.

When we came out into the open, wide waters of the Halls Bredning fiord, where there was quite a sea, the women inflated eight sealskin bags and tied them to the hull outside the boat, four a little aft of the bows and four a little forward of the stern. This was to prevent the boat from being swamped. With so little wood in the frame, if she were swamped she'd go down like a brick unless she had buoyancy. The sealskin bags gave her an added 250 pounds of buoyancy each. I watched carefully, storing all these ideas at the back of my mind. As the roughness of the sea increased, a sealskin flap, which had been hanging down all round the inside of the freeboard, was raised and tied to the wooden rail fixed round the boat above the gunwale. They had even thought of the weathercloth! The dodger!

Once up, the weathercloth flaps were held in place by sticks jammed between the gunwale and the rail. All very seamanlike and simple.

But the most original thing about the skin boats is that if someone is stranded in one, or wrecked on one of the many rocks or ice floes, he need not starve. He can eat the un-cured hide of which the boat is made! There's enough food in an umiak to last ten men for a month! True, it would be tough and taste like old rope, but hunger knows no taste.

There were only three huts in the Eskimo settlement, and these were almost completely surrounded by walls of turf bricks, about five feet high, acting as windbreaks. On ar-rival a meal was prepared of the two large codfish caught on the expedition. As guest of honor, following the Eskimo custom, I got the head. This I ate with relish. It was the first warm food I had had in over ten days.

The proper name of the people of the East Greenland Arctic is *Kalatdlit,* and this is how they refer to themselves. The meaning of *Kalatdlit* is not clear, but the meaning of *Eskimo* is. It means "eater of raw meat," and the Kalatdlit find this very insulting.

After the fish head, which I ripped from the bones, eyes and all, boiled salmon was served by the women, but I thought it unwise to eat too much after having had so little for so many days. I therefore asked for only a small portion. The Kalatdlit understood my reasons for this, and also for turning down an offering of raw narwhal blubber.

Around the inside of the wooden hut, there were pictures from Danish magazines and newspapers. Three small stone oil lamps burned seal oil, with a little wisp of black smoke rising from each one into the rafters above. There was a fairly large potbellied stove of iron, the only white man's influence I saw in Syd Kap, with the exception of the magazine pictures. Everything else had been made, caught, killed, or grown there.

Untuk, the chief, told me that caribou head and fish head are the best food, rabbit the worst. He gave me to understand that if one eats nothing but rabbit for six weeks one will die. Of course he's right. There's no fat on a rabbit. He showed me a caribou head ready for eating the next day. It had been skinned and two rawhide sinews threaded through the nostrils, from which it could be hung over an open fire outside.

It was interesting to see the Kalatdlits drying the fish in one of the other huts. They had mainly cod and salmon, which they first gutted, then took out the backbone with the head. The rest of the fish was split and the two halves tied together with sinew at the tail. The head and backbone were hung separately, those of the small fish for the dogs to eat and the larger ones for the old people. They did not salt the fish because any flesh, meat or fish or fowl, which is salted soon loses its antiscorbutic power.

Scurvy results partly from not eating enough food with the necessary antiscorbutic ingredients. Salt kills these. This is probably the reason for the many cases of whole ships' crews' dying of scurvy in the old days. Their main diet was salt beef and pork. Their main antidote to scurvy was lime juice, which is just about useless for anything except a thirst quencher! The way to combat scurvy is to cook food only as long as is necessary to make it digestible, or to make it taste pleasant, and to eat only enough salt to replace that lost by sweating. The cures for scurvy are many. If fresh fruit and vegetables are available, they will do the trick (if only because they do not have the antiscorbutics cooked out of them); but if, as in the Arctic, fruit and vegetables are not readily available, then raw meat (except rabbit) or bone marrow will serve the purpose.

Death by scurvy is by no means the most unpleasant death, at least with respect to pain. There is, in fact, hardly any suffering right up until the last few hours, except perhaps a mild form of toothache. But the last hours are distressing, as death is usually from internal hemorrhaging caused by broken blood vessels flooding the stomach and lungs, thus causing you to drown, as it were, in your own blood. The first symptoms are purple gums, loose teeth, and muscle ache. There are few other signs until close to death, for bowel elimination and even digestion remain normal throughout the whole process.

During the four days I stayed with the Kalatdlits of Syd Kap I learned many things: how to find a seal under the ice and harpoon him; how not to set my dog onto a bear (a live dog is much more useful than a dead bear); how to trap and kill arctic foxes; where the fishing was best around where the boat was hidden; where to find blueberries in the early spring; and a lot more advice on how to live in intense cold without a gun.

No matter how interested I was in their culture, it was tiring to be among people whose language I did not understand. Besides, I was concerned about *Cresswell* and anxious to get back to Nelson. So on the fourth "day" Untuk gathered an umiak paddling party of eight women and four men to return me to the boat, promising that he would send a party to visit me every month, if the weather was good.

I said my goodbyes to Untuk and his family, which was a big job, as he had eight children and six grandchildren, and returned in the umiak to *Cresswell* beach, where, after sliding along in the dark across the sea ice and brash, I donned

the snowshoes which Untuk had presented to me and
sloshed away up to the boat. The breeze was onshore, and
as I said goodbye to the women, who stayed in the boat, I
could hear Nelson barking, almost a mile away. He had my
scent and knew I was returning.

As the four men and I clambered around the gap in the
rock line, I had a shock, for at first I could not see the boat.
Then a piece of sailcloth caught my attention. She was
almost completely buried in a snowdrift. There was only a
slight rise in the snow to show where she was! I scrambled
along the top of the drift and up to the fluttering sailcloth.
There, inside, on deck, Nelson was jumping up and down
with joy and relief.

I made the Kalatdlit men some tea, gave them ten cans of
corned beef and some sugar, then, as they tied on their
snowshoes, bade them goodbye. They all grinned and
waved as they disappeared around the gap between the
boulders.

I surveyed the scene. I had chosen my hibernation hole
well, for on the seaward side of the boulders great hummocks of ice had been forced up the beach by the pressure
of the icebergs calving off the Elv glacier to the east. But the
boat lay peaceful and unharmed, under three feet of snow. I
cleared a hole for the stovepipe chimney, then went below.
It was mid-November.

For the whole of the arctic winter I ventured very little out
of the boat. When the wind dropped I would go out on the
drift in my snowshoes, for exercise, or, if it was calm
weather, to perform ablutions. The rest of the time I carried
out boat maintenance chores inside the boat, in the
warmth, slept, ate sparingly, and read a great deal (I went
through the whole of Shakespeare twice). I listened to the
radio for a couple of hours each day only, as I had to
conserve the batteries. I also knitted two pairs of socks and
one jersey. I had brought back from Syd Kap a stone seal-oil
lamp and some oil, and this I rigged up, with a chimney

passing through a wooden porthole "dummy" shield, to give me longer hours of light, for my kerosene ration only allowed four hours of lighting per twenty-four.

Sometimes I would see the awesome sight of the aurora borealis, the northern lights, great streaks of colored lights shooting through the blackness of the arctic sky, and I learned to watch for high cirrus clouds after the northern lights, which always indicated a storm pending. Then, cozily tucked up in my warm woolen indoor clothing and insulated by the mutton cloths tacked around the cabin and the yard-deep snow outside on deck, I would read by the light of my seal-oil lamp. Every few weeks, just as Untuk had promised, the Kalatdlits would come in their umiak to see me—sometimes only two or three, sometimes six or seven—and we would sit around for a few hours talking in poor Danish or sign language. But I learned to make them laugh, and they seemed to enjoy their visits as much as I did.

December came, then January and February and March. By early April the snowdrift around the boat had mostly blown away. In late February the sun reappeared—a wondrous sight, the first rays of light in the southeast sky, after almost four months of absolute night—and the ice out in the fiord started to break away from the shore. It was time to think about refloating the boat.

But first I delved into the chart locker and studied all my Arctic charts. I had failed to beat Nansen by going up the Greenland coast; now I would try the same route as he had.

The Gulf Stream, as it passes northwestward across the North Atlantic, sends an offshoot into the Arctic between Iceland and Britain. The warming effect of this water, coming all the way from the Caribbean, makes for much less ice to the north of Norway than is the case off Greenland. The ice line is much further north, and there are drastically fewer icebergs.

The warm current gradually cools as it heads north of Norway, then passing around the islands of Svalbard (or

Spitsbergen), it turns north, then northwest, towards the very high latitudes near the pole, moving the vast ice fields with it. If I could get *Cresswell* onto that ice field, the chances were that the movement of the ice would carry her further north than Nansen's ship *Fram* had reached. The estimated rate of current is twenty-five sea-miles a day, with the ice drift a good deal less, about six miles a day, and so if I wintered out over 1960 to 1961 on the ice, I would stand a very good chance of getting beyond latitude eighty-four north. The current from the Norwegian side of the pole turns southwest somewhere due north of Iceland and joins the southbound Greenland current, upon whose ice pack I had already had one free ride.

I made up my mind to get out of the Scoresby Sund as early as possible in May and to make for Svalbard. It would be somewhat risky passing through the eastern Greenland ice floes, but once out and as far east as the eastern tip of Iceland, the Gulf Stream offshoot would take me rapidly to Svalbard. Then I could tackle the Arctic region from a point further north.

I turned to find Nelson lying on the floor looking at me. He was absolutely fed up, as his only exercise had been walking round and round the deck under the tent and jumping up and down the companionway ladder. He could not go out in the snow yet, for fear of sinking into a hole. As I looked at him, his tail thumped on the floorboard. I patted him. "One good thing about not being able to go 'ashore,' mate; you won't get a bloody tapeworm!"

Nelson got up slowly and walked to his favorite spot, between the table and the forward bulkhead. Then, with a sigh, he laid his head down to doze again.

The next day, with two visiting Kalatdlits, I started digging a passage through the packed snow, now about three feet deep, and prepared to move the boat out of her nest. We unfroze the blocks and set the masts and spars out, then reversed the earlier hauling procedure. By April fifteenth we were hacking away at the small hummocks of ice down by the shore, then, on the eighteenth, at the sea ice to clear a passage through. When she was sitting with her bows over the fiord edge, we took the long storm line out and tied it right around a small berg about as big as a house. Heaving against that, the berg was soon aground and we had a good "deadman" to haul the boat against. By April twentieth *Cresswell* was back in the water, and on the twenty-first we hauled up the masts and rigged her for sailing.

Then, after resetting the stove up in the engine compartment, I rested three days, before setting off to try to reach the radio station at Scoresby Sund. The first place I made for, however, was Syd Kap, where all the Kalatdlits came onboard, men, women, and kids, and bade me a grand farewell. Their umiak escorted me about ten miles down the fiord, and then they turned and waved through the pale twilight of the weeks-long arctic dawn.

They were the last human beings I was to see for another fifteen months.

*I met an ancient man who mushed*
  *With Peary to the Pole.*
*Said I: "In all that land so hushed*
  *What most inspired your soul?"*
*He looked at me with bleary eye,*
  *He scratched a hoary head:*
*"You know that Sourdoughs jest cain't lie,*
  *So here's the dope," he said.*

*"I saw it clear, I raised a cheer,*
  *I knowed the prize was won;*
*The huskies too, like wind they flew—*
  *Them critters sure could run.*
*The light was dim, the site was grim,*
  *But sunshine swept my soul,*
*To see—each husky lift a limb*
  *And . . . irrigate the Pole.*

Robert Service
from "My Husky Team."

# 21

## *Across the Arctic Ocean*

It is estimated that more icebergs flow out of Scoresby Sund than out of any other stretch of coast in the world. But in late April, with the spring thaw not yet set in, there were very few, and they were fairly small, not more than half-a-mile long and around four hundred feet high, moving slowly out to sea. The shore and pack ice, however, were jammed up solid against the coasts, out to a distance of ten miles or so; further out, the great flat floes and mighty bergs moved across the horizon. It was light for most of the twenty-four hours, a grey, funereal light as the weakling sun tried to penetrate the thick cloud cover. Low clouds hovered halfway up the giant cliffs, obscuring the peaks six thousand feet above the grey waters and dull ice.

When I reached the northern exit of the Sund, I found that the ice stretched out even further to sea than it had back in October—so far that there was no chance at all of communicating with the Danes. I was not too concerned, as I had sent a message to them through the Kalatdlits that I would try to get out of the Sund and make my way to Jan Mayen Island at the end of April. They, in turn, had sent a message advising against sailing too soon, as the exit from the great fiord was almost blocked by ice. But I realized that they were accustomed to dealing with the movement of much bigger craft, and, as they had said that there were leads through the blockage, I decided to have a go at escaping from the Greenland fiord. If I could get far enough to the east, beyond the ice line, and pick up the offshoot of the Gulf Stream, I stood a good chance of getting much further north, to Svalbard. There I could wait a while; then, in the late summer, when the ice line had receded to its northernmost point, I could emerge from hiding and head into the pack for the winter.

I rested the "night" under the lee of the ice piled up off Kap Brewster. It was far too deep there to anchor, so I landed on one of the floes, jumping from the boat onto the slippery ice in my sealskin boots, a sledgehammer tucked under my jerkin and an iron spike tied to my shoulders. Slithering around in the slushy snow, I drove the spike two feet into the ice, then tied the boat up. The wind held the boat off the floe; if another floe did touch *Cresswell*, she just swung around out of the way, sometimes quite violently, sometimes softly. With the southwest breeze, bitterly cold, blowing stronger as *Cresswell* sailed out of the lee of the mountains of Knud Rasmussen Land, I started to pick my way through the ever-increasing number of huge floating floes, swirling round slowly as the Greenland current picked them up and pushed them south.

Way out on the northeast horizon a great gap had shown in the southward-advancing ice field, so on the second of May I made my way out to sea. There was a good, strong, thirty-knot wind blowing from the southwest, and with all sail crowded, I made swift passage. Out to the north, through the grey gloom, I could see distant icebergs, mighty masses of ice, like mountains, under the low, black, heaped-up clouds. But when the sun shone it was gloriously free sailing.

My plan was simple. If I got stuck in the ice, the current would carry me south. When the Greenland current met the Gulf Stream, the ice would break up and I could escape. If I was too far south, I would head from wherever I escaped to Iceland, and so on north from there. But if I could avoid being trapped, I would keep on eastward and meet the

warmer Gulf Stream current in the waters northeast of
Iceland.

After all the maintenance work done while she was
aground in Schuchert Elv, the boat was in good shape, and
I was well rested. The Kalatdlit had carried in stores for me,
bought from the wireless station, and so there was now
many months' supply of food onboard, plus fifty pounds of
seal blubber and a hundred pounds or so of dried frozen
fish—cod, halibut, and other kinds. My water supply was
no problem, as the tops of the ice floes were almost devoid
of salt. I was well rested, in fact too rested—for the last
month or so, before launching the craft, I had been hard put
to find enough work to fill my waking moments.

The wide, eastward-running gap turned north on the
fourth of May. It was about eight miles wide. Here I was
forced to make one of those decisions which a skipper has
to make and which makes him a skipper. The question was
whether to head north along the lead, or south, with it. I
was now, by dead reckoning, about 150 miles east of the
Liverpool Land coast of Greenland. All the ice, floes, bergs,
and brash were moving south at a rate of around one knot.
The patch of open water I was in was also moving south or
southeast. To the east, the horizon was one solid line of ice.
There might, or there might not be, a gap leading eastward
further to the north of me. This was not certain.

I made the decision. I handed all the sail except the
mizzen and turned the boat's head to point in line with the
middle of the lead, southeast. She drifted on the current at
almost the same rate as the ice surrounding her. By fiddling
around with the mizzen and rigging the storm-jib forward,
together with lashing the wheel, I arranged it so that the
boat would hold herself roughly on course. Then I settled
down to bide my time.

On the eighth of May I celebrated my thirty-sixth birthday by baking a small cake, which Nelson shared. As the
heating stove was set up in the engine compartment, I was
sleeping and warming myself there. Only six feet by five, it

was nowhere near as roomy and comfortable as the cabin, but I managed to make a cozy enough berth by taking up the cabin floorboards and fixing them up across the beam of the engine room. In the cabin, with only the kerosene cooking stove to heat up the compartment, I found that water vapor formed on the top and sides of the cabin. Once the stove was turned off, this turned to ice, and when cooking recommenced and the cabin warmed up again, the ice melted, making everything damp—the bedding, my clothes, books, charts, everything. Then, when cooking was over, this dampness again turned into ice. It was like living alternately in a meat-market cold room and a Turkish bath. The most time I could spend on deck in one spell was about fifteen minutes in my normal seagoing, cold-weather clothes. Otherwise, it meant donning the full arctic Eskimo suit, which had to be removed below when I was in the engine compartment or I would start to sweat. This was dangerous, because as soon as I had been on deck for a few minutes, the sweat would start to freeze.

While the boat drifted in the calm water between the distant ice fields, I rigged the solid fuel stovepipe to pass through the cockpit. Now I could at least warm part of my body even when on deck. The extension to the stovepipe I made with cans, wired together and stuck with strong glue. During the winter months I had collected a great pile of driftwood and this kept dry in the bottom of the engine compartment, as an emergency fuel supply. I reckoned that if I kept the stove going for two spells of three hours each over the coming winter, I would have enough fuel to last for one year, possibly more.

The next few days were pleasant enough, despite the snow. There wasn't much movement inside the floating ice fields, and though the wind blew hard, there was a flat sea.

I drifted with the Greenland current for eight days, keeping an eye astern for floes and bergs which might overtake my rate of drift and collide with *Cresswell*. I spent much of the time fishing, but caught only two small halibut. My attempts at shrimp-catching were no more successful—out this far from the coast the shrimp are much deeper—but I managed to catch about one plateful in a week.

A very careful eye had to be kept on the ice growing on the masts and rigging, especially when any kind of wind was blowing. When sleet and snow fell, ice grew on the rigging wires at the rate of about a quarter of an inch a minute. Then I had to climb the main and mizzenmast every hour or so with a small ax and chop loose the ice, to prevent too much weight accumulating aloft. If this was not done, the "black ice" (as it is called) would continue to grow around the wires. The weight of the ice eventually would be greater than the weight of the keel and ballast, and the boat would overturn. No one can live for more than a few seconds in the icy cold water of the Greenland current.

I lashed a small hammer to a long pole and, in calm weather, used that to knock the black ice off the rigging. But in heavy wind it was impossible to use, and then it was a matter of slowly and carefully hauling myself up with the mainsail halyard on a bosun's chair, knocking the stuff off as I ascended. I dared not start at the top, in case the extra weight of my body at the masthead, along with the ice, should cause the boat to capsize. Climbing up a wildly swinging mast covered with ice, in a high wind, is a real circus performance.

During sleet and snowfalls, which were often heavy, the snow would land on deck and, unless shifted immediately, would turn into ice. It was a continuous effort. But most of the time the wind was slight, and it was a matter of clearing the rigging only twice every twenty-four hours.

On about the eighteenth of May I got a sun sight which put me 250 miles east-southeast of Scoresby Sund. The ice to the east was loosening up. I decided to have a go at following a long eastward gap. The wind was in the northwest, and again I crowded sail. The next day at 0400 hours, under the light of the midnight sun, I saw ice only to the west of me. After another twenty-four hours with no sight of anything but small floes, I realized that I was in the clear.

I had broken through two hundred miles of massed, moving ice. Immediately I changed my course northeast, for Jan Mayen Island.

By this time it was daylight for twenty-four hours. The skies had cleared, and the wind was from the southwest. I stayed in the cockpit, huddled against the stovepipe when it was warm, two blankets thrown over my Eskimo suit when it was not. It was good sailing, except for the cold. In fact it was so good that when I reached the point where I could have headed north, on the meridian of Jan Mayen, I decided to press on to the northwest. I could have done with the rest and human contact in Jan Mayen, but I wanted to reach Svalbard while this rare good weather persisted, so as to get to the edge of the ice field before the summer retreat north commenced. In this way I anticipated good prospects of reaching further than eighty-four degrees north.

Out of the ice-field area, the seas were now lively again, and *Cresswell*, with her shallow draft and narrow beam, was boisterous. It was, however, warm enough in the engine cuddy, and when the horizon was completely clear of any ice, I set the sails to self-steer and, together with Nelson, would go below. He would lie at the end of the shelf I had made, and I would take off the sealskin boots and stick my feet in between his legs and his belly. He made a grand foot-warmer.

By the eighteenth of May I was 130 miles to the west of Jan Mayen Island. Way out on the grey horizon I saw the smudge of smoke from a ship, but heard nothing on the radio. She was too far over the horizon to see me, but I could tell that she was heading to the east. I stared for two hours at the thin discoloration in the sky, thinking of all the millenia of effort and struggle it had taken to put her there, and wishing she were nearer, just so I would see somebody, and perhaps have a word with them. But she went on her way, unaware that I was there, and I settled down again, pushing north.

On the twenty-fifth of May I sighted, right across the

northern horizon, a long line, like a low shore. First it was grey, then, as the sun rose high in the south, it changed to deep blue, to aquamarine, then white, and finally gleaming silver—the edge of the ice pack! Soon, all around me, there were loose floes, but they did not seem to be moving. At first this puzzled me, until I figured that the southwest wind was holding them back from flowing southwest with the current. But then a question loomed. Was that the case, or was the ice, in fact, moving north?

I dropped the sails and hove to, under mizzen only, to wait a few hours and find out exactly what was happening. By noon I knew. The ice was actually moving north, but very slowly, and the edge of the ice field dropped back to the northeast. I decided to follow it, at a distance, just far enough away that I could see it, low on the horizon.

On the thirtieth of May I reached latitude seventy-six degrees ten minutes north. This was the furthest north I had reached in the previous year. I was elated. It was only the end of May, and I had clear water still to the north of me and all the months of June, July, and August for the ice to melt and break up, before it started to solidify again in September.

The wind increased that "night," and soon I was shortening sail. Under spitfire jib, trysail, and mizzen I headed due east, for I wanted to be far away from the ice should heavy weather blow up.

I switched on the radio, but got nothing in English. Back topsides, it seemed that a regular dusting was in the offing. I steered as straight as I could in the ever-steepening seas, to get clear of ice. By midnight it was blowing a twenty-four-carat bastard, with the wind howling, black clouds racing across the sky, and the sea getting up into a short, steep frenzy. I carried on to the east, staying on the wheel for a solid fifteen hours, unable to leave the helm for more than a few seconds at a time.

Eventually, with no sign of the storm abating, and with no ice having been sighted for twelve hours or so, I hove to, dowsing the spitfire jib and the trysail. Then I went below, to try to rest for a couple of hours and warm up a little. Sleep, in that sea, with the boat jerking and plunging, was impossible, but I did doze for a few minutes at a time. The smells from the diesel oil and lubricating oil in the engine compartment were sickening, and so I moved my blankets into the cabin, getting a great slop of icy cold Arctic Ocean water all over them in the process. But this soon froze, and I was at least warmer under the frozen blankets than I was outside. It was so cold during this storm that even Nelson, who was keeping watch while I rested, came down below every few minutes to warm himself up for a spell.

The storm raged for six days. It slashed, it howled, it screamed, driving the seas before it like berserk monsters. Soon the tops of the seas were so white with driven spume that it was impossible to tell if there were ice floes anywhere near the boat, and for a week I existed with the ever-present threat of death right in front of me, staring me full in the eye. To touch a floe with these seas running would be the end. Instant and very, very final. The great twenty-foot-high mountains of water would pick the boat up and throw her against the ice. She would be crushed like a matchbox. The only thing I could figure out as a possible safeguard was to slow the boat down to what I estimated would be the speed of a floe. Being low in the water, they move before the wind much more slowly than a boat. If I could stay at the speed of the average floe, chances were that I would not overtake one and drift close to it.

With the boat bouncing up and down like a crazy yo-yo, I delved into the after cuddy and dug out the long storm line. This was six hundred feet long. After leading the rope outboard through blocks on the gunwale at the chain plates, I secured both ends around the mast tabernacle, then cast the bight into the roaring sea, over the bow. The woven nylon line floated, and the bight created enough resistance to stop the boat drifting. However, the strain imposed on the hull, every time the sea lifted it up then dropped it forty feet, was *shocking*. She would rise up slowly, hover for about ten seconds as a great long, grey, icy sea ran under her, then slam down into the trough with force enough to lift me clear into the air if I was not securely tied down to the wheel binnacle. Where the storm line imparted the shocks to the hull, through the chain plate blocks, the sudden judders were great enough for me to wonder how long she could stand this treatment, strong as she was. But I had to accept the risk of the boat shaking to pieces as better than the risk that she would hurl down onto a floe.

During the storm I had not been able to get any sun, star, or moon sights to enable me to estimate my position, but by dead reckoning (that is, calculating the direction of course, drift, and the current, together with the speed), I had a rough idea. I was about 200 miles to the west-southwest of Prins Karls Forland, an island in the Svalbard group, and my latitude was approximately seventy-seven thirty north. Only 390 miles from the magical eighty-four degrees!

With the wind dropping and swinging to the southeast, I determined to head northeast. On the fifth of June I sighted, through a gap in the cloud cover, far away, the black mountains of the Barentzburg, on Spitsbergen. I got a bearing and went below. Checking up on the chart it was soon obvious that my previous dead-reckoned position had been way out, because I was only now at seventy-seven degrees forty north. When the horizon cleared up, it showed that the line of the ice field went clear across to the coast of Spitsbergen, and through the binoculars I could see plainly the settlement smoke of King's Bay. The entrance might be clear. I made sail again and headed for the smoke. The wind continued to swing to the east, and I was soon sailing in long zigzag tacks against the wind. Within six hours all hell broke loose again, with a fifty-knot wind blowing straight out of King's Bay dead against me. Before the sleet began to slash down, a quick gaze at the far-off shore showed that I must be around twenty miles off. The engine's ten-horsepower was useless against such a wind and sea, so I continued patiently and wearily, tacking all day. But the wind rose even more, and finally I had to admit defeat. After I had seen King's Bay and safety! I hove to. Again. All day on the sixth, the seventh, the eighth, and the ninth. Despite the storm line slowing her progress, the wind was blowing the boat away from Svalbard towards the ice field. Anxiously I watched astern, through the sheets of freezing hail and sleet, hour in, hour out. I had no idea what I would do if the ice field showed up, except perhaps rig the trysail and attempt to head south. But even with those sails up the wind would still blow the boat sideways, and the chances were that she would end up being flung against the awful ice. The only thing that I could hope for was that there was enough sea room astern of me, to the west.

Then I saw it; after many long, freezing hours of anxiety. I saw it, through a momentary clearing in the sleet, a great piled-up hump of frozen slabs, all thrown up into the air, this way and that. A mile long and seemingly a thousand feet high, glowering over the lashed, grey waters of the Arctic, and to each side of it, the frozen wall of the ice field, stretching back from here right across the top of the world, all the way to Alaska and the Bering Strait. Dead astern right in the way of the boat.

"Holy Jesus Christ Almighty!" I murmured to Nelson, as I crawled forward over the icy deck to hoist the trysail in a sixty-knot wind. "It looks like we've had it, old son."

Little by little, with the wind flogging the sail as I let go of the tiers and started to haul, up went the trysail. Then, hanging onto the ice-festooned boat with one hand, getting the spitfire jib up with the other frozen hand and my teeth, I struggled like a maniac. Then back to the cockpit, where I unlashed the wheel and heaved her over.

In a few seconds the wind picked up the sails and she was crashing over the immense moving mountains of white spume and grey green heaving water, straight for the ice.

After the first few minutes of shock, I peered again at the ice field, through another clearing in the sleet. Then, wiping the cluttered ice off my face, looked again. Another wipe over my eyebrows and lids, heavy with fluffy ice from my frozen tears. I looked again. There was an inlet behind the mountain of piled floes! There was a gap between the south end of the berg and the ice field. It was my only chance. I rammed the boat through the wind; she refused to go. I wore her, that is, turned off the wind; the trysail slammed across with a juddering shock, the spitfire came about with an explosion of ice particles and cold water, and she was over, heading for the gap!

*And now the storm is over,*
*And we are safe and well;*
*We will walk into a public house*
*And drink and drink our fill;*
*We will drink strong ale and porter*
*And we'll make the rafters roar,*
*And when our money is all spent*
*We'll be off to sea once more!*
*(FINE GIRL YOU ARE!)*
*Ye're the girl I do adore,*
*And still we'll live in hopes to see,*
*The Holy Ground once more!*

Old Liverpool halyard shanty. The Holy Ground was the Scotland Road brothel area, the landowner of which was the Roman Catholic Church.

# 22

## *In the Arctic Icecap*

The sail for the gap behind the iceberg was the kind I never want to make again as long as ever I live. To keep the boat moving northwest, beam onto the switchback seas, she had to carry all the sail she could. The course was uncertain. I did not know if there was submerged ice between me and the gap; I did not know if there was shallow water or other underwater hazards, such as protruding ice, near the ice field. All I knew was that this was a God-given chance of survival. I pushed her on, with the freezing spume off the tops of the seas blowing right over the boat, the spitfire jib dipping into the tops of the seas, picking up whole buckets of water and flinging them aft with the wind from its slipstream, the droplets freezing into hail as they flew with the wind straight at me, turning into a thousand burning daggers.

As visibility improved, I saw that the berg was, first of all, not as far away as it had seemed and, secondly, not as big as it had first appeared. Two hundred yards off the gap, I let fly the spitfire jib-sheets, to slow down the boat, and took stock, balancing myself up high in the mizzen shrouds. What I saw was incredible. There was a good clear passage, about forty yards wide, between the "hill," which rose about two hundred feet, and the piled-up pack ice on the other side. It all seemed to be clear of obstruction. Beyond the mouth of this inlet was a bay of flat water. I hauled in the sheet and steered a course right for the middle of the gap, bashing away over the great long thrusts of angry green seas.

*Cresswell* shot into the gap like a rat up a drainpipe. One minute she was in terrifyingly high, steep seas, with frozen spray flying all around, and the next minute she was becalmed, in the lee of the hill of ice, floating in calm water. Ahead was a small bay, reaching about two hundred yards deep between the hill and the ice field. The little bay was about one hundred yards wide.

I let go the sheets again and clambered below to start the engine. It had been shaken clear off its bed and was lying in the bilge, on its side. The strain imposed on the propeller shaft by the shock had bent the shaft like butter. I took one look below, then climbed aloft. I tested for depth with the sounding lead, all eight hundred feet of it. There wasn't any bottom! I could not drop an anchor (useless anyway, with the ice field moving over the top of the world). I had to make the boat secure to the ice!

I inflated the rubber dinghy (try getting rubber bungs into the air inlet valve holes while wearing two pairs of mittens!) and threw it over the side. Then I hopped into it with a long crowbar, a hammer, the mooring line, a small block, and the oars. Towing *Cresswell* almost a hundred yards was agony, for I was using up my reserves of strength, but eventually I made it to the middle of the bay, where the "shore" of the berg fell back. I rowed ashore, axed out footholes in the side of the berg, to get about ten feet above sea level, drove in the crowbar, and made fast the line. Then back to the boat to shorten the line and secure it to the knightheads. Over the side again with another line, I rowed over to the ice floes on the western side of the bay, clambered up the eight-foot sides, drove in a spike, made fast, and returned to the boat. Shortened up on the after line, and that was that, the boat was tied up secure, in flat calm water. I crawled down below so tired that I could not even find the strength to make a cup of tea or dish out some burgoo. I collapsed in the cabin, fully dressed, and fell asleep, to the noise of the wind, the ice floes grinding against the field, the seas crashing onto the ice floes, and Nelson padding around on deck. It was the tenth of June. In Britain the flowers were blooming; there was green, green grass, and trees, and towns with electric lights and buses. I drifted off. Outside it was broad daylight. Inside, with the felt pads over the decklights and portholes, with the companionway hatch shut, it was dark. Dark and cold, though under the blankets crackling with the cold as I moved in my sleep, it was warm enough. I was so weary I could have slept on a clothesline.

When I awoke, shivering, it was 0600 hours the next day. I lit the cooking stove, then carried it outside on deck and made a fine breakfast of corned beef hash and cocoa for me, the remainder of the burgoo, boiled up, for Nelson. Around, the wind was dying, but the seas were still colliding heavily with the floes outside the little bay. I lit the stove in the engine compartment, then sat down to smoke one of my six-a-day cigarettes and have a think.

There was plenty to do. But the first thing was to make sure that the boat was safe. This is always a skipper's highest priority. I made ready to climb the ice nearest to the boat and from there survey the scene. It was now obvious that what I had thought was one hill, was, in fact, three. These piles of ice did not look like the type of berg I had seen off Greenland. I concluded that this was a great chunk of ice which had escaped from the coast of Siberia, and was not a glacier-spawned berg, but in fact sea ice which had piled up on the coast far away somewhere.

Again, I gathered my ax, hammer, two spikelike chisels, rope and oars, and paddled over to the berg. The face at sea level was an overhanging wall of ice fifteen feet high. Climbing it to get a spike into the ice on the top of the wall took four hours. By the time that was done, and I had secured a block and rope onto the spike, I was about half-frozen, so I dropped into the dinghy and headed for the boat, to warm up for half an hour. Then, packing some food, corned beef and beans, with a block of freshwater ice in a small shoulder bag, I set off again.

From the overhanging edge of the berg's side, on top of which I had fixed the block, the hill overhung a platform, rearing up one hundred and eighty feet. To one side there was a slope of ice rising about fifty feet to a shoulder between two small peaks. The slope was at an angle of thirty degrees. Cold, shiny bright ice, with no handholes. Getting up the slope, driving one chisel in while standing on the one just driven in, was purgatory and it took three hours. When I got to the shoulder, I found myself once more in the wind, although by now it was down to about ten knots. Looking out "to sea," to the east, there was nothing but ice. To the north, the west, to the east, and as far as I could judge, to the southeast as well. To the south the broken ice floes were piled up against the bottom of the berg. Directly to the southwest the slope of the hill rose at around twenty degrees to a height of about two hundred feet. I started climbing, every now and then looking down. Thin ice was already forming a dull grey sheen all across the bay. It took another four hours to get to the top of the hill, the most southerly of the three. I promptly made a note to name them, from south to north, "England," "Wales," and "Scotland." The whole ice-mountain I christened "Brittania-Berg."

The scene from the top of "England" was astonishing. To the north, right around from east to west, there was nothing but ice. Most of it was flat, but at intervals other great hummocks appeared, similar to the one I was on, though not as big, except for one, in the far-off, hazy distance to the northeast, which was a giant. On the other side of the bay was a great jumble of ice floes, all heaving up and down separately as the monster sea-swell rolled in from the east, crashing, groaning, wheezing, and sighing. Then I looked at the mouth of the gap. It did not seem as wide as it had the day before. I made a note to check it in a few days' time. On top of the hill I firmly set a broom handle with a red ensign nailed to it to signal any searchers.

It took much less time to climb down "England" hill, as I had chopped out footholds in the ice. I was very careful though—one slip would mean death in the freezing water. I resolved that next time I climbed up I would bring a rope up all the way with me. I had chipped some of the ice and tasted it. Right on the top it was fresh, but on the shoulder it was salty. This confirmed my suspicions about the berg's origin.

By the time I got back down into the dinghy I was sweating. Supporting myself on a frozen line, over murderously cold water, I kicked out with my feet to bring the wildly swinging dinghy underneath me, so I could drop into it. Then, on my way back paddling over the bay, I hit ice. It was thick enough to support the weight of a man, whereas when I had left the boat it had been very thin. Weighing up the risks involved in heading out to sea with another easterly brewing as against being frozen in here, in what appeared to be a safe place, the answer was obvious. I would stay. A couple of hours later, when I paddled out to reconnoiter the entrance to the bay, I found that it was jammed solid with pack ice driven in by the wind.

Back on board, I set to making the boat shipshape for the coming months. I could not lower the mainmast, as there was nothing to rig a lowering line to. I unshipped the booms and slackened off all the standing rigging, so that by shaking it hard I could remove any ice which might accumulate. With the booms I made a frame for the old mainsail and the big canvas awning to act as a tent. These I lashed down firmly, at a steep angle, so that any snow falling on them would slide over the side. I made sure that the cockpit was well covered, so as to prevent snow from entering, thawing, and getting into the bilges. Then, after shifting the heating stove once more back into the cabin, I let the stove really rip, trying to drive out all the dampness.

After this I could once more live comfortably in the cabin.

My cooking stove I moved into the cockpit, so that the humidity from the burnt kerosene would dissipate in the open air.

By the time the "tent" was rigged, the weather was at storm force. Again hail and sleet slashed down. I rested below in the dry cabin, and let it scream overhead. Much better here than out at sea I thought to myself, as I set to, repairing the torn sails, cozy and warm.

It took three days for the storm to pass, and at the end of it the ice around the boat was a foot thick. I decided to lighten her as soon as the ice was strong enough to bear the weight of the stores. Meanwhile, I secured the engine back on its bed—hard work, as it weighed well over 180 pounds.

By the middle of July the days were getting shorter. I had seen very few signs of life—a seal, far away on the ice floes; one or two birds high up; and while out surveying the western floes, a few fish—nothing more. It was nowhere near as lively as the Greenland side.

When the weather was calm, I gingerly felt my way over the bay ice to the western side and made a sketch map of the ice floes, giving all the larger ones names, mainly from the alphabetical Morse code. If any wind was blowing, or if there was any sea movement, this was too risky, as the whole bed of ice would move around violently, like an animal in pain, and great long crevasses would appear and disappear continuously. By the end of July the ice in the bay was around two feet thick. By taking sun and moon sights, I knew that the drift of the ice was to the northwest, and it was obvious that we must be in a part of the Arctic Ocean where the Greenland current doubles back, counterclockwise, onto itself, which was why the cold water formed ice so rapidly.

I started to lighten the boat, unloading the ship's stores and food stores onto the ice, at the same time digging a narrow trench around the hull, so that as she lightened she lifted. Then, when I had her lightened by something like three tons, with the stern and bow almost out of the water, I let the ice freeze again. As soon as the boat was frozen into the ice, but eight inches higher than before, I started to load her once more, at least with the stuff I needed daily and for routine jobs. The rest I left out in the open, covered by the spare mainsail, well pegged down.

As her frames were on nine-inch centers, four-inch balks, the two feet of the boat's bottom now gripped in the ice was almost solid wood. *Cresswell's* bottom was round, and if she was gradually squeezed by the ice, she would lift up, vertically.

With the boat clear of gear inside, I started to clean her up. It proved impossible to get good fresh water, except when snow fell, which was not regular until late September, so I scraped and painted all the blocks instead, took weather observations, and navigated. With the awning over the boat, not much light got in, but I used my seal-oil lamp, with its chimney fixed up again in the porthole, so I could read by its glare for a few hours a day.

By the end of September the "days" were much shorter and it was obvious that the gap at the mouth of the bay was closing up rapidly. Every time there was a wind, any wind, except from due north, the ice floes would start to move and twist, crushing up against each other. The "Scotland" hill was breaking away from the main ice field, while "England" was steadily and surely heading west. In other words, the iceberg was revolving very slowly in a clockwise direction and making one hell of a noise doing it.

On 30 September my latitude was seventy-eight degrees fifty minutes north, 310 miles south of the *Fram's* furthest north! I was jubilant, for it seemed that at this rate I should pass the eighty-four-degree mark well before the ice turned with the current towards the southwest.

When the weather was calm, now that the dark hours were lengthening, I wandered out on the ice and watched the northern lights shining through the ice of the piled-up floes. A wondrous sight to behold. The great streaks of pure power and energy streaming across the night, right across the star-laden, blue black velvet sky of the Arctic is a vision which still comes into my mind every time I hear someone talk of miracles. But generally, the nights were far too cold to go out for more than a short while, so most of the time I was inside the cabin performing necessary chores. Alone, and having no idea if you are going to survive or not, the main thing is not to think about it too much. All the thinking in the world will not change the circumstances. Self-pity is the harbinger of despair, which, in turn, brings panic and fear. There is only one thing to do in these circumstances—think about and perform only the jobs in hand. If something I was reading dealt too heavily with the more profound aspects of existence, I put the book down and baked some bread, or repaired another sail, or had another go at straightening out the engine propeller shaft. A strict routine helped make time pass. Every "day" at 0900 I was up. Breakfast before ten, then repair and maintenance jobs until noon in clear weather. Then the latitude sight, then lunch until 1300 hours. Next, maintenance again; then tea and a longitude sight. Then read for an hour or so. Then a walk out on the ice with Nelson, or, if it had snowed, shoveling out the walkway. Later in the winter, of course, the snow became too thick for Nelson to walk very far safely, but I would still slog out there in snowshoes, in a wide circle, looking for tracks or anything else.

As the weather became colder, the simplest activities became more difficult. With very low temperatures it was no longer possible to have a shit on the ice. Instead it had to be done in the bucket down below, then carried out onto the ice. One minute's exposure in those temperatures was enough to cause frostbite.

Being alone is not being lonely. If you know there is no other human within a few hundred miles, it is much easier to accept than if there are millions and you know no one. Sex becomes very unimportant. I personally have not, during my long spells of being without relief for the sex urge, found that deprivation had any effect on my performance once back in the green pastures. In fact, the case is the exact reverse, or at least so I am told by impeccable authorities on the subject.

This seems to be the story with most of the other solo sailors that I know, and they all agree that the further away one is from possible partners, the less important sex becomes.

By mid-October the mouth of the bay was completely closed, both by the steady movement of the iceberg's southerly end in a westward direction, and by a jumbled mass of piled-up sea ice, stretching four or five miles to seaward. By the end of October, I hibernated inside the cabin, emerging only on clear nights to take star and moon shots.

So the weeks passed, with both Nelson and I eating sparingly from our diminishing food stocks. By mid-November all was darkness, and I was at latitude seventy-nine degrees fifteen minutes north. Only 285 miles from the target.

Again, on clear nights, when there was no precipitation in the form of falling ice and snow, I would sometimes watch the northern lights for a few minutes at a stretch, filling the whole sky with a display of wonder. I kept notes on how often this phenomenon was followed by strong winds and heavy weather. These events occurred about 90 percent of the time after the appearance of the aurora borealis. I came to the conclusion that there must be some connection between the northern lights and the weather, especially in the Arctic regions. The arctic wind-pressure system has a great bearing on the rest of the world's weather; if someone could find the connection, and the reasons for it, there might be a new, more accurate way of foretelling long-range climatic changes.

The boat was now completely frozen in. There was nothing but ice and darkness in all directions. Once, back in July, I had heard, far away, the drone of a plane, but there was no time to arrange a smoke signal as the ice was not then safe to step on. It had come, hummed for a few minutes in the cold clear air, and gone away again. That was the only sign of human presence in the world that I saw for ten months. Just a slight noise, anything up to forty miles away.

December 1: latitude seventy-nine, thirty-five.
December 18: latitude seventy-nine, forty-two.
December 25: latitude seventy-nine, *thirty-two*!
December 31: latitude seventy-nine, *sixteen*!

The direction of the flow of ice had changed! I was heading southwest! By January 10, 1961, I knew for certain: latitude seventy-eight, fifty-five. I had failed to beat the *Fram* by 285 miles! I had failed to get nearest to the Pole in a sailing craft. I had failed to beat Nansen! I had failed to reach nearer than 618 miles to the Pole!

I bent over my calculations, tears of defeat misting over the scribbled figures on the tattered page of my logbook. I stared, half-blind, at my grimed fist tightening over the pencil, squeezing it until it splintered into three shattered stubs—broken, like my dreams. I opened my palm and glared silently, bitterly, at the fragments. I threw the splinters down onto the table. Then, as I groped for my mug of tea, I glanced at the broken bits of wood and lead. I stared from one to the other and back again, like an idiot. I wiped my eyes, then stared again. A moment passed, then I picked up one of the pieces of wood.

The pencil, the *artifact*, the *result* of some man's dreaming effort somewhere, was destroyed, fragmented. But the man's dream survived! I stared closer, turning the splintered shard of wood around and around. The atoms of wood, the molecules of lead were still there; I could touch them. I could see them . . . only the man's dreams, only his ideas I could not see. Yet I could see the results of those dreams lying before me shattered. Yet the dream was not shattered, and *that's what mattered*!

Slowly I began to see that the realization of a dream, an ambition, was not of itself *essential*. It is the *conception* and *survival* of the dream, the idea, the ambition, that matters. But dreams, ideas, unlike atoms, cannot survive of themselves. The dreamer himself must survive to pass on his dream! Then, in the survival of my dream, in *my survival*, would lie my victory!

I picked up the shards of wood and lead and placed them carefully, reverently, in the pencil box. I would repair that bloody pencil!

Then I finished my tea and turned in.

Nelson stirred in his sleep, dreaming of some faraway bitch.

*Everything that happens either happens in such a way that you are formed by nature to bear it or not to bear it. If what happens to you is within your strength to bear, bear it without complaining; if it is beyond your strength, do not complain, for it will perish after it has destroyed you. Remember, however, that you are formed by nature to bear everything which your own opinion can make endurable and tolerable, by thinking that it is either your interest or your duty to do so.*

Marcus Aurelius, *Meditations* 10. 3.

# 23

## An Embarrassing Predicament

During the eternal darkness of deep winter, on the edge of the icecap (although by now *Cresswell* was ten miles "inland"), the weather was calm for about four "days" out of ten. Then, the skies would clear and millions of stars shone bright, casting a diffused luminescence over the barren, cold, dead world of ice. High overhead Alkaid, Alcor, Alloth, Dhube, and Muscida, great blobs of shining light, delineated the backbone of the Great Bear, Ursa Major, while to one side, his cub, Ursa Minor, the Little Dipper, balancing on its unsure backpaws Kochab and Perkhab, pointed a grubby little claw-nail through Yildun at the paralyzed fish around which the whole sky revolved—Polaris—the pulse of the heart of the universe at a spot almost directly above my head.

To the east, the low horizon was obscured by the three mountainous humps of the Brittania-Berg thrusting their gleaming, pale white sugar loaves into the black velvet sky. In every other direction, north, west, and southwest, I could see stars so low in the firmament that they looked like ships passing by far away on a silver sea. Slowly they passed around the rim of the ice world—Vega, the lonely, shy virgin with her lyre, accompanied always by her handmaidens, Shelyak and Sulafat, tripping lightly along the dark corridors of infinity to escape muscle-bound Hercules. Cygnus, the Swan, his regal head picked out by

248

Deneb, with Gienah and Delta Cygni worn, jewellike, on the ends of his wings, led Vega to the court of Queen Cassiopeia, sitting regally in her celestial chair. Toward her, Perseus, the messenger, flew out of the ice horizon, bearing in his right hand the great flaming torch of Algol, the star of knowledge. This arrival of the light of learning at the feet of the eternal queen was watched joyously by her hand-maiden, Capella, together with Betelgeuse and Bellatrix, the two lovely wearers of the diamond-studded belt of Orion. Outside the palace door the gallant gladiators, Castor and Pollux, made way through the crowded lanes of the sky for beauteous Athena, while ahead of their proud progress, Leo Minor, the Lion Cub, scampered by the clumsy feet of the Great Bear.

As I stood, transfixed by the wonder of this sparkling spectacle, with my arms withdrawn from the sleeves of my jerkin to warm them against my chest, it was sometimes difficult to pick out the familiar stars against the sequin-spangled backdrop reaching to the other side of infinity. Draco, the dragon guard of the Little Bear, the playful favorite of the queen of the skies, was almost impossible to distinguish. Yet there he was, as faithful as ever, with his great tail flailing out from AlSafi, through Eta Draconis and Thuban, millions and trillions of miles across the reaches of space to his tail-tip, Giansar. While at the other end of his twisted frame, his fiery eyes, Eltanin and Alwaid, stared with defiant challenge at lovelorn Hercules wearily plodding through eternity after his virgin Vega.

All the themes of human emotions are shown in the sky. If a man can but tell a thousandth as much as the faintest, most obscure pinprick of light, as it shows its reflection of life, love, and hope to us from the nethermost corner of the most remote galaxy, he will have told more than all the greatest of men that ever lived here on earth.

Most of the moonrises I could not see, for they were obscured by the Brittania-Berg. But on two memorable occasions I did see the full moon rise in a calm arctic night,

with not a sound except for the faint, faraway gnashing of
the sea ice on the edge of the death white field. I was out on
the western side of the bay, mapping the floes which had
piled up there, watching for signs of possible leads opening
up. This was a job which took twelve hours at a stretch, for
the "terrain" over the floes, all jumbled up, was extremely
difficult and hazardous. Some of the floes had frozen solid
at an angle of sixty degrees from the horizontal. Often there
was no way around these capsized slippery surfaces, and it
was hard and heavy work to climb up glassy slopes the size
of a soccer field. Then, having reached the top, I would
have to sling a rope through a block and lower myself down
the underside of the floe, which sometimes overhung the
next floe. I always had the dinghy compass with me, for
once beyond the "shore-side" floes, the frozen-in boat was
completely out of sight. Snowstorms often closed in very
suddenly, limiting vision to a matter of yards.

One night I reached the southern edge of the Brittania-
Berg, or Gibraltar Point, as I called it. I was attempting to
climb up England hill from the south, but this proved
impossible. It was far too steeply angled and absolutely
smooth. I was resting before making the four-hour scram-
ble back to the boat, when, looking to the southeast, I saw
the sky light up, very slowly. The horizon turned a cobalt
color, then electric blue, next powder blue, shot with silver
rays streaking up through the stars. A little while after, with
the whole sky in the east gleaming with shot-silver, the ice
accepted, like a woman handling a rich brocade, the moonlight. The tip of the moon's upper arc was actually shining
through ten miles of piled-up ice! The light rays glittered,
splintered, and slithered at odd angles, flashing right
across the horizon. These shocks of pure silver were reflected on the base of the low, slow clouds over the sea, far
away. It was as if the world would crack asunder with cold
beauty. Then, slowly, the moon showed herself, her light
shining horizontally over the cluttered masses of ice, casting long shadows. The whole surface of the world, as far as

my eyes could see, became a vast panorama of speckled silver and black while the sky above was black with the speckled silver of twinkling stars. The moon seemed about twice the size she appears in the temperate zones, and the air was so clear I could see every freckle on her pockmarked face. Then, as she rose higher and higher, the shadows of the ice piles withdrew, and soon all was pale white and black again, with the moon's face cold, ghostly, and deathly alone as she became smaller and smaller, to hang in the sky like a crystal ball of ice, under the cold curtain of stars.

I shuddered, then put my arms back in the sleeves of my jerkin and headed off for the boat. Hours later, back over the ice barriers, onto the flat surface of frozen *Cresswell* bay, trudging wearily through the recently fallen, powdery snow, I saw a black shape advancing towards me. It was Nelson. Once alongside, he jumped up to greet this apparition. "I know, old son, it's alright. I know I look like a bloody Christmas tree!"

I hurried back to the warmth. There were a couple of dead spots on my cheeks, which did not feel my tears as I thought of other Christmases and the cheerful company of my sailor mates and the lasses we had loved.

Back in the galley, with the stove lit, I removed my goggles and warmed up my face. I inspected myself in the small looking glass. I looked wretched. Then I looked down at Nelson. Looking into the mirror, I said, "Right, you bastard, less of that crap, there's things to be done."

"What?" I asked myself.

"Well, for a start, feed the bloody dog."

"Right." I was getting to know me alright, and I was getting me shaped up, keeping control. But it was hard; it was terribly difficult to hold back the floodgates of self-pity and awful, soul-shrinking loneliness, and I took more and more to watching the stars and listening to their message in the stillness between raging blizzards.

After hot tea, ground-up peanuts, and porridge, I turned in, my head feeling the bump of the loaded Very pistol, broken at the breech, under the pillow. The whole time the boat was in the ice I was wary of a bear attack. If the bear off Greenland had been so aggressive while there was plenty of food available to him in the shape of fish and seals, what the devil would they be like out here, where there was apparently nothing?

All the time, in the ice, I was never very far from my ax, my hammer, a rope, and the Very pistol. Every time I left the boat, for whatever reason, even if it was only for ablutions on the calm, clear nights, my ax, my compass, the Very pistol, snowshoes, and two days' food went with me. Thick sheets of slashing snow and ice came down so fast that even yards away from the boat it was easy to be caught out and not be able to find the way back. Then it was necessary to find some kind of shelter under a cocked-up ice ledge and await the blizzard's tempering. But every move more than two yards from the boat was studied, every direction noted. I could not leave a lamp lit on the boat. For one thing, my fuel stock was low; for another, it would hardly show more than ten yards in a blizzard. Also I did not want to attract any possible prowlers, especially if I was absent from the boat. My shelter, my food, my warmth, my life. The center of my icy cold world. Each time I left the boat, I unwound a long line behind me, to show me the way back.

So the long, long procession of dark hours passed, week after week. I made it a rule to go over to the western ice-floe field whenever it was calm. Now it was a half-solid frozen mass, and I tried to follow the movement of the ice. It was always moving, not only en masse, everything together, but also bits and pieces, some as big as a city block, against the others. The Brittania-Berg moved clockwise, crushing into the western floes, which in turn had slowly transmitted the tremendous pressure of the berg onto the flat ice steppe beyond. Cracks and crevasses changed continuously towards the west of the boat, and this was where my attention was riveted, because I reckoned that when the breakup came (if it ever did), it would loosen the heavy floes and open a passage to the southwest.

Nine times out of ten, storms and blizzards were introduced by a display of power and light beyond imagination, as the northern lights flashed through the sky, like the fireworks of the gods, sending showers and fountains of streaking, liquid sparks across the black arch of the arctic sky. Hours later the wind started up—first a low moaning in the rigging, then rising to a whistle. This was the signal to batten everything down. Then the roar built to a scream of satanic anger. The vessel shook as the wind tore at the masts, trying to pluck them out of the snowbound hull. Now and again I peeped through the doghouse portholes, lifting the inch-thick felt insulators. Outside, a blinding white sheet of the wall of hell was zinging past the ice field, with the top ice breaking off under the strength of the mighty wind. On rare occasions I would brave the blast, well shielded with two extra blankets tied around my caribou-skin clothes, and through a tiny gap for my eyes, watch the ice blow over the top of Brittania-Berg, like a continuous spray of steam, clear over the top of the boat, onto the western side of *Cresswell* bay, where it filled the recently opened crevasses, changing the whole appearance of the ice-floe field.

Then I lit the seal-oil lamp and, putting some of my rapidly diminishing charcoal on the heating stove, settled down to read. This was my only relief from the arctic conditions of cold, anxiety, loneliness, and, when the weather was bad, idleness. My radio had given up the ghost just after Christmas, and though I fiddled with it for hours, it simply refused to speak to me any more. I came to the conclusion that the severe dampness in the cabin had got to one of the transistors. But after drying out all my volumes, I had plenty to read, and I was cozy enough, with the little stone lamp sending up its slow, tiny, wavering column of black smoke into the corned-beef-can chimney, and Nelson lying under the table, against my feet, with a

bone held between his good paw and the stump of the
missing limb.

Tiring of reading by the fitful lamp, I made plans for the
long dawn, due to arrive about the end of February. I made
ready a long line and a block, to fix a pulley up the steep
northern slope of "England" on the Brittania-Berg. I made a
new signal flag out of an ancient cockpit cover which I
painted yellow and nailed to a frame. I hammered all my
old empty food cans flat, then wired and glued them together, to make a sun reflector, a sort of heliograph. This
was about a yard square, and I made a hole in it so I would
be able to sight it at an airplane, and polished it, with emery
paper and sand out of the bilge, until it shone like a mirror.
When the sun rose high and the temperatures climbed, I
planned to paint the big boat cover yellow and to make a
separate signal to peg down onto the ice, away from the
boat, out of the old awning. The food stores, in their boxes,
together with the empty boxes, I pegged out in groups on
the western side of the bay, while the ice held, to spell
S.O.S. in Morse code, so it might be sighted from afar in the
air.

Once a month, when the weather was calm, I baked
bread, using the pressure cooker as an oven. I became quite
expert at this, and the snow mixed with evaporated milk
seemed to give the bread a good, light texture.

I do not know exactly what the lowest temperature I
experienced was, as the alcohol in my outside thermometer
had dropped out of sight by October, but I did find out
later, from the Norwegian air force, that a plane within a
hundred miles of my estimated position on New Year's Day
of 1961 had registered, very close to sea level, something in
the region of sixty-four degrees below zero Fahrenheit!
Inside the cabin, with a domestic thermometer, I was able
to raise the temperature as high as thirty-eight degrees
Fahrenheit, but this was only for about five hours out of
twenty-four. The rest of the time the temperature averaged

around twenty-five degrees Fahrenheit.

The effects of cold and enforced idleness resulted in a slowing down of my whole system. I was not aware of this until one day I noticed that Nelson seemed to be moving much faster than he normally did. He was like a beast in an old-fashioned silent movie, jerking around, very fast. I stared at him for a while, then at myself, in the newly made sunlight reflector. It occurred to me that what had happened was that it was I who had slowed down; everything about me. This was interesting, and I lumbered over to the navigation cupboard and, after a few moments' thought (actually it was more like an hour), took out the chronometer to wind it up. I stared at it. Not only could I see the second hand moving fast, but I could see the minute hand moving quite steadily, and the *hour hand* moving! Time had warped my senses! I put the chronometer back and sat down to think this one out.

Was it the cold that was slowing me down? The loneliness? The enforced idleness? The diet? I puzzled out the reasons for a while, then decided to tackle the problem from another angle. Did the slowing down matter? Not if I was idle; in fact it was probably a good thing. Yes, if I had to get something done, and double-yes when and if the time ever came to get the boat out of this deathtrap.

From then on I made a conscious effort to increase the speed of all my movements and tried to vary my diet. Daily, I ate about eight ounces of greasy, rubbery seal blubber, raw. If it kept the Kalatdlits from getting scurvy, it would do the same for me. I left off frying food, even though I had still a good supply of lard on board, and tried to eat as much canned food as I could stomach, merely thawed out in the frying pan. I did these things by instinct, for I had never studied dietary rules, apart from getting hold of enough food to stay alive.

One thing I did learn during those months in the ice: the average westerner eats far too much and overcooks his food. I learned to eat what the body needed and no more, and to expend the energy given by the food before the next meal.

The other thing I learned was to play chess against myself without cheating. I had had a game going ever since I settled down in the ice, back in August, but it had been desultory, for I had to leave the board after each move and wait a week until I had forgotten the moves that I:a was going to make, then tackle the last move of I:a with I:b's fresh approach. The snag was that by the time I:b was ready to play his move, I:a had forgotten the moves in his future sequence of play. Gradually, however, over the weeks, the forgetting period of both the I's shrunk, and by December I could completely separate the two sets of tactics, blocking out I:a or I:b at will. At first this frightened me, and I gave up the game for a few days. But then I came to the conclusion that no human is only one "set of thoughts," that there are many sides to us, and so set to finish the game. Then a further complication arose, disturbing the first, until I became used to it. Not only were I:a and I:b well matched, but I was completely unbiased to either of them, merely watching the game from a spectator's point of view, objectively, forming separate and distinctive ideas as to what the future moves should be, yet not giving I:a or I:b a clue as to these thoughts. I cast encouragement or disapproval on both I:a and I:b as the move was made, without fear or favor.

One night, in between watching I:a form his strategy against the wily countermoves of I:b, I had to clamber topsides and shake the black ice off the loosened standing rigging wires, perform ablutions, and take my ghostly trek around the ghastly perimeter of smoking ice, watching the shooting stars fall from the heights of my mind and the stars and moon reflected on shining . . . shoulders . . . soldier boulders armies . . . dark winter's general campaign . . . over frozen steps . . . stepping-in-step across instant . . . bleached white covers . . . coniferous Conestoga wagons . . wagons-lits . . . no wheels wheeling . . . blue shadows

lined . . . maligned . . . tramlines . . . butcher's apron . . .
ridged ice below . . . five-day growth . . . frostbitten jaws . . .
skull . . . icy white frozen . . . skull . . . icicles upside-down
in the empty eyesockets staring at bicycles cyclic cyclops . . .
traffic lights . . . policemen's whistles gristle . . . southwest
blizzards . . . gizzards, fried fish . . . chips smell . . . smelt . . .
from the . . . Brittania-Berg, Nelson limping after me
through the knee-high sheet of blown snow, beast snapping at my idol's legs with . . . walrus teeth and wasn't . . . it
. . . hot . . . in . . . the . . . bath tonight . . . because Ulli is
waiting . . . in the cabin . . . game just go on play up play up .
. . I:a will move this pawn into *that* floe *there* . . . capture the
queen-boat . . . *Cresswell-Andromeda* . . . two ice chisels . . .
whoops! don't lose the hammer . . . Christ that's a hell of an
angle . . . it will need two . . . hundred . . . feet . . .
inch-and-a-half-nylon-line-in-the-spring, tra-la-la . . .
"I:b, you fucking idiot, why did you move that bloody rook,
your knight is day and day is night" . . . cold . . . cold . . .
and—"Jesus Christ!" I must have fallen flat on my face into
the bilge of the cabin, onto the slushy ice in the bilge,
hot-shocked into sanity with heart-freezing fear. Nelson
gasped—the boat was moving upwards and onto her side!
Outside the sky seemed to be caving in with noise! The deck
shot up, lifting me bodily.

"Holy fuck!" I staggered, drunkenly, to the hatchway,
trying to keep upright in the wildly heaving cabin. Then,
turning around and screaming, I grabbed the chessboard as
it slid across the table and heaved it against the forward
bulkhead. Now the boat was rearing up, *up* by the bow,
sinking down, *down* by the stern. Out in the cockpit after
what seemed like an aeon, I ripped the snowcover to one
side.

The ice field was in a frenzy of movement all around, as
far as I could see through the driving snow. I shook my
head and looked again, horrified, just in time to see all the
food boxes, two-thirds of my meager stock, slide down a
tilted floe into a widening crevasse and disappear as if

swallowed by some murderous, greedy beast. The noise was deafening. Cracks, thunder, explosions, then great loads of falling ice, in barrowloads at a time, truckloads, falling vertically down from the sky onto the heaving hull.

*Barrowloads? Truckloads? What in the name of God?*

I looked up. The sight I saw will haunt me until the last flicker of light leaves my weather-wracked soul. *The Brittania-Berg was capsizing!* It was turning over on its side, with "Wales," a great mass of ice, thousands of tons of the stuff, slowly falling, two hundred feet above the boat. Directly above the boat, and coming straight down onto the top, while *Cresswell* was being dragged by the shifting ice under her, right into the maw under the mountain of ice!

Was I going crazy? I shook my head as the boat was flung forward and upward again. *No, I wasn't. This nightmare was for real!*

*What is a woman that you forsake her,*
*And the hearth-fire and the home-acre,*
*To go with the old grey Widow-maker?*

*She has no house to lay a guest in—*
*But one chill bed for all to rest in,*
*That the pale suns and the stray bergs nest in.*

*She has no strong white arms to fold you,*
*But the ten-times-fingering weeds to hold you—*
*Out on the rocks where the tide has rolled you.*

Rudyard Kipling,
from "Harp Song of the Dane Women."

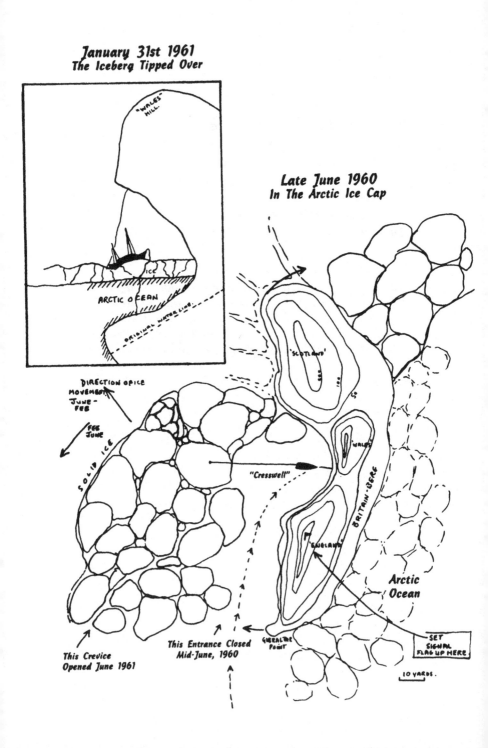

January 31st 1961
The Iceberg Tipped Over

"WALES" HILL

ICE

ARCTIC OCEAN

ORIGINAL WATER LINE

Late June 1960
In The Arctic Ice Cap

"SCOTLAND" BERG

"WALES"

"Cresswell"

"BRITAIN" BERG

"ENGLAND"

DIRECTION OF ICE MOVEMENT JUNE—FEB

FEB JUNE

SOLID ICE

GIBRALTAR POINT

Arctic Ocean

SET SIGNAL FLAG UP HERE

This Crevice Opened June 1961

This Entrance Closed Mid-June, 1960

10 YARDS.

# 24

## Under the Ice

How long I stood gazing straight upwards, horror-struck, I do not know. By the time I came to what senses I had left, my mittens were frozen to the guardrail and the ice on my snow goggles had completely obscured my vision. I remember thinking that this was death, this was the end. I just stood there, unseeing, with *Cresswell* steadily tilting up at the bow, waiting for her to go right over, hoping she would, before the great ice-crash came and blotted out the world, but this was more of a vision than a thought, more like a sideways glance than a direct stare.

Suddenly *Cresswell* gave a great lurch downwards at the bow, then froze. The racket around me was mind numbing; it was as if all the tortured souls in hell were screaming for mercy at the feet of Almighty God. It was not only the volume of noise, it was the awful agony, the groans, the crashes, the grinding *suffering* of it all.

I found myself working to free one hand from the rail, which took a century, then fisting the ice from my goggles. Just as they were clear and the world changed from dirty black to blinding white again, the boat gave another lurch, again the bows were thrown high up, and again they smashed down. Even through the roars, bangs, and groans of the ice my ears picked up the splintering crack as the bowsprit smashed off, and the clatter of the forestay as it swung wildly, free now, and smashed against the doghouse. But I was not looking at the bow; my eyes were riveted on the berg. It suddenly stopped dropping and, with an almighty lurch, reared back again, hesitated for two or three seconds, then slowly settled down, coming to a halt with the peak of "Wales" at an angle about forty degrees from the vertical. There it hovered, 150 feet over the top of the masts. And stayed there! Bobbing.

Slowly I became aware of Nelson's whimpering and agitation, as he valiantly tried to keep his balance on the ice-covered deck of the heeled-over boat. I looked again at the berg around the boat. It was a shambles. The capsizing of the berg had meant that the wide ledge below the "Wales" peak had left a great gap under the overhanging summit. The pressure of the ice floes piled up against the western steppe had suddenly been released, and the whole mess had moved to the east, to take up the vacant space under the ice. With it, the boat had moved, the after line snapping like a piece of knitting wool. The forward mooring line, pegged to the edge of the berg's lower edge, had gone completely slack and was now hanging down vertically. With the pounding and smashing of the ice against the boat, the propeller, useless anyway with a bent shaft, had been snapped away. Fortunately, I had been able to unship the rudder before the boat had iced in. Now she was lying on her port side, at an angle of thirty-five degrees from the vertical, with her bow flung up, and the deck about forty degrees from the horizontal.

All around the ice was settling down again, and I realized that it would soon solidify into a frozen mass once more, until the berg moved over again onto the boat. My first resolution, once sanity returned, was to shift out of the boat as soon as the ice froze and make a refuge on the flat frozen steppe over to the west, from where I could watch both the berg and the boat. My second resolution was to cut my daily food ration down by a half. That would give me supplies for six months. I looked quickly at Nelson. "Then it'll be your

turn, old son," I thought. He rubbed his good paw over his
eyes. His tears were freezing, too.

Aware of the bitter cold, and giving one last look up at the
tip of the ice peak hovering right overhead, I clambered
below to survey the scene. It was chaos—clothes, books,
charts, chess pieces, pans, cutlery, everything, lying wet in
the icy slush of the bilges.

I set to picking up the bits and pieces of civilization out of
the mucky slush. The first thing I did was to make a horizontal platform for the heating stove. Using the floorboards from the engine compartment, I wedged them up
with emptied boxes. Then I shortened the smoke-pipe and,
finding some dry charcoal, soon had a little fire going to dry
out all the gear. Then I mustered all the available food and
worked out how to make it last for eight months. The
collection was pitiful. Some seal blubber, six twenty-pound
bags of peanuts, four pounds of sugar, twenty pounds of
rice, thirty pounds of porridge, a block of salt, eighteen
pounds of flour, twenty pounds of tea, ten pounds of
cocoa, twenty cans of evaporated milk, twenty-four small
cans of sardines, and eighteen large cans of beans, with
twenty-two medium-sized cans of corned beef. I noted it all
down, then, looking up at Nelson, thought *"and you."* He
wagged his tail. And I did something I thought I'd never do
again. I grinned at him. His tail bumped the deck.

I set to, tired and worn-out as I was, to tidy up the cabin.
"Bugger it, mate," I said to him, as he lay down by the
stove, out of the way. "If we're going to go, let's bloodywell
go shipshape and Bristol fashion." I found that some sugar,
out of the ready-use tin, had fallen under the navigation
shelf, into the bilge. I spooned it out and set it on a tin plate
to dry.

Then, when the cabin was squared away, I clambered up
the crazily leaning companionway for a last look around.
The first thing I looked at this time was not the ice around
the boat. That had subsided now, and all was quiet, except

for the faint hum of a low breeze through the rigging. My
eyes went straight up vertically above my head, to the three
thousand tons of hanging death hovering there. Polaris had
shifted on its two-degree circular course around the celestial pole. Now it was over the peak of ice and shining
*through* it. I gazed at the sight, fascinated.

As I watched, the first glares of the northern lights shot
through the sky right above the hanging ice. Again I was
petrified; would a strong wind blow the berg right over?
Then the pyrotechnics of the heavens played across the
night sky, sending sharp stabs of light into the Brittania-
Berg, spears and daggers of pure energy. These, once they
hit the ice, changed direction, scattering into the heart of
the mass. I was fascinated, then wonder-struck, then delighted, so much that I yelled with pure joy at the sight, at
the thought that the Spirit of the Universe was sending me
this signal, this life, right across the vastness of space, just
for me!

How long I was up there, gazing like an idiot at this
display of awful power, I will never know, but finally I
made my way below, intoxicated with the visual poetry of it
all. Nelson opened his eye as I slithered down the drunkenly leaning hatch. "Well, old son, to die after seeing
that—fuck it, *it's worth it!*"

Then I lay down on the level planks in front of the warm
stove and went to sleep, thinking how beautiful, how very
beautiful life is, so full of wonder.

The next "morning" was the twenty-fifth of January, and
after the initial shock of finding the boat on her side and
remembering the nightmare of the previous hours, I again
stepped outside.

The berg was still there, all that ice straight overhead. It
was steady and the ice all around was frozen solid, from the
base of the berg to the ice field in the west. It was fairly clear
by the starlight, and I looked over to the southwest. There,
far up on the tilted ice mass of "England" hill, drooped the
signal flag, hanging down right over the ice two hundred

feet below. What had once been the high peak of the berg was now the side, fifty feet below the new peak! I grinned at the memory of having risked my life to reach the peak to plant the signal so many weeks before, when there was light in the world—and—I looked again at the peak of "Wales," then at the gap between it and "Scotland," to the north.

I peered, then removed the goggles.

There was—there was—light in the sky! A faint yellowish tinge, a mere touch of a glimmer of a glow! Not silver this time—gold! It was the sun, though still below the curve of the world. It was sunlight! It could not be the moon, for she was low in the ice rim to the west. It was Sol, it was light, and warmth; and the same light shone so far away on trees and unimaginable green things, grass and hedgerows, houses and—people! And it made the sea blue and green and the corn waving gold in the fields, and it was shining here, in this frozen hell of slow death, and it was shining for me! It was telling me that I would live and that I would follow it again and again, just as other men would follow other stars until the very hem of time turned into itself. The sight moved me to dance a slippery jig on the crazily canted deck. I shook the black ice free of the shrouds, shouting for joy. I rushed back, slithering, to call Nelson out. As he hobbled up the ladder, I grabbed his head and faced him to the whisps of gold in the black, star-studded sky. "There, it's there, old son, bloody daylight. We'll get out. We'll sodding well get out, I know we will!" Nelson jumped up and down as best he could.

By this time my position was approximately seventy-eight, forty latitude and one degree ten minutes east of the Greenwich Meridian. The whole ice mass was moving slowly but steadily southwest. I considered to myself that at this rate something was bound to happen during the next four months, as long as the direction and speed of the flow were maintained, and that that something was the gradual breakup of the ice floes on the edges of the field, then of the field itself. But if the direction changed to north again, I was probably a dead man, unless I could attract attention from some stray plane during the daylight season. Chances were that I was a dead man anyway, because if the weather deteriorated and piled more snow and ice on top of the Brittania-Berg it would capsize onto the boat. There was not much point in making a camp on the ice, because if the boat went I would not survive more than a few days in the ice. I had to stay with her and build a stack of wood close to her, laced with oil and covered from the snow, ready to light as a signal should I hear a plane.

I came to the conclusion that my best chance of getting out of this mess was to stick with *Cresswell*, keeping a close eye on the berg, and then if it seemed ready to capsize further, try my luck on the ice. But the dice would be loaded against me down to the quick.

I reckoned that February fourth would see the actual sunrise, and to watch it I scrambled for sixteen hours over the new jumble of piled ice, to a position north of "Scotland" peak. There I sheltered from the westerly wind and patiently waited for four hours until I saw the blood red glow, a tiny sliver of light, over the vast ice field to the southeast. Then, exhilarated, I clambered and slithered back for ten hours to the boat, and slept.

I made my mind up not to neglect the gear on the boat, and the first task towards this end, as soon as twilight filled the eastern half of the black dome of the sky, was to repair the bowsprit, which I did by gluing on a scarf made from one of the floor boards, and refix the spar to the knightheads. As the repaired sprit was slightly shorter than the original, I then had to shorten the forestay, which took several days, as it was difficult to splice wearing two pairs of mittens and working on a frozen wire. I could not get the forestay down to work below, because the mast was canted at an angle, and I dared not try climbing it as it was slippery with quick freezing ice.

By March first, twilight was upon us, and the ice mass

was moving faster. My position was now seventy-eight, fifteen north; zero degrees, sixteen minutes west. After a storm which lasted from March tenth to the fifteenth, I clambered out onto the western floe field and, looking far to the south through the binoculars from a high hummock, saw that the edges of the mass were indeed starting to break up. By March thirtieth, as the warmer water of the Gulf Stream offshoot passed under the ice field, the breakup began in earnest. From my lookout point, I found that the distance from where I stood, just near the southern tip of the Brittania-Berg, out to the "open" water (that is, ice with leads running between the floes) had diminished to approximately six miles. By April fifteenth, with the sun higher in the sky and more accurate sextant shots possible, the distance to the nearest open lead was about three miles from Brittania. The explosions of the separation of the floes could be heard from every direction around the clock. By May first, with the floes on the eastern side of Brittania-Berg opening up and drifting away to the south, the pressure was off the berg. It started to move, slowly at first, no more than a couple of feet a day, then more rapidly, two, four, six yards a day, in a counterclockwise direction. I was out at all hours, taking bearings on Gibraltar Point with the hand-bearing compass and noting the great mass of ice overhanging the boat gradually moving to the east. By the twenty-fifth of April the ice-in-the-sky was clear of the bow of the boat, and by the first of May the ice around the boat began to break up. On the eighth of May I celebrated my thirty-seventh birthday with an extra ration of seal blubber.

On the fifteenth of May, *Cresswell* suddenly fell down into a crevasse which opened below her. The shock was not too great, for, pitched bows up as she had been during the great upheaval, the stern was close to water level. The crevasse opened up from the west, and when it reached the stern, the boat, with a rumble, slid down into water. I anxiously searched below for leakage, but there seemed to be none or very little. The hull had held! I set to rigging spars and sails, tightening up the shrouds.

All this time I had been scrimping on food, eating no more than one small meal daily, with Nelson the same. It was no good getting out of the ice only to starve to death at sea. But now that the ice was breaking up, with cracks leading right out of the "bay" to the open sea only two miles away, I needed to build up my strength. So I increased my seal-blubber ration from eight ounces to ten, and the porridge from four ounces to six, while halving Nelson's ration of porridge for burgoo.

On June third, with a southeasterly storm heaving up the western floe field, it started to break up. The noise was enough to prevent any sleep; warily I watched for the slightest chance of springing the trap. By the tenth of June, after a long spell of high wind, which changed to a northerly, the ice floes southwest of *Cresswell* opened up and floated away like fishing boats leaving harbor on the evening tide.

The next day I managed to drag *Cresswell* astern by jumping onto the loose ice floes and pulling her with a mooring line, after cutting the bowline loose. Gradually, I maneuvered the boat until the bows were facing southwest. Then, driving the crowbar into a football-field-sized floe, I secured the boat's bowline and waited for the floe to move out when the wind dropped or shifted. The boat was a lot higher out of the water, for the food stores and ship's gear lost in the upheaval, together with food consumed for the past year, accounted for well over two tons. But weight lost meant easier hauling, and I soon had her ready to exit.

The southwest wind persisted for three days, pushing back loose floes into the open lead and jamming up the escape route. For three sunny days I waited patiently, willing the wind to change, while Nelson moped on deck, hungry on short rations. I put two lines over the side, baited with seal blubber.

Suddenly the wind dropped. We waited. One more day, the whole sunny night, half the next day. I was asleep in the now much warmer cabin when it happened. A slight judder on the bowline. I was awake instantly. I crowded up the ladder. She was moving—she was heading out—with the great silver gleaming ice floe blinding me until I got the goggles over my head. She was moving out! Ahead of our "tug" the whole ice floe pack was shifting forward, away from the great ice-field plateau. Behind us were a hundred smaller floes, one of which was pushing against our rudderless stern. I didn't care. We were moving.

At the moment we rounded the south end of the Brittania-Berg, one of the fishing lines jerked. With a muffled whoop, I leapt for it. There was a nice fat cod. Nelson scampered for joy as I held it up, shining in the sunlight. "Bugger it, old son, underway or not, this is going in the pot!" I left the boat to fend for herself and lit the stove. With the pot steaming merrily, I dashed topsides to look around and found we were going at a surprising rate away from the ice field, at least a knot and a half. The smell of cooking fish wafted through the companionway. Soon the pan was out on the bridge deck, with the pair of us scoffing cod-flesh straight off the bone. We finished it all—flesh, eyes, head, liver, fins; the whole fifteen pounds of it—the finest meal we had seen for months. We drooled over it, tearing the flesh away from the bones. The berg, and the three hills of death, dropped astern. We were still surrounded by great ice floes on all sides, and our position would be highly dangerous if a storm blew up, but I wanted to be well clear of the berg before turning to the southeast, to thread a way through the massive jigsaw of floes.

"Well, mate, that's that!" I said to Nelson, as we glanced back at the monstrous gravestone we had so narrowly escaped. "Now we'll get some sea time in!"

*Come cheer up, my lads, 'tis to glory we steer,*
*To add something new to this wonderful year,*
*'Tis to honor we call you, as free men, not slaves,*
*For who are so free as the sons of the waves?*

*Chorus: Heart of oak are our ships, heart of oak are our men;*
*We always are ready, steady, boys, steady;*
*We'll fight and we'll conquer again and again!*

Royal Navy song, eighteenth century. It is
the lower-deckmen's marching tune.

# 25

## *By the Skin of My Teeth*

Being underway was the most immense relief imaginable. Free at long, long last, after one year and a day locked in the ice field, 366 days—staring death right in its grisly skull-sockets. Even though the chance of collision with a floe was possible if a heavy wind piped up, I felt so unburdened, for the first three or four days, that I found myself taking risks which normally I never would dream of, steering straight for a floe, missing its leeward side by a matter of feet, and crowding on sail in forceful gusts.

The boat leaked like a sieve. The whole line of the garboard strake, where the hull joined the keel, had had the caulking shaken almost completely out of it during the wicked battering by the ice in the Brittania-Berg capsize. I had to pump her out almost continuously, though in calm weather I could take a rest, letting the boat take in two feet of freezing cold water. Then I would don my sea boots, reaching up to my thighs, go below the cockpit floorboards, and bucket the water out. It was heavy work and left no time for desperation or fear.

As soon as the wind picked up, I inflated the rubber dinghy below in the cabin, for extra flotation, just in case I fell asleep or was knocked unconscious. This made life below difficult, with a seven-foot dinghy stuck into the living space, but somehow I managed. It was cold, wet, miserable work, a great expenditure of my body's strength, meager as it was by this time. Mainly, it was willpower that enabled me to start bucketing once again.

I looked up at Nelson sniffing around the horizon during one spell of backbreaking bucketing. "Yes, you old bugger," I yelled at him, "and if you had two bloody forelegs, you'd be down here too." He frowned and again turned his snout to the far horizon, pretending to ignore me.

My position, when I broke out of the ice, was about 185 miles west-southwest of the main settlement of Svalbard, Kongsfjorden (King's Bay). As this was the nearest human abode, this is where I steered for, with a slight to moderate southwest wind pushing *Cresswell* before it over a kindly sea. On June thirteenth, four days after emerging from the ice trap, I obtained a position fix. I was only fifty miles from safety! The weather was much warmer now, some degrees above freezing for hours at a stretch. Becalmed from the thirteenth to the sixteenth, I managed to bail enough water out of the thawing tanks to wash three shirts, together with underwear and long sea-boot stockings. I used salt water to get the worst grime out, then rinsed them in fresh water. Then I trimmed my beard, which was all of nineteen inches long. It had served as a chest-warmer during the winter! Then my hair, which was down around my shoulders. It took me hours to unmat the hair and wash it before I could cut it, as the scissors were blunt and the whetstone was worn away entirely. The spare knife sharpener had gone to a watery grave with the other lost stores under the Brittania-Berg. This was the first time I had doffed the Eskimo-rig since entering the icecap, except for the three times I had had to remove it to peel off a sweat-frozen shirt. The fawnskin underwear came off like it was my skin itself peeling from my body, and underneath I was lily-white, while my face, around the eyes, was almost black. Naked, I looked like something out of a nudist-camp harlequin party. My weight had diminished, of course, but what I had been eating must have been good, for I'd no sunken gums, loose teeth, or falling hair, sure signs of scurvy. I was eliminating liquids about an hour after drinking and solids about twelve hours after eating, and my body muscles were like high-tensile steel wires. At first, my normal sea vision suffered. This ability always surprises landsmen (I can, after a day or two at sea, read a ship's name from four miles' distance). I knew this was the result of being in the dark cabin, straining my eyes with the seal-oil lamp, and, outside, wearing the snow goggles. But slowly my vision returned. My hearing was most acute. I was so accustomed to listening for the slightest boat noise or other unnatural sound, such as a possible airplane, that I could hear every one of the hundreds of separate wooden joints working in the hull. My sense of smell was almost as good as Nelson's. I was well rested, the boat steering herself, now clear of ice floes except for the odd maverick. I was warming up some porridge for peanut burgoo, when I smelt fish. It could not have been from the shore, as the wind was still southwest. I hopped topsides and looked around. There was nothing but a lone ice floe to the north. But I clearly smelled fish! Nelson was straining his nose around the compass, and finally settled for a direction to the west-southwest-by-west from our position. I stared hard, but, seeing nothing, went below to finish cooking the scrimpy meal.

By this time all the canned food had been eaten, with the exception of six cans of corned beef and six of sardines. We were down to porridge, peanuts, flour (I was out of yeast), and lard, together with the remnants of the seal blubber, about twelve pounds, stinking to high heaven. I fished diligently the whole time after leaving the ice, but caught only the cod on the way out and two small, poor-looking creatures the names of which I know not. They were so ugly that I was suspicious of them. I fed a boiled morsel of one to Nelson. He got sick, and I threw them back into the Arctic Ocean and gave him an extra helping of peanut burgoo.

Eating solids in the form of seal blubber, we both had the runs, but the color was not bad, and now that it was warmer, we could shit over the side, to leeward, without fear of frostbite, which was a great luxury.

One good thing about being alone in the Arctic, or out in the oceans anywhere, is that there are no cold germs, no lice, and no fleas. All the time I was up in cold latitudes I never had a headache. Nothing but my regular bouts of rheumatism when the weather gauge dropped and a stiff blow was on its way. Also "chinky toe-rot," as sailors call athlete's foot. How this came about I've no idea. It must have been from the previous owner of the sealskin boots, but the itch was murderous at first, until I finally ground up some chalk and cured it by that method.

But mentally and spiritually I had changed. The man who went into the ice was not the man who came out. Going in, I had not known the true nature of fear. I had not known, that is, the natural *animal* part of man, always lurking, waiting for the slightest chance to overcome his intelligence; always lurking in the shadows of man's mind, to spring upon him and drag him so easily, should he not purposefully resist, back into the murky dark cave from which he has so painfully, so slowly, so bloodily, so heroically, dragged himself over the millenia of human history.

When I went into the ice I had not known, either, the true nature of loneliness. Over the months of waiting for death, I had realized that the emotion we know as "loneliness" is, in fact, learned. *If there were no one to tell us we should be lonely, we would not be.*

Animals herd together for two main reasons: for protection and for procreation. Along with these two instincts man adds another: to try to hide from himself the fact that everyone, in the long run, is alone. *Absolutely alone.* In the whole vastness of the wastes of space, every human is on his own. To admit this, and to accept it, is the key to freedom from so-called loneliness. The more it is accepted, the more the company of other, likewise "alone" people can be appreciated, and the more they can be respected, liked, and even loved.

The intelligent man need never be "lonely." We can, if we are prepared to make the effort, keep the company of thousands of other intelligent men who have gone before us. We can learn from them, cry and laugh and hope with them, and recognize our places in the thrust of humanity from the corner of the cave to the outermost reaches of the firmament. Then we need never believe that any one of us is useless, disdained, or unwanted, for as long as there is blood in our veins, or a dream in our hearts, or a thought in our heads, we are, each one of us, an inescapable part of humanity, part of a whole. We are all a part of a spirit, a force, a *will*, which is irrepressible. A spirit which, even after inconceivable aeons of time, even after the whole universe collapses upon itself, will continue *to be*. A spirit the form of which is unknown to us; we have only an inkling, about which we can only guess.

It is towards this spirit, this unity, that we all strive. All humans, regardless of our faith or our political colorations, strive towards the eventual unity of the human spirit in eternity. We strive towards this, consciously or not. Some of us fail, some of us lean on others. Those of us who can perceive the paradox of our *alone-ness* and yet at the same time our *unity* with the Whole can defeat fear. We can triumph over the worst death of all, the death of the human spirit!

As *Cresswell* neared the haze of land to the east, I reflected on all that had passed, and wondered if I could rejoin the human race.

On the sixteenth of June, anxious and hopeful, I saw land. Magic, wonderful, solid, faithful, eternal land. True, it was the silver white, snow-topped peaks of the Barentz-burg, but under the sinister white there was a glimpse, a shivering smudge of darkness down on the horizon. Rock! Terra-bloody-firma!

Excitedly, I trimmed the sheets and fussed about like a weekend racing man, even though the wind was very weak and the boat was hardly moving. I grabbed the bucket and the deck scrubber and went to it like a maniac, scrubbing the ice-gashed, torn canvas deck covering, wiping the spars, washing down the porthole lights, fussing and tidying the grubby, stinking blankets below, squaring up the oil-smeared books in the repaired library, nailing down the floorboards, a mass of broken wood, and running up the red ensign, hardly recognizable, just a pale pinkish yellow shaggy-edged rag. The treble-stitched cross and triangles of the Union Flag, now pure white, bleached out of their colors, were still whole and sound.

It took another thirty-six hours to reach the lee of Prins Karls Forland, even though the wind was up to gale force three hours after I sighted the land. I dared not push her too hard, for fear of opening the garboard strake even more. There was a serious risk that the amount of water leaking in would be more than I could get rid of, so I made my way into the channel between the Forland and the mainland of Spitsbergen under spitfire jib only. Of course this tiny sail would only move her very slowly, no more than two knots, but at least she was only pounding the seas, not dropping off them, as she would under the normal gale rig of mizzen, trysail, and spitfire.

On the evening of the eighteenth of June, I found myself in flat water, in the shallow sound east of the Forland. While I worked the boat through the fluky winds as they swept round the island, I stared about in wonder and delight. There were beaches, and rocks, seals, walruses, birds, and in the calm water by the shore of the island, hundreds of jumping fish. The temperature was just below freezing, and there was ice and snow to within yards of the beach. Above, the sky was black with storm clouds charging for Siberia. Rain stabbed down at intervals, but now and again sun-rays slanted down through the gaps.

No tropical island with white sandy beaches shining beyond the dazzling surf under the high sun of Capricorn ever looked to me as sweet, as inviting, as beautiful, as did this Godforsaken hump of half-frozen primeval rock, sitting in the raging, ice-spume-blown Arctic Ocean. The sound of the anchor chain coming out of the hawsepipe for the first time in fourteen months was to me like all the trumpet blasts of the heavenly hosts; the wind-torn wisps of ice-laden clouds whistling over the high ground of the Forland seemed like the very banners of Caesar's triumph; the walruses snouting out of the knife-thin ice by the shore and the birds gliding up on high, like a vast crowd of welcome. As I gazed around the small bay through the sleety rain, waiting to see the anchor dug in properly, I could feel the life force in everything about me. Suddenly my eyes blurred and I lifted my gloved hand to wipe away the sleet from my wet cheeks. But it wasn't raining.

I staggered down below, to sleep on the makeshift shelf I had fixed six inches below the top of the cabin, so that the rising water would not reach me if I overslept. Pulling the blankets, still damp from the washing, over me, I cried myself to sleep like a baby. I was safe from the clutches of death. I was back among living things, that swam and flew and *dreamed*.

Two hours after I fell asleep I was awakened by a far-off noise. It was an engine. I scrambled out of the blankets and clambered aloft. There, away to the south, was a boat, coming towards me. I delved into the after dodger for the siren and started to hoot. Then I realized that this was futile. They would not hear me at this distance, above the noise of the engine. Nelson jerked up and down on his foreleg, yelping a welcome. Sadly, I sunk down into the cockpit bilge to bail out two feet of icy water.

When the boat was only a mile away and I could sense the human presence, could feel the nearness of their souls, I hooted the siren, again and again. The answer came loud and clear through the now dying wind. I saw a figure waving from the small wheelhouse. It was a man! It was that wonder of all the wonders of a wonderful world—a human being!

I could not speak as they came onboard, and I could hardly see for the tears. The skipper sang out something, but I could not understand. In that state, at that moment, I would not have understood the Lord's Prayer in plain English. A crewman, a large, ruddy-faced, cleanshaven, blue-eyed giant, jumped onboard with a line, his heavy weight thudding on the deck. He looked at me and said quietly, "My God!"

He walked along the deck, to where I stood clutching the mizzen shrouds, tears streaming down my face, sobbing. He put his arm around my shoulder and spoke again. The sound of his voice, this rough fisherman on one of the most forlorn, remote, cold islands in the world, was overwhelming. He held me for a full minute, while I struggled to put a round turn and two half-hitches on my emotions.

It is said that when a man drowns he sees all his life flash through his mind's eye. The moment Olaf touched my shoulder, it seemed as if I could feel all of humanity, past, present, and future, pass, like an electric shock, through my whole being.

Then the skipper of the boat leaning through the wheelhouse noticed my ragged flag. He spoke to me in English—the first time I had heard it since Reykjavík, two years before. He called the time-honored words of welcome the world over.

"Hey, where you come from, friend?"

"Reykjavík, by way of Greenland!" I croaked.

The skipper repeated this in Norwegian to Olaf and the other two crewmen, who stared at the boat in disbelief. There was hardly a patch of paint left on her hull, she was all dirty grey wood where the ice had scraped and hammered her. Her wounds and gashes seemed to bleed.

"When you sail from Reykjavík?"

"July 1959!"

"Goddamn!" the skipper ejaculated, then turned and spoke rapidly to Olaf. Another crewman jumped onboard my boat. I was feeling claustrophobic with two other highly complex nervous systems observing, computing, and analyzing, so very close to me that their thoughts, as they silently poured out, almost seemed audible, touchable, and visible, like the balloons of speech in the cartoons of kids' comics. It was as if, all at once, I could feel every sensation, every emotion, that these men had felt all their waking lives, and see before me all the visions of their long-past dreams.

The voice of the skipper broke through. "I put Olaf and Gudar onboard your boat, and I tow you into King's Bay. You come onboard, come, eat, drink!"

"No, captain."

"It's okay. They good seamen, they bring her safe—come onboard, bring the dog!"

I shook my head. I wouldn't leave my boat until she was safe and sound at her destination. I wouldn't leave her, even if she sank under my feet. She was my vessel, she was my responsibility. That is the hard law of the sea, immutable and fixed. I came to, squaring my thin shoulders, and nodded to Olaf as he fixed the towing line around the tabernacle. I could see, as soon as he picked up the line, that he was a fine boatman. His mate looked horror-struck at the Arctic Ocean creeping up through the boat. Grabbing the pump, he worked away at clearing the bilge. I'd not been able to completely clear the boat of water for days. He did it in fifteen minutes flat.

I steered *Cresswell* in, with the fishing skipper taking it very slowly and easily, right down the deep fiord of King's Bay. There were all of twenty wooden structures! There were houses and buildings, and a church steeple even, and although it was lightly snowing, it seemed to me like we were going up under London Bridge, with the great city all around, or up the Hudson into New York harbor.

Olaf anchored the boat, while I deflated the dinghy and dragged it out of the cabin. Then Olaf reinflated it for me. But I went ashore in the fishermen's jolly boat, which they drove straight up onto the pebble beach. I didn't weep for joy as Nelson and I stepped our five feet onto the scrunching pebbles, but I surely felt like it. Instead I glanced back at wounded *Cresswell*, looking battered beyond belief.

All the inhabitants of the small outpost were on the beach to watch us go ashore. Within the hour I was sitting in Olaf's house with an electric light bulb shining miraculously over roast beef and creamed potatoes, cabbage and, the running gift of a breathless lady, Colman's Mustard! And the miracle of a hot bath with water from kettles boiling on the big potbellied stove.

During the three weeks in King's Bay I tried to explain what I'd been doing, but it came hard, because for the first days my mind simply refused to remember. I would try to recall a date, or the weather, and a curtain would drop, and then I could think of nothing but the immediate present and the future. Above all, I could think of little else besides getting away from the Arctic.

The Norwegians of Svalbard are quiet, sturdy, stolid folk, and they understood well enough how the long, long solitude had affected me. By instinct, for the first few days, they confined their solicitude for me to the needs of the moment. Did I sleep well enough? (I was sleeping dreams of relief.) Did I have enough to eat? (I was eating enough to feed a horse.) Was I warm enough? (I was warmer than I had been for many months.)

The rest of the time they left me to sit in a corner, silently drinking in the sights and sounds of human interplay, like a thirst-crazed man sipping cool water at an oasis. Then, little by little, I talked to Olaf and his mates, at first babbling away incoherently in basic English, about the Kalatdlits and the bear; about the stars and the ice; about escaping from the Arctic and the everlasting numbing cold, away from the ever-present threat of a soul-freezing death in the cold, cold darkness of glittering ice. I told them how I longed for warmth and the sunshine and gentle seas, and waving palm trees in the clear, starlit heavens of the tropics.

The Norwegian air force ran a weather station at King's Bay. Their doctor, when he examined me, was amazed at the complete absence of any fat on my body; yet, though skinny, I was very strong. He pronounced me fit and gave me some lotion for my rheumatism. Then he asked me what I was going to do.

"I'm sailing as soon as I can, before the weather closes in

again, before there's any chance I might get stuck here for a whole winter."

"But you can winter safely here. You have your boat up on the beach. You can take off in the early summer next year. We can even arrange work for you here, if you are concerned about earning money."

"No, doctor, I have enough money to buy five weeks' food. With what I already have, there will be enough to reach Canada, or, if worse comes to worst, Iceland. At least I'll be out of the Arctic Circle. I can work there a season, then sail on for Canada."

"Why Canada?"

"Well," I said, "look at all that bloody marvelous boat-building timber, pitch pine, Douglas fir——"

He patted my shoulder. "I know your type. We've got them, too. I won't try to stop you. You sense your destiny and you follow it."

I bought food: potatoes, dried egg, canned milk, canned meat, flour, sugar, chocolate, and canned vegetables and fruit. The kind folk of King's Bay, together with the air force men, donated another six cases of canned goods, and Olaf, with Gudar, helped me paint the boat and test the engine. On July tenth all the good folks in King's Bay turned up at the jetty to wish *Cresswell*, Nelson, and me farewell and Godspeed for Canada.

"Send me a card!" cried Olaf.

"A card?" I called back. "I'll send you a book!"

"When?" He and all the crowd were laughing.

"When I've something to write about!"

I patted Nelson. The breeze picked up. *Cresswell* lurched to the first wavelets beyond the pier. The new, blood red ensign fluttered. We were off on the long trail again, across the ocean!

Envoi: A last thought from and for America—

*Wild Nights—Wild Nights!*
*Were I with thee*
*Wild Nights should be*
*Our luxury!*

*Futile — the Winds—*
*To a Heart in port—*
*Done with the Compass—*
*Done with the Chart!*

*Rowing in Eden—*
*Ah, the Sea!*
*Might I but moor—Tonight—*
*In Thee!*

                  **Emily Dickinson, "Wild Nights."**

Made in the USA
Las Vegas, NV
23 May 2023

72412276R00173